THE PROSPECT OF INTERNET DEMOCRACY

In memory of David Resnick
Scholar, Author, Friend

The Prospect of Internet Democracy

MICHAEL MARGOLIS
University of Cincinnati, USA
GERSON MORENO-RIAÑO
Regent University, USA

Routledge
Taylor & Francis Group
LONDON AND NEW YORK

First published 2009 by Ashgate Publishing

Published 2016 by Routledge
2 Park Square, Milton Park, Abingdon, Oxon OX14 4RN
711 Third Avenue, New York, NY 10017, USA

Routledge is an imprint of the Taylor & Francis Group, an informa business

British Library Cataloguing in Publication Data
Margolis, Michael.
The prospect of Internet democracy.
1. Internet--Political aspects. 2. Communication in politics. 3. Democracy.
I. Title II. Moreno-Riano, Gerson, 1971-
321.8'02854678-dc22

Library of Congress Control Number: 2009932736

ISBN 9780754675143 (hbk)

Contents

Acknowledgements

Plato's understanding of everyday life as a world of becoming and passing away is an apt metaphor for writing a book about the Internet and e-democracy. As we wrote this manuscript, the Internet continually expanded and morphed as did its political uses—they became and passed away before our very eyes. We are greatly indebted to those who kept us anchored amidst a dynamic intellectual sea. First, our collective thanks go to the editorial staff at Ashgate Publishing for their patience and advice. And thanks as well to the anonymous reviewers of this manuscript who provided expert suggestions to improve the final product.

Michael Margolis thanks the University of Cincinnati (UC) and Professor Joel Wolfe, Political Science Department Head, for providing the facilities and support to complete this research; additional thanks to Sally Moffitt, Head of the UC Library's Social Sciences Reference and Research Services, for the help she has provided with this and related projects over the years. Finally, thanks (in the first person) to my wife, Elaine Camerota, whose patience, encouragement and editorial advice are just a few reasons why she is the first person in my life.

Gerson Moreno-Riaño thanks Regent University and the Office of the Vice President for Academic Affairs, Regent University, for a research grant that greatly facilitated the completion of this project; additional thanks to Hanisha Besant and Crystal Pough for their research assistance as well as to Augustina Amakye for all of her help in the copy editing of the final version of the manuscript. Special thanks to the staff at the University Library, Regent University, and especially to Harold Henkel, Reference Librarian, for all of his expert assistance. Lastly, a very special thank you to my wife Ellen whose continued love, support, and patience never cease to amaze me—*nihil amori iniuriam est.*

Michael Margolis
University of Cincinnati

Gerson Moreno-Riaño
Regent University

Introduction

The adage that you never can step into the same river twice applies to any attempt to describe the current state of the Internet. The Internet's information flow, augmented by ever increasing rainfalls of data, constantly alters people's knowledge of public affairs and more broadly the political relations of citizens within and between societies, much as a river's flow constantly alters the depth of its channels and the topography of the surrounding shore. *The Prospect of Internet Democracy* aims to draw back from the shore and to discern how the flow is altering the political landscape. What changes has the Internet wrought, how have these changes affected the conduct of democratic politics, and what are their likely consequences for democratic politics in the future?

Politics comprises one of the key avenues through which people define themselves and their cultures. Yet politics itself is continually re-defined through human interaction and cultural influences. Advances in digital technologies affect the transactional process between politics and culture. Indeed, numerous scholarly and popular observers contend that politics has ceased to be local and boundary-centered. It is now global and universal. Moreover, citizens have become active consumers and "shoppers" of political commodities rather than passive recipients of political goods. Governmental bureaucracies in turn have assumed more "customer service" orientations in order to satisfy their citizens' demands. The concept of democratic citizenship is also changing from its nation-centered roots to a more transcendent "Globalism." As such, the Internet holds promise for bringing about a broader political community with increased international solidarity, and greater human empowerment.

Others, however, contend that this promise is unlikely to be fulfilled. These observers argue that established powers (e.g., governmental officials, CEOs of multinational corporations, media moguls, leaders of mainstream political parties, interest groups and religious organizations) have captured key elements of the Internet. They "own" its backbone, they determine how citizens can access the Net, and they monitor citizens' usage. They also maintain a great deal of influence over the "independent" rule-making bodies and the protocols that all users must follow. In short, the Internet provides them with another tool that they can use to direct and control politics. As a consequence these observers expect that the Internet will lead neither to significantly greater empowerment of the people nor to significant furtherance of democratic politics.

Scholarly and popular observers who hold conflicting visions of the Internet's likely impact on democratic citizenship tend to talk past one another. Those who remain optimistic generally see the Web 2.0's interactive and broadband features as providing the information and communication technologies (ICTs) necessary for professional public administrators to assure efficient delivery of governmental goods and services to citizens in accordance with transparent rules and regulations. Elected officials and bureaucrats can employ these ICTs to exchange relevant information with their peers as well as with the citizens individually or in groups. As a bonus these exchanges cut costs by reducing duplication of records and services among agencies and increase satisfaction by giving administrators better feedback regarding the effectiveness of the policies and services. Governmental services can be rendered with the efficiency and panache of much admired customer oriented business models. Although this vision emphasizes aspects of "e-governance" over a more participatory vision of "e-democracy," advocates point out that citizens participate indirectly in rule-making through feedback to administrators as well as periodic election of representatives who determine the policies and oversee how administrators implement the rules and regulations.

Critics disparage this bureaucratic e-democracy model as barely changing the status quo. In their view, the model ignores the crucial concern that modern democracies ought to encourage citizens to employ new ICTs to deliberate and determine which policies and services governments *should* provide. Using ICTs to encourage greater citizen participation in deciding policies would be the very embodiment of robust political engagement. If citizens of a democracy are supposed to exercise the ultimate authority to choose and to dismiss those who decide the great political issues, shouldn't their roles in governance be more than those of customers? Businesses, after all, encourage customers to satisfy their private demands and those of persons or groups they hold dear. They generally do not ask them to consider how their private transactions might help or hinder resolving broader problems that affect the quality of life—perhaps even the survival—of their society as a whole. For these critics little will change unless or until democratic theorists figure out how to use ICTs successfully to implement deliberative policy processes in which all interested citizens can readily participate.

This book examines the empirical and philosophical arguments that engage the strengths and/or weaknesses of these two visions. It also looks at the extent to which changes in ICTs like those associated with Web 2.0 require that western democratic theorists revise not only the 18th century institutions associated with democratic governance, but also the philosophical assumptions that those institutions were designed to implement. Modern democratic political institutions in the western tradition, for instance, incorporate philosophical assumptions of the Enlightenment. These include faith in citizens' ability to think logically and rationally, and the belief that they will exercise their reason for the general good, not merely for their own selfish gain. In a globalized world where citizens of non-western democratic tradition far outnumber those of established democracies, and where citizens of western democracies increasingly prefer flashy multimedia presentations based on Internet ICTs to complex logical arguments based upon printed words, the assumptions of the Enlightenment may be obsolete. Similarly, in a global community where governmental, corporate, and other interest groups, as well as clever—and often nefarious—individuals can monitor virtually any citizen's activities, democratic assumptions about personal privacy may need revision.

While many positions lie between these opposing visions regarding the distribution of political power, each encapsulates moral and empirical considerations. For instance, persistent socioeconomic inequalities within and among polities produce differential rates—digital divides—that hold back poor and otherwise disadvantaged citizens from access to and adoption of ICTs. These inequalities are compounded by diverse societal norms that hinder democratic deliberation and participation, such as traditional dominance of men over women regarding public affairs, or of well established political, economic, ethnic and religious groups' resources and abilities to use ICTs to mobilize their members and to sway public opinion. Another hindrance stems from the ongoing replacement of traditional mass media that provided common sources of general information and viewpoints about public affairs with more narrowly focused partisan media like Newscorp's Fox News Channel, *The Wall Street Journal*, MSNBC or *Al Jazeera* or even with ideological forums like Townhall.com or Huffingtonpost.com. Given the propensity of busy users to prefer short message services (such as Twitter), video clips, instant messaging via social networks and the like to traditional discourse, the public commons of the future may consist mostly of audio/video clips augmented with graphic designs and PowerPoint outlines. The ability to read or to write a clearly articulated logical argument, much less a scholarly essay, may soon become a quaint reminder of the ancient pre-digital era.

In fairness, even though the popular inception of the Internet stems only from the introduction of graphic browsers in 1994, the exponential growth of users and types of usage, the scale of technological innovation, and the rapidity of events threaten to render social scientific observations—let alone generalizations—outdated before they can be published in print. It follows that researchers, journalists and other social observers need to augment books, magazines, newspapers and other printed publications with digitized media that include text, audio, video, and graphics. Nevertheless, we must remember that oratory and graphics originated with, and still remain the fundamental means of mass communication for illiterate and semiliterate peoples. Their content cannot (as yet) replicate or replace the complex properties of written language.

We employ several strategies to meet these research problems. First, we assume that most readers are familiar with the Internet's basic characteristics and have some experience using it. Second, rather than overburden readers with multitudes of citations, we point out major sources—online and offline—that compile and update the latest empirical and theoretical social scientific studies of politics and the Internet. Third, we utilize the observations, interpretations and generalizations of researchers who preceded us in order to discern these patterns. Fourth, we rely upon classical theories of democracy to inform and structure our own interpretations, theories and expectations about the prospects of democratic governance.

We invite readers to draw back from the minutiae of everyday usage and join our quest to discern behavioral patterns within an ever-changing online environment.

Chapter 1

The Internet and the Prospect of Democracy

Does the Internet Foster Democracy?

The Internet is the stuff of dreams. It has sparked visions of a new information economy in which citizens enjoy unprecedented levels of prosperity and democracy, and it has been hyped as the means to realize both. In this work we explore the prospect that the Internet will enable the USA, and eventually the world, to realize these long sought goals. The enthusiasm for the Internet's revitalization of democratic politics stems from two expectations:

1. Public officials will use the Internet's information and communication technologies (ICTs) to elicit citizen input about public policy decisions and to deliver public services with greater equity and efficiency; and
2. Citizens will use ICTs to acquire knowledge about civic affairs and public policies and to organize themselves to communicate effectively to policy makers their informed opinions and desires.

But what do we mean by prosperity and democracy? While dictionary definitions of "prosperity" usually refer to general good fortune, we commonly use the word to denote wealth and affluence. In contrast, even though dictionary definitions of "democracy" usually emphasize government by the people, exercised either directly or through elected representatives, in popular parlance we use the word as a catchall for nearly everything that is good or desirable in society. For many, democracy is not merely one criterion among others that we use to adjudge an ideal society: it *is* the ideal society. Americans in particular often proclaim that democracy facilitates—perhaps even produces—widespread prosperity. People's conceptions of democracy generally incorporate whatever values they yearn for, whether these values entail justice, freedom, liberty, religion, equality, community, prosperity, or some other desiderata. Scratch beneath the surface of these values, however, and great differences emerge. Does justice include capital punishment for criminals? Does freedom mean people seeking work can move to wherever they can find employment both within and across national boundaries? Does liberty include the right to post whatever one pleases on the Internet? Virtually every society values religion, but are all types of religiosity (or atheism) tolerable? Notwithstanding the complexities these differences entail, people ask: "How can a nation call itself a democracy if it fails to promote our particular list of cherished values?"

Obviously, we cannot resolve these questions in this chapter nor even in this book. We can begin to evaluate how the Internet affects a nation's politics, however, by considering a less exalted notion of democracy. An ideal society implies perfection, a worthy but unreachable goal. To start with, therefore, we will use a conception of democracy that reflects its dictionary definitions. We will consider democracy as a method of governing an association, a form of governance through which the people rule by means of political procedures upon which they commonly agree. We view rule by the people as a necessary, but hardly sufficient, condition for an ideal society. Unfettered majority rule, for instance, can be used to suppress the opinions and values of those in the minority. Finding an agreeable balance between the power of democratically designated majorities to rule but still preserve the power of opposing minorities to replace them leaves a great number of social and political values and procedures to explore.[1]

Political theorists who emphasize democratic procedures for decision-making argue that such procedures should provide all adult citizens with substantially equal opportunity for effective participation in politics. "Effective participation" implies participation that demonstrably has more than a negligible probability of influencing the outcomes toward which that participation is directed. Voting in an election in which no candidates appear on the ballot other than those nominated by a governing elite, for instance, does not constitute effective participation. Neither does expressing an opinion about any question of public concern for which the most relevant data remain classified as secret or otherwise as the exclusive property of a governmental or technological elite (Dahl 1989, 106-118; Margolis 1979, 156).

The procedures must presume modern governmental institutions that are capable of dealing responsibly with complex problems in a democratic fashion. That means citizens or their elected representatives must be able to control governmental bureaucracies, the military and large private corporations, whose officers are not directly responsible to the people. This power should include both the ability to protect traditional liberal democratic concerns, such as guarantees of due process or enforcement of contracts, as well as the ability to address informational, social and economic concerns, such as setting standards for protecting sensitive personal and governmental data and for utilizing human labor and natural resources. Otherwise unelected bureaucrats, military leaders, and corporate officers can freely exploit their informational and economic advantages to dominate a nation's governance.

American democracy has emphasized liberal values like individual freedom and liberty for all. Liberal democratic procedures, therefore, should facilitate

1 There is of course a large literature on the moral basis for "democratic values" deriving from (God-given) natural law/natural rights discoverable by faith or reason. Social contract theory also arises from the idea of people forming societies and governments in order to protect these rights. For classical statements see John Locke's *Second Treatise on Civil Government* (first published in 1690) and Jean-Jacques Rousseau's *Social Contract* (first published in 1762). For an overview, see Barker (1960).

diverse lifestyles and individual self-development. While individual liberties must accommodate the social concerns of others and the limitations of the society's natural resources, liberal democracies are distinguishable from those that consistently rank communal values over individual concerns. When communal values preclude the ability of ordinary citizens to place alternatives they favor onto the political agenda for public consideration, or when only an elite sets the political agenda, liberalism is absent.

Lastly, democratic procedures must not demand a level and quality of participation that exceeds people's capabilities and willingness to participate. Reformers who desire to "improve" these procedures must take into account social science research results about citizens' knowledge, attitudes and behavior regarding public affairs.[2]

To what extent have these procedures been put into practice? The USA tends to present itself internationally as an exemplar of democracy, but like any human society it falls short of fulfilling its democratic ideals. Many who recognize the imperfections of American and other self-proclaimed democratic governments have looked to the Internet as a means for remedying their procedural and institutional flaws (Chadwick 2003 and 2006; Watson and Mundy 2001). In truth, our hopes that the Internet's powerful capabilities would improve the conduct of democratic politics in the United States and possibly throughout the world originally inspired our research.

Two aspects of democratic theory suggest that American society is inadequately democratic. The first concerns the process by which the American political system implements popular rule. While the process formally embodies the rule of law and the values of a democratic constitution, its practices are largely controlled by socially and economically privileged elites. Citizens have the right to participate in politics, but many believe their participation is ineffective and they choose not to participate (Sullivan and Riedel 2001). To make matters worse, many who chose to participate either lack the knowledge to act rationally and responsibly or find that the elites control access to the information necessary to acquire that knowledge. (Barber 1984 and 2007; Fishkin 1992; Gilens 2001). Scholars and critics who favor widespread but limited democratic participation see the Internet as a vehicle for educating citizens to make more informed choices among competing slates of leaders (for example, Kobayashi 2006; Kaye and Johnson 2002). Those who favor widespread active participation look to the Internet as a vehicle for providing information on demand sufficient for citizens to make informed policy choices (for example, Deibert 2000; Coleman and Gøtze 2002). In either case the Internet holds the prospect of improving democratic governance.

---

2 On the general problem of melding democratic theory and practice, see Duncan (1983) and Dunn (1999). On recent trends in political behavior, see Caplan (2007); Pew (2007) and European Commission (2008). We shall have more to say about this in later chapters.

The second aspect concerns the scope of democracy itself. The Internet advances the prospect of extending and deepening citizens' involvement in public affairs. Why restrict democratic participation to formal aspects of governmental decision-making? Why not use the Internet to extend democracy to other areas of decision-making, which heretofore were considered private, yet demonstratively have profound effects on civil society? The affluence of modern society supposedly fosters individualism, yet people turn over control of significant areas of their lives to assorted professionals and bureaucrats. For example, to what extent can a government call itself a democracy yet remain largely indifferent toward regulating the decision-making processes of giant corporations like Wal-Mart, Exxon-Mobil, American International Group (AIG) or Toyota?

The Internet provides opportunities to create innumerable virtual communities in which the people can take charge of various aspects of their own lives and work out their own collective fates. These range from creating online extensions of real world organizations to creating new interest groups online that can reach out to the real world. Social networks can range from gargantuan communities like Facebook and MySpace to modestly sized family groups. Cyberspace also allows people to create new identities that are recognized almost exclusively in virtual communities like Second Life. People can control aspects of their personalities in online communities that were never thought subject to individual choice. Some theorists claim that democracy online is often superior to the mundane democracy available in the real world. "The cybercitizens of virtual communities can establish forms of interaction and self-government that are more meaningful to the participants than citizenship is in either ethnically or territorially bounded nation-states" (Vandenberg 2000, 289). While mundane reality has always frustrated those who sought the democratic ideal, perhaps they have been looking in the wrong place. The Internet and related ICTs present limitless arenas within which each citizen can realize the democratic prospect (Castronova 2005, 205-226).

To what extent can these virtual communities overcome democracy's limitations? Why, despite all efforts to promote democracy, do great swaths of our common physical and social environments remain exempt from the democratic will? Traditionally the nation state has been the locus of democratic practice. Democracy tries to control the power of the state, but what if the state is subject to forces beyond itself, to the flows of international capital and freewheeling transnational corporations? Can hundreds of millions—potentially billions—of e-citizens use the Internet to organize popular pressure to meet the challenges of the international political economy?[3] Can the Internet serve to extend democracy beyond the nation-state?

3 See *Internet World Stats* <http://www.internetworldstats.com/stats.htm> for current estimates of Internet users.

The Democratic Process

The procedures alluded to in the previous section represent a first approximation of a democratic process of governance. Robert Dahl, a leading political scientist and democratic theorist, has influenced our view. He argues that for a process to be truly democratic, it must meet five criteria. There must be *effective participation*. By this he means that all the members must have a chance to make their views known about a proposed policy before it is adopted.[4] There must be *voting equality*. Each member must have an equal chance to vote, and all votes need to be counted honestly, accurately and equally. There must be *enlightened understanding*. This means that all members must have an opportunity for learning about alternative policies and their possible outcomes. The members must have *control over the [political] agenda*, and membership must be based upon the *inclusion of adults*. Dahl argues that nearly every permanent adult resident should have full citizenship rights as delineated by the first four criteria. He also observes that this last criterion was not acceptable to most advocates of democracy before the twentieth century (Dahl 1998, 37-38).[5]

Effective Participation

We need not agree with Dahl's understanding of these criteria to find them useful and suggestive. For example, some critics of contemporary American democracy argue that *effective participation* means more than simply the right to make one's views known. Effective participation requires not merely a chance, but rather an equal chance to voice those views. But what constitutes "an equal chance" in modern society? The right of free speech affirms people's right to air their views, but the overwhelming majority does not exercise this right. In contrast, the views of some are not just voiced, but also amplified millions of times via the mass media. Critics of modern democratic practice point out that the marginalized in society—the poor, various ethnic, racial and religious minorities, and women—suffer from this lack of political equality. The problem of inequality is exacerbated when we consider the enormous divide between the resources available to citizens of rich versus poor nations (Norris 2001). The principle of political equality is violated when effective participation is denied to so many.

The Internet has been heralded as a way of creating a space in which all voices get an equal chance to be heard, and all views can be expressed effectively. Technically, for a modest investment every citizen can become his or her own publisher. All

4 This characteristic actually reflects the Roman legal principle, *quod omnes tangit debet ab omnibus approbari* (what touches all should be approved by all) that was later incorporated into medieval canon law.

5 Certain groups of adults, such as incarcerated felons, the mentally ill or mentally incapacitated are of course excluded from full participation.

one needs is an Internet Service Provider (ISP) and a digital communication device with which to access the Net. One can use the Net to communicate with many others simultaneously as well as asynchronously, a feature that facilitates group organization and coordination. Moreover, as the information packets that comprise each user's communications traverse the Internet, the transmission control protocols assures that they are treated equally and relayed without regard to their contents, origins or destinations (Margolis and Resnick 2000, 25-52). While this "Net Neutrality" represents good news for democrats who advocate equal opportunities for extensive political participation, it does not sit so well with commercial Network Service Providers that own and operate most of the major routers and backbone connections, which provide the Internet capacity that ISPs purchase. They would rather establish something akin to tiered levels of service, where well-heeled users can pay ISPs to give their information packets priority.[6]

Out of the welter of democratic theories we can distinguish two major models: classical democratic theory and elite democratic theory. Classical democratic theory envisions democracy as a form of self-government that entails the public's direct participation in political life on an ongoing basis. It harks back to the understanding of democracy in ancient Athens where citizens were seen as active participants in their polity's collective fate. In contrast, elite democratic theory describes democracy as essentially a system of government in which political leaders periodically appeal to citizens who have the right to chose those who will govern them. As Joseph Schumpeter, a leading exponent of this view, put it, "the democratic method is that institutional arrangement for arriving at political decisions in which individuals acquire the power to decide by means of a competitive struggle for the people's vote" (Schumpeter 1950, 269). Elite democratic theory claims to be more realistic than classical theory, and more suited to modern conditions of mass society and representative government. It assumes that citizens act mostly as consumers of public policies. Rather than creating the policies directly, they prefer to elect those who they believe will create the policies they favor. Elite democratic theory tries to explain how responsible and responsive government, which has long been the aim of democratic theory, can be realized without requiring citizens' direct active participation in governmental decision-making.

---

6 As *Wikipedia* ("Net Neutrality," 2008) defines it, "Network neutrality (equivalently net neutrality, Internet neutrality, or simply NN) refers to a principle that is applied to residential broadband networks, and potentially to all networks. Precise definitions vary, but a broadband network free of restrictions on the kinds of equipment that may be attached, on the modes of communication allowed, which does not restrict content, sites or platforms, and where communication is not unreasonably degraded by other communication streams, would be considered neutral by most observers." Zuckerman and McLaughlin (2003) provide an overview of the Internet's structure and network "peering" arrangements. *Savetheinternet.com* (2008) tracks the ongoing controversy.

Dahl's understanding of effective participation leans more towards classical democratic theory, but it is still compatible with elite theory. Effective participation can mean that the citizens have a right to publicly express their views about politics, to tell political parties and political leaders what policies they would prefer prior to elections. In fact modern political leaders are highly attuned to what the people prefer. An entire industry has developed that attempts to discern public opinion. For advocates of classical democratic theory, however, making views known by speaking to pollsters, voicing opinions through mass media or contacting officeholders or office-seekers is inadequate. "Real" effective participation means taking an active role in policy making. Participation cannot be limited to expressions of opinion and voting (Chadwick 2006, 83-113; Berthon and Williams 2007).

Unless citizens engage directly in the political process, classical democrats believe that politics cannot yield the psychological and moral benefits that a democracy should provide. Considerations such as these lead to the belief that the Internet can renew democracy. Citizens can do more to affect public policy than simply to choose one set of candidates over another. They need not be passive spectators to distant contests that may hold little meaning for them. Citizens can learn about policy alternatives, and they can debate them with fellow citizens. The Internet creates an accessible public sphere for citizenship where deliberations can raise the quality of public discourse. For advocates of the classical ideal of active political participation, the Internet demonstrates that we need not accept the limited view of participation prescribed by elitist democrats. Elite theories of democracy may not be as realistic as their adherents believe.

Anthony Downs, in his model of democracy, modified Schumpeter's elite model. He elaborated upon how competition among political parties provides the means by which people can exercise the power to decide upon questions of public concern. Political parties, by offering slates of candidates who articulate competing principles and policies, enable citizens to use their votes to express their policy preferences effectively. If we accept Downs' focus on the centrality of party competition for democracy, then the principle of political equality entails not only that each citizen has the right to participate equally, but also that each political party or group has the right to espouse popular principles and to compete in a fair and equitable manner (Downs 1957; Dudley and Gitelson 2002; Lowi 1994; Schattschneider 1942). If the voices of a few major parties drown out the appeals of minor parties or groups, electoral competition is rigged and the democratic process is defective.[7]

The elite theory of democracy raises another problem. Democracy means popular rule, but the business of formulating public policies and implementing them actually is done by the government in power. In a modern mass democracy such things are done in the name of the people and hopefully for the people, but

7 Consider Democrats and Republicans in the USA or Labourites and Conservatives in the UK, for example.

most assuredly, they are not done by the people. Elite theory denies that the gap between the people and the officials who carry on governmental business can be eliminated in any populous modern nation. Through voting in elections or through voicing opinions to governmental officials, people can provide input for making public policies, but they cannot implement them. What may have been possible in democratic city-states of the ancient world is impossible in the mass societies of today.

Many adherents of classical democratic theory believe that the Internet can permit the people to rule more directly than they do now, but few believe that the people can make decisions collectively and then take actions on a continuing basis to carry out their decisions. Their hope is to assure that democratic government responds to the will of its citizens, a hope that is compatible with some elite theories of democracy. Democratic governments must be accountable to the people, and classical and elite models both assume that the people will hold public officials responsible for their actions. Elections are the most visible public occasions when the people exercise their power to call their leaders to account, but there are other occasions and other ways to make government more responsive.

Dahl describes the democratic process in terms of popular participation in formulating public policy, but governing is more than making political decisions. Forging a responsive government requires more than bending to the popular will at regularly scheduled elections or at extraordinary times of great national debates about issues and policies; it also requires continuous adjustments and refinements. Much democratic theorizing has focused on the input side of governance, concentrating on the process of translating popular will into authoritative decisions, laws, and policies. But citizens also must deal with the output side of government.

Citizens of a democracy are both rulers and subjects. They have the ultimate power to decide the great political issues of the day, but they are also subject individually to the authority they wield collectively. As subjects they face the authoritative rule of officials and bureaucrats. Governments enforce laws and implement public policies. They collect information and taxes, and they distribute permissions and benefits. How genuine is a democracy in which the citizens are collectively all powerful, but individually subject to capricious, rude, or indifferent treatment? Democratic citizens should expect their government to be responsive to them in their everyday transactions with it. Considerations such as these have led theorists to extend the idea of democratic responsiveness to the administration of governmental policies. Citizens are not only franchise holders who ultimately exercise political power; they also are the government's clients and customers (Jaeger 2003; Howard 2001; Weling and Wei 2004; West 2007).

Reformers have seen the Internet as a means of moving toward the ideal of responsive democratic governance in the area of public administration. They view the burgeoning presence of government on the Internet as an attempt to respond to citizens as clients and customers. They believe that conducting public business online provides many of the same advantages as conducting private business online. Information can be accessed and services can be delivered at the convenience of the citizen. No standing in line at a government office, no trying to reach a bureaucrat by telephone, no waiting for forms to arrive in the mail. Just as the Internet has brought dramatic changes to e-commerce, so advocates of e-government, the provision of governmental information and services online, see the Internet as a way to modernize the public sector and democratize the relationship between individual citizens and their government. (See West 2005, Appendixes I-III.)

Voting

While political participation in general is a contested concept in democratic theory in that people mean different things by it, we might expect that voting as a particular form of political participation would generate less controversy. Yet the right to vote has been a prime focus of the struggle for extending democracy. When the U.S. Constitution was written, the franchise belonged almost exclusively to white property-owning male citizens. In time property requirements were eliminated, and eventually the franchise was extended to blacks, women and Native Americans. If a functioning democratic process simply requires laws that decree equal and effective opportunity for all citizens to vote and that all votes count equally, then for the most part the United States has achieved it. As the disputes about the casting and counting of ballots in the Presidential elections of 2000 through 2008 aptly illustrate, however, the conduct of American elections is far from perfect. And while nearly everyone supports refining the mechanics of voting in principle, implementing systems that assure the fairness and reliability in registering voters, casting ballots, and tallying outcomes remains controversial (HAVA 2002; Caltech/MIT 2008).

The American situation is not an isolated case. Studies show that voter turnout in numerous countries around the world has been in decline since the mid-1980s. Moreover; this decline includes both "new" and "established" democracies (López-Pintor and Gratschew 2002). If voting is the central symbolic and political act in a democracy, how can the USA and other countries be called democracies when, in some cases, barely half the eligible voters cast ballots in national elections, the fundamental occasions when the public demonstrates its power? Proponents of classical democracy argue that once security problems are resolved, the convenience of voting online at home, at work, or in accessible public places can make it so easy to vote that nearly every eligible can easily take part (Alvarez and Hall 2004).

Classical democrats believe that the people can, and ought to play a greater role in determining the course of public policy. They question the assumption that voting should be restricted to choosing political leaders who in turn choose policies. It is well and good to say that democracy requires voting equality, but on what should the people vote? In the 19th and 20th centuries the main struggle for democracy was to include all citizens equally in the electoral process. One of the great efforts of the progressive period was to get the initiative, referendum and recall. Why not make the 21st century the one in which citizens will at last extend the power of their ballot to more and more political issues?

Those who feel that democracy requires more power to the people than they exercise under existing election rules see the Internet as a way of extending democracy. Why must citizens rely so heavily upon political representation when it is possible for them to vote on policies directly?[8] Why can't we extend the fight for democracy that animated the Progressives? The Internet can free us from the sorts of constraints that were necessary when communications and transportation were primitive and inefficient. We could not expect our forebears to devise a true system of popular democracy when it was impossible to assemble a large citizenry in one place at one time. Cyberspace eliminates the problem of geographical location, however, and the Internet provides instantaneous communication. Citizens can access all the politically relevant information they need to make wise and informed decisions. A new agora awaits, a democratic public sphere created by technology. It is not just utopian fantasists who are enamored of the democratic potential of new technology. Presidential candidate Ross Perot pledged to give more power to the people by adopting a form of teledemocracy. Dick Morris, political commentator and former adviser to President Bill Clinton, champions using the Internet to conduct continuous online polls. President Barack Obama has converted his official campaign website into "Organizing for America" and similarly updated his YouTube channel, his Facebook and MySpace pages.[9] Internet polling, cyber-democrats argue, can shift power to the people and away from political elites and the powerful interest groups with whom many of them are allied (Etzioni 1992; Morris 1999; Schudson 2000). And such global efforts as that of e-democracy, headed by Steven Clift, seek to build local democratic initiatives and expand online citizen engagement not only in the USA but also in the UK and New Zealand through a number of ICT strategies and tools. As we approach universal access to the Internet, how—and upon what—citizens should vote seem likely to remain contested issues, especially between those who adhere to the purest forms of classical and elite democracy.

Enlightened Understanding

One of the common arguments against democracy has been that ordinary people—the masses if you will—are too ignorant to be trusted with the power to rule. Most people are by nature creatures of appetite who fail to see the long-term consequences

8 Urbinati (2006) and Mansbridge (2003) defend representation as intimately related to a sound democratic life.

9 The extent to which the websites will be used for two-way communication remains to be seen.

of their actions. Whenever a governing elite has proposed making concessions to include a greater portion of the people, those who oppose broadening democracy have trotted out this argument in one form or another. Proponents of democracy have always assumed that the people are wise enough to exercise their power in a responsible manner. The notion of enlightened understanding as a criterion for a truly democratic process, therefore, points to the importance of education for all. To provide "education for all" in the modern world, however, requires—at the very least—a commitment of public resources sufficient to overcome the disadvantages that economic inequalities inflict upon the children of the poor (Dewey 1916, 94-115; U.S. Dept. of Education 2006; Carey 2008).

Most agree that participants in a democratic process need opportunities for learning about alternative policies and their consequences. But exactly what does this mean in the real world where deciding complex political issues require informed sophisticated judgments? Can the participants understand them? Democracy requires that the people be educated, but how much education is enough? Advocates believe that widespread access to the Internet will bring enlightened understanding by lowering the cost of higher education and making it available to those who otherwise would have to work inordinate hours in low paying jobs to earn tuition. Why must the best education be limited to the wealthy who have the time and resources to devote a significant portion of their young lives to study? Can't ordinary citizens make use of networked ICTs to further their own education? In fact, frequent retraining and updating of skills have become necessities in the 21st century world of constant innovation. Education already can be accessed on a 24/7 basis via the Net. People can enroll in a variety of courses throughout the year to accord with their individual schedules. When these developments become commonplace, won't that finally realize the democratic dream of an educated citizenry, able to rule themselves and function in an increasingly complex world?

Yet even if people are capable of understanding alternative policies and their consequences, will they be able to exercise informed judgment under contemporary conditions? Critics claim that most people cannot get the information they need in order to make crucial political decisions. The information is controlled by government itself or by special interests that dominate traditional media. Proponents of classical democracy see the Internet as a source of politically relevant information that can prevent powerful elites from manipulating and distorting the will of the people. The Internet enables ordinary citizens to gather information for themselves without relying on commercial news organizations, special interest groups, governmental officials and traditional political parties. Classical democrats argue that citizens who possess politically relevant information, unfiltered by these elites, will increase their levels of political participation, realign the balance of power between rulers and the people, and move closer to achieving enlightened political understanding. They see the popularity of political blogs as a promising step in this direction. (See Lenhart and Fox 2006 and Internet Public Library 2008).

Control over the Political Agenda

While initiatives, referenda and recalls give citizens power over important aspects of the political agenda, exercising these powers requires mass support. Such support usually remains beyond the reach of marginalized groups, which the democratic formula of majority rule continually consigns to minority status. These include gays and lesbians, undocumented immigrants, members of unpopular social groups and ethnic minorities, atheists, adherents of peculiar religious dogmas and felons who have served their time.[10] Ironically, mainstream groups sometimes use their agenda-setting power to undercut the rights of these marginalized minorities. In recent years majorities in various American cities and states have voted to deny some of these groups protection from discrimination in jobs, housing, and marriage benefits, or to deny them access to medical care or public education. Minorities in the USA and some European nations have been forced to support the mainstream's religious principles, symbolically through icons placed (or forbidden) in public spaces or concretely to programs that appropriate their tax dollars. Mainstream groups in the USA have also initiated recalls to remove elected judges whose decisions have protected the rights of unpopular minorities.

The Internet has the potential to alleviate some of these problems. Minorities can develop and organize support for proposals they favor by taking advantage of its relatively inexpensive communication capabilities. They can pool their resources and coordinate their efforts via the Internet in order to tap into support from established groups. If members of the minority coalition can demonstrate that their relatively small numbers are nonetheless widespread, this can be effective in breaking down their separation from the mainstream (Noelle-Neumann 1992).

Critics of American culture contend that privileged groups control the mass media and dominate public discourse and popular culture. They argue that people of color, women, the poor and other disadvantaged groups can use the Internet to foster stronger self-identities and group consciousness. Heightened identity and consciousness will enhance their ability to recognize potential allies, build alliances and mobilize coalitions via the Internet in order to overcome the cultural hegemony of the privileged (Chadwick 2006, 289-316; Graber 2006, 33-55; Norris 2001, 17-21).

Regardless of whether we have mainstream or marginalized groups in mind, the Internet affects which questions of public policy are considered. If, as some critics allege, media moguls, managers of multi-national corporations, and leaders of military and civilian bureaucracies control access to information from traditional sources, then the Internet remains one of the few independent sources that is critical for citizens' enlightened understanding of public problems. The people can rule democratically only if they or their elected representatives have sufficient

---

10 In most states those convicted of a felony forfeit their right to vote for the duration of their sentence, including probation and parole. In eleven states they forfeit the right to vote for life (Dudley and Gitelson 2002, 14-15).

information to determine the problems that need to be addressed and the policies that ought to be adopted to solve them. What information should be placed online? Who should control its access, and how? These are fundamental questions that theories of democracy must answer as Internet access becomes ubiquitous.

The Prospect of Internet Democracy in the 21st Century

Extensive claims have been made about how the Internet changes nearly everything, including politics. Enthusiasts have speculated that this medium will at long last eliminate the dominance of the established mass media, create an engaged and active citizenry, and redistribute power in more egalitarian ways. They assert that we should free democratic theorizing from the constraints of advanced industrial or post-industrial society and replace liberal democratic pluralism with direct democracy, strong democracy, deliberative democracy or more radical democratic theories. They presume that citizens' desire for and support of participatory forms of democracy includes their willingness to commit the time and to assume the responsibilities that such participation requires.

Our purpose is to examine the likelihood that the Internet will fulfill this promise. It is not too early to tip our hand about this matter. The evidence so far suggests that the radical democratic potential of the Internet will not be realized in the manner that its proponents expect. We acknowledge that the Internet has brought about significant political changes in how national and international politics take place, but we expect that its long term consequences will be more evolutionary than revolutionary. Indeed, we will argue that revolutionary changes in democratic political participation are unlikely to occur not only because they make extraordinary demands upon ordinary citizens but also because the established political elites will use their superior resources to structure the Internet to reinforce the current distribution of political power in manners analogous to those they have used in the past to tame each new mass medium that has appeared.

But we also caution that even if revolutionary changes were realized, the probable consequences would not be as desirable as proponents claim. The bulk of western democratic theory suggests that mass participatory democracy never has existed and that replacing representative institutions with direct democracy has little to recommend it. Representative institutions are not second best, makeshift solutions to the problem of self-rule created in the technological dark ages because it was impossible to assemble everybody and have true direct democracy (Urbinati 2006). We are hard-pressed to find convincing evidence—theoretical or empirical—that millions of e-citizens continually researching, debating and voting on public policies via ICTs would be preferable.[11]

11 Budge (1996) is an exceptional attempt to justify direct democracy both theoretically and empirically.

Looking Ahead

If our aim is to assess the prospect of Internet democracy, our first task is to examine the recent origins of that prospect. Chapter 2 investigates the radical impulse in democracy in order to understand what fostered the belief that Internet democracy would change society profoundly—and change it for the good. Cyber-democrats of this ilk view democracy as more than a set of procedures for determining how people decide their common affairs. Achieving true democracy would fulfill their dreams of an ideal society. What are these dreams, and why has recent speculation focused on the Internet for their realization? Democratic idealists have long envisioned a vital egalitarian society, and for them the Internet represents a means to implement classical participatory democracy.

The advent of the Internet signaled the most significant rebirth of utopian democratic thought since the radicalism of 1960s and 1970s. We trace the intellectual roots of those who believe that Internet democracy will initiate radical change and pay particular attention to the proximate connection to both the "New Left" and the "Counterculture" movements of that time. After the decline of support for such radical change in governing institutions in the United States and Europe proponents of elite democratic theory seemed to have been vindicated. The Internet has revived some of these radical democratic beliefs. We set out the main arguments of those who believe that the Internet will reform and revitalize American democracy, but we also show why these arguments remain highly speculative. True, Internet based ICTs facilitate citizens' access to and communication about (political and non-political) information on virtually any subject. But why should we expect citizens who previously had little interest in participating in political and civic affairs to become political activists just because the Internet makes it easier?

In Chapter 3 we turn to an examination of democratic theories that draw upon elements of radical democratic theories, but attempt to realize classical democratic ideals without promising they will cure all the ills of the world. In their zeal to transform society radicals often show impatience with the niceties of democratic procedures and propose utopian solutions. In contrast, scholars like Jurgen Habermas, Benjamin Barber, James Fishkin and Darrell West attempt to overcome the objections of elite democratic theory by combining new ICTs with democratic procedures.

For the new democratic theory to be more than simply another critique of the inadequacies of modern democracy, it is necessary to turn theoretical arguments into concrete political procedures and practices. The Internet represents a means for transforming democratic participation by creating a new public arena for popular discussion and enlightenment. Yet technical possibility is far from historical inevitability. We argue that despite the sophistication of new democratic theory, the complexities of life in a modern society are likely to vitiate reformist impulses. Well-informed and well-intentioned citizens may still decide not to participate in public affairs because they have more pressing obligations or priorities. But even if the Internet were to move politics in a more populist direction, we question whether the results would prove as salutary as these theorists anticipate.

Regardless of whether it succeeds or fails to create an active participatory citizenry, the Internet could still create a more tolerant society. In Chapter 4 we investigate this potential. Democracy is a means for large numbers of citizens to settle disputes peacefully, and to function smoothly and effectively it requires that citizens respect the rights and opinions of others. Democrats believe that mutual understanding will overcome deep-seated divisions and conflicts. Liberal democratic theory, as classically formulated in the works of John Stuart Mill, asserts that the way to deal with differences is not by repression but by airing them in a public forum. The Internet has become the most accessible forum ever through which people can express the variety of views, opinions and emotions that exist in modern mass societies.

Early advocates of the Internet were very optimistic. Cyberspace would be a realm divorced from the restrictions and censorship of ordinary society, a realm where people could express themselves freely. Access to the Internet would provide something for everybody. It would help resource poor groups to cut communication and organizational costs and thereby allow them to participate more effectively in civil affairs. Political radicals saw it as providing a means to overcome the established media's disdain. Adherents of identity politics thought they could use it to increase group consciousness. But as the Internet has matured its dark side also has emerged.

The Internet, like other ICTs, is an ideologically neutral medium. The same access it provides to adherents of egalitarian, pacifist or socialist values also permits racists, terrorists and hate groups to flourish. Adherents of diversity imagined that the Internet would strengthen the identities and organization of oppressed groups, but it can also strengthen the identities and organization of their oppressors. We must consider the likelihood that the Internet will foster intolerance more than tolerance, that it will facilitate a fragmented politics beset by self-absorbed and narrowly focused groups and individuals who can choose never to talk to one another. Worse yet, their circumscribed goals may lead to criminal or even terrorist activities. The events of September 11, 2001 and their aftermath highlight these dangers. Far from solving the problems of democratic governance, the Internet can be used by anti-democrats who aim to exacerbate those problems and ultimately to destroy democracy altogether.

Uncertainty remains about how—or whether—the Internet will affect overall levels of tolerance, but there remains little doubt that the Internet has already affected how information is disseminated to citizens, both informally to the general population and formally to those enrolled in courses of study. First and foremost, the Internet has been touted as a wonderful new source of information, one that provides ordinary citizens access to field observations, laboratories, and libraries formerly available only to the privileged few. Moreover, compared to other communications media, such as telephone, radio, broadcast and cable television, DVD and the VCR, the household penetration of the Internet has been astonishingly rapid. In Chapters 5 and 6 respectively we consider the Internet's impact on the mass media and education.

As we show in Chapter 5 the optimistic fervor that surrounds the Internet is nothing new. Every mass medium introduced since the Industrial Revolution has occasioned philosophers and pundits to proclaim new opportunities to achieve a more democratic society characterized by an active, informed, enlightened and sophisticated citizenry. The emergence of cheap newsprint, film, sound recording, radio and television in turn would not only provide the populace with information on public affairs but also expose them to foreign cultures and to humanity's great artistic achievements. While each of these media, from the popular press to community access cable television, has had some impact on political and civic life, none has brought about the enlightened democratic participation that its boosters prophesied.

By the time most people have adopted the new medium, the lofty goals of civic enlightenment largely have been cast aside. High production costs favor content that attracts a mass audience to whom investors, advertisers, or sponsors can be sold access. Producers assemble this audience by responding chiefly to popular tastes, not by attempting to raise civic, cultural and educational standards. Popular tastes tend to reflect the prevalent norms, which usually include the unenlightened selfish interests and the vulgar intellectual and artistic preferences that the philosophers and pundits proclaimed the new medium would elevate. We show that the pattern of media usage in cyberspace is no exception. Despite important differences between the Internet and previous communications technologies, especially regarding each user's power to publish or exchange information rather than merely to receive it, the dominant social, political and economic institutions of the real world have largely extended their primacy into cyberspace. Moreover, just as they require those who access their information in the real world to foot a portion of the costs of producing it, so too they strive to charge users for access to their proprietary information in cyberspace (Wingfield 2003). While the battle is hardly over, the evidence suggests that the Internet's impact on who controls the preponderant share of the content and distribution of information regarding public affairs will be far less radical than classical democrats had expected.

Ironically, the plethora of online information sources and related technologies can encourage less rather than more exposure to new information and ideas. Most people have neither the time nor the inclination to gather sufficient information to make intelligent decisions about most questions of public policy. For most of the 20th century they tended to rely upon newspapers, news magazines, broadcast radio and television news, and similar sources that catered to general audiences nationally or within particular regions, states, or localities. The likelihood of inadvertent exposure to information about unexpected topics or discomfiting points of view was always present. Opinionated Internet users have greater ability than previous generations to focus solely upon ideas that reinforce their ideological predispositions: My *Fox News*, My *New York Times,* My religious network, My partisan listservs and My favorite blogs. The Internet means never having to ponder an idea I really don't like.

Regardless of the extent to which the real world institutions predominate in cyberspace, the Internet provides diligent researchers and students with unprecedented access to databases. Chapter 6 examines how the Internet affects public education. The Internet and associated instructional technologies provide the opportunity to alter, enhance and otherwise improve traditional forms of instruction and research. Beyond placing syllabi and assignments online, using e-mail, online discussions and visual presentations can improve communication with traditional students on campus and can also reach new students at a distance. Websites and courseware can deploy digitized audio and video as well as automatic feedback and asynchronous communication for teaching or wikis for facilitating research. Online courses can extend from preschool through postgraduate education. Remote access to digitized libraries and databases can provide resources, both for coursework and for original research, comparable to those once available only at elite governmental, corporate, or university research centers.[12]

In a perfect world these resources would be used to enhance and enrich each student's educational experience from preschool through graduate school. In the real world, however, these technologies provide a means for new enterprises to upset the near monopoly that traditional institutions have enjoyed as providers of education. For better or for worse, these developments may force public institutions to replace their traditional models of research, teaching and service with business models in order to cut their costs. Will extending Internet facilities to all K-12 public schools improve education enough to obviate increasing appropriations for school buildings, textbooks, libraries, or salary and training for teachers and staff? As a new communication technology the Internet holds great promise, but so too did previous technologies, such as slide and overhead projectors, sound recordings, films, radio, television, video and computers. Will governmental institutions, such as state legislatures in the USA, which control the bulk of public funding for education, allocate sufficient money for otherwise poorly financed school districts and poorly endowed post-secondary institutions to adopt the new ICTs and to assess the results? At the post-secondary level, will adopting ICTs for instruction via the Internet provide the means for administrators to respond to pressures from politicians, taxpayers, and students-cum-customers to decrease the cost of delivering higher education? To what extent will new types of higher learning enterprises—private and public; for profit and not-for-profit; national and international—that strive to deliver higher education via the Internet at less cost than traditional institutions succeed? (Arnone 2002; Bromell 2002; NASULGC 2007; Odin and Manicas 2004; Arneberg et al. 2007). Will the liberal democratic ideal that higher education develop the leadership ability and civic character of the students survive the pressures to deploy ICTs primarily to provide students

12 See Arneberg et al. (2007) and Peterson's (2009) and related links for the features of distance learning programs in the European Union and the USA.

with skills to meet the job requirements of the business world? (Resnick 2000). The Internet is likely to force a major reconsideration of how North American and Europe institutions of higher learning operate.

As the Internet would facilitate challenges to traditional educational institutions, especially those devoted to higher education, so too would it facilitate challenges to traditional political parties and interests. Indeed, many classically inclined democrats expected citizens to utilize the new ICTs' capabilities to reshape the balance of power among competing interests in our social and political world. Interaction among citizens in cyberspace would enrich public opinion and bring about more effective participation in democratic politics. In Chapter 7 we examine these expectations.

Advocates of classical democracy point out that Internet-based ICTs afford ordinary citizens opportunities to become their own publishers. Political activists—"netizens" if you will—can employ them to reduce the costs of forming new political groups and building new coalitions. Indeed, as the Internet began to receive popular notice, cyber-democrats like Howard Rheingold, Rhonda and Michael Hauben, and Andrew Shapiro heralded its promise for realizing heretofore utopian visions of informed engagement in political and civic affairs. At the very least, they expected reduced costs of organizing to foster viable new parties and interests to challenge the dominance of traditional political parties and established political interest groups (Hauben, M. and Hauben, R. 1997; Rheingold 1993; Morris 1999; Shapiro 1999).

When we began our studies of the Internet's impact on democratic politics in the early 1990s, we too hoped to see unprecedented levels of intelligent democratic participation. The openness of cyberspace seemed to present a way to liberate electoral and interest group politics from many of the constraints, pressures, conventions and procedures which had made it fall short of the promise of democracy. The practice of democracy online could renew and deepen the conduct of democratic politics in the real world as new political parties and interest groups emerged. Our investigations have made us skeptical that our original hopes will be fulfilled. The evidence indicates that far from political activity in cyberspace revolutionizing the politics of the real world, the established organizational and behavioral patterns of that world have invaded cyberspace. The tactics have changed—for instance major political parties, their candidates and established interest groups use online communications to distribute information, to recruit, organize and mobilize supporters, and to raise a good deal of money—but the distribution of power as measured by amounts of money raised, traffic to websites, ownership of the most popular Web services and the like largely replicates the power structures of the real world (Margolis and Resnick 2000, 53-116).

Notwithstanding its origins as a vehicle for research, originally underwritten by the U.S. Department of Defense, the Internet has become largely a privatized worldwide vehicle for commerce. In Chapter 8 we show that the Internet has facilitated citizens' roles as consumers of government services and policies, but it has done far less to enhance their roles as participants in the formulation of public policy. While many political scientists, philosophers, politicians, and citizen activists have concerns about the Internet's prospects for improving democracy, most people are far more interested in using the Net for personal concerns from everyday shopping to entertainment of the highest and lowest forms. The minority that monitors or participates in politics offline tends to be the same people who monitor or participate in it online. As in the real world, many more people follow news about stock markets, business, sports, weather, crime, scandal, hobbies, entertainment and myriad interests other than politics. People also rely upon the Internet to keep in touch with friends and family or increasingly, to make new "friends."

Most citizens' concerns for the input side of governance—making specific demands or proposing public policies—are largely undeveloped and limited to a narrow range of issues. While government could use the communication capabilities of the Internet to encourage more interaction with and input by citizens, surveys of websites that we review in this chapter indicate that elected officials, legislative committees, and bureaucratic agencies make considerably more effort to communicate information to citizens about public policy than to solicit their participation in public policy formulation.

We find far greater opportunities for citizens to interact with government as customers or consumers of government services than as policy-makers or even policy-reviewers. Government, like most private enterprises on the Net, seeks to use its technical capacities to make it easier for its customers to conduct business. Rules of eligibility and applications for various government services or programs, licenses, and permits, even various forms for filing fees or taxes, obtaining records, registering to vote, and a host of other products and services can be accessed online, downloaded, and in some cases filed via the Internet. Increasingly such usage extends all the way down to local levels. If the privacy of personal information and the security of sensitive records can be assured, we expect that most transactions between citizens and government will take place via the Net.

In our final chapter we assess the implications of the above-described developments for the conduct of democratic politics in the early decades of the 21st century. Our analysis suggests that even though the Internet will hardly revolutionize politics, it will increase the leverage of those citizens who actively participate. While the patterns of dominance on the Net are likely to reflect those of the real world, various measures indicate that the relative strength of this dominance appears to be weaker in cyberspace than in the real world. Citizens will enjoy greater access to governmental information, particularly with regard to the output side of public policy. We are hopeful that citizens will use their own experience regarding the consequences of public policy together with unfettered access to digitized information about those policies to evaluate their leaders' claims of the successes or failures of those policies. And second, we hope that citizens will evaluate the information and will vote to oust incompetent or unscrupulous public officials and return responsible ones. We are doubtful, however, that their influence over the detailed formulation of public policy will increase dramatically. Should the global economy truly encompass all countries, we expect that the Internet will play a significant role in spreading the gospel of democratic prosperity.

Nevertheless, the dark side of the Net cannot be ignored. Just as the Internet can provide citizens with information about public policy, it can provide governments and other powerful interests with information about citizens' private lives. Just as it can provide citizens with the means to communicate their reactions to public policies, so too it can provide the means for governmental officials and other established groups to distort, manipulate or otherwise control accessible information. Realizing this dark potential could produce a totalitarian nightmare like Orwell's *1984* where citizens fear or revere an all-seeing Big Brother, or a seemingly benign hedonistic society like Huxley's *Brave New World*, where a conditioned citizenry happily accepts the existing social order. In short, the institutional arrangements for managing the Net greatly affect the extent to which citizens can use it to exercise democratic control (Gibson, Römmele and Ward 2004, 1-16; Fountain 2001, 193-206).

If the response to expanded terrorism becomes an excuse to impose secrecy or to restrict access to information, the dystopian nightmare of government and big business controlling private stores of information, including intimate details of citizens' every move, could be closer than we think. Worse yet, political leaders could assuage citizens' fears of terrorism by imposing restrictions that destroy the civil liberties that democracy purports to protect.

In the end, we fall back on the Enlightenment philosophers' faith in the collective reason of the people. No set of institutional arrangements can guarantee that citizens fulfill the prospect of democracy through effective political uses of the Net. In the real world a viable democracy requires that its citizens pay attention to the quality of governance and to the consequences of public policies for the polity—online and offline—not merely to how easily they personally receive governmental services and how well public policies affect their personal interests.

Chapter 2
Impossible Dreams: The Radical Roots of Cyber-Democracy

As we mentioned in Chapter 1, the hype that surrounded the initial popularization of the Internet promised a radical renewal of American democracy. The Internet would remake our social and political world. Interaction among citizens in cyberspace would enrich public opinion and increase participation in democratic politics. "Netizens" would employ email, newsgroups, and websites to reduce the costs of forming new political groups and building new coalitions. Activists argued that the reduced costs of organizing would foster viable new parties and interests to challenge the dominance of the Democrats, Republicans and established political interests (Hauben, M. and Hauben, R. 1997; Morris 1999; Rheingold 1993; Shapiro 1999).

When we began to study the Internet's impact on democratic politics, we shared the hopes that cyberspace would inspire more intelligent citizen participation and lead to a renewal of democracy. Now we are more skeptical of realizing these hopes. Instead of revolutionizing the politics of the real world, political activity on the Internet has tended to reflect and reinforce familiar patterns. The real world's political parties and interest groups, together with the candidates, officeholders, and the established public and private institutions they control dominate political activity on the Internet. The World Wide Web, which for many users is synonymous with the Internet, has been largely appropriated by "dot-coms." Cyberspace is replete with heavily advertised websites of familiar commercial enterprises and political interests, websites that mirror their prominence in the business and civic affairs in the real world. In this chapter we investigate why e-democracy has not fulfilled its advocates' expectations.

In the next section we trace briefly the intellectual roots of e-democracy paying particular attention to their proximate connection to both the "New Left" and the "Counterculture" movements of the 1960s and early 1970s. The third section compares the emergence of the Internet as a vehicle for remaking democracy with the cycle of soaring promise and failed fulfillment that each new mass medium has engendered since the Industrial Revolution. We conclude with a discussion of the likely effects of the Internet for the conduct of democratic politics today.

E-Democracy's Roots

Conditions in the 1960s in the USA fostered the growth of two distinct but interrelated radical movements, the New Left and the Counterculture. They shared a number of fundamental values, but had separate political agendas. Both were anti-elitist and egalitarian; they valued openness, sharing, community and cooperation rather than competition. They opposed the manipulation of wants and desires that characterizes a commercial society. Many who participated in them shared similar musical tastes, clothing styles and recreational drugs, but the two movements differed in political strategy. The New Left's notion of participatory democracy was a way for citizens to reestablish control of their lives. Citizens would become aware that their private problems had public causes and political solutions. Americans would shed their apathy and build a new democratic movement for social change. They would transform the bureaucratic, impersonal society that had pacified them. Participatory democracy would provide the means for the people to wrest power and control from the corporate and governmental elite, from the "Establishment."

Adherents of the Counterculture (a.k.a. "New Communalists") also rejected the Establishment, but unlike the radical political activists of the New Left, they did so by dropping out rather than engaging in political struggle.[1] They created alternative communities or communes in which they could live as they pleased, unconstrained by the values, assumptions, material possessions, and the laws that governed the rest of society. They aimed to build a new way of life based on joy and liberation, and a new politics worked out directly by the people themselves without interference from the repressive structures of traditional American society. While the New Left saw themselves as struggling to radically transform American society through organized political activity, the Counterculture saw themselves as subverting society by creating freer and more attractive alternatives.

Of course neither of these movements rose whole like Aphrodite from the foam of the sea. The radicalism of the 1960s had roots in previous radical movements. Many of the early leaders of the New Left were so called "red diaper" babies, children of radicals who had been members of left wing parties and active in the trade union movement. The Students for a Democratic Society (SDS), which issued the Port Huron Statement and helped found the New Left, had ties to the democratic socialist tradition. It was born in 1959 when the Student League for Industrial Democracy (SLID), the campus auxiliary of the League for Industrial Democracy, a socialist group that went back to 1905, changed its name to the SDS (Davis 1996).

The New Left attempted to revive progressive politics after the conformity of the 1950s. A new generation of radicals would leave behind the bitter ideological conflicts of the previous generation, as well as its reliance on the industrial working

1 Turner (2006) traces the roots of the Internet and its cyberculture to the rise and influence of the "New Communalists" over 1960s Countercultural movement.

class as the engine of social change. With the civil rights movement and the idea of non-violent democratic change energizing many students, it was time to challenge the Establishment. Even though it opposed the Cold War and the anticommunist crusade of American liberalism, the New Left did not believe that the Soviet Union was better than the USA, let alone the vanguard of the revolution. Old-fashioned Marxist-Leninist theory could not be applied to American society. The New Left embraced the works of other postwar radicals, such as C. Wright Mills and Herbert Marcuse, one with intellectual ties to American Progressivism and the other to the Frankfurt School.[2]

The New Communalists were also connected with earlier forms of protest. One of their most popular gurus, the poet Alan Ginsberg, came of age as a leading member of the Beat Generation. The Counterculture's rejection of repressive American cultural values also owed much to the revolt against the moral, sexual, and artistic conventions of bourgeois society proclaimed by a variety of 19th and early 20th century European avant-garde movements. To the extent that it tried to establish alternative societies, the Counterculture also owed something to the anarchists and to the Utopian Socialists. While utopianism was an anathema to the Old Left, a deviation to be avoided, the Counterculture gave it a positive spin. To be utopian was to be realistic: one could reject corrupt society, drop out and join a commune (Reich 1971; Roszak 1969).

Seen in hindsight both movements were excessively utopian, and neither produced a radical democratic transformation of American society and politics. The New Left was mostly an avant-garde of campus intellectuals organizing students and poor people to struggle for self-determination and participatory democracy. It never successfully allied itself with organized labor, nor did it develop a third party to challenge the established two party system. As a result, it hardly altered the nature of corporate power in American society, nor did it fundamentally change the established political order. The Counterculture or New Communalists did not create alternative ways of living for the masses, nor did it replace the norms of hard work and conformity.

Yet both movements left their marks on the United States, and by dint of the international prominence of American mass media, they served to bolster political and cultural protests abroad (Tunstall 1977). While it may be difficult to ascertain how much to credit changes to these radical movements and how much to credit other social, political and demographic factors, the United States—at least until the events of September 11, 2001—became a more democratic and inclusive polity than it was in the 1960s, as did Japan, Australia, New Zealand, Mexico, and most European nations where political and cultural unrest also took place in the late 1960s ("1960s," *Wikipedia*; Charlton 2008; Tusa 2008).[3]

2 On American Progressivism as a response to Socialism, see Zinn (1999), 321-358. For an introduction to the Frankfurt School and Critical Theory, see Stephens (1994).

3 See Lichtblau (2008) on the erosion of due process in the United States following Al Qaeda's attacks of September 11, 2001.

Beyond the possible linkage of cultural change and democratic improvement, it seems clear that the New Communalists' values influenced the design of the Internet as well as alternative ways of understanding the relationship between technology, information, community, and human development (Turner 2006; Markoff 2005). The New Left's pursuit of a radical and activist struggle for democracy and the Counterculture's creation of alternative rival models of social order did not become extinct with the end of the 1960s. The desire for liberation, emancipation, and social meaning at the heart of both of these movements was deeply enshrined in the personal computer, the openness of the Internet and the rise of such organizations as the Electronic Frontier Foundation and the WELL (Whole Earth 'Lectronic Link), one of the Internet's first online communities. The Internet's noncommercial beginnings, a paradoxical fusion of "tribal technocracy" and "informatics anarchism," has transformed various aspects of everyday life (Rothstein et al. 2003; Mooney and Evans 2007). In the realm of political and civic affairs, the cyber-democrats of the 1990s and contemporary advocates of e-democracy owe a considerable debt to the radical movements of the 1960s.

Margolis and Resnick (2000) proposed using three categories as a helpful way to think about the influence of the radical movements of the 1960s upon contemporary Internet politics: intra-Net politics or politics within the Net; political uses of the Net; and politics that affects the Net. Politics within the Net encompasses the political life of virtual communities and other identifiable online groups that develop their own norms, regulate their own affairs, and settle their own disputes. We already mentioned the WELL as one of the earliest of these communities (WELL). Moreover, we find that today's vast and growing array of formal and informal networked groups—even centrally directed and commercially underwritten ones like MySpace, Facebook, Friendster or YouTube—still retain aspects of the original community-based intra-Net politics to establish norms for interaction among their members. Political uses of the Net refers to the ways in which the Net can be used by ordinary citizens, political activists, organized interests, political parties and governments to achieve their real world political goals, which often have little to do with the Internet per se. While community networks like the Blacksburg Electronic Village (Virginia), Ennis Information Age Town (Ireland), and E-Democracy.org (USA, UK and New Zealand) exemplify ordinary citizens using the Internet to increase their participation in political and civic affairs, we shall see that established interest groups, familiar mass media, political parties and their affiliates tend to dominate political uses of the Net. Politics that affects the Net refers to the host of public policy issues and governmental actions that arise from the Internet having become a new form of mass communication and a vehicle for commercial activity. The first two types of Internet politics are relevant for sorting out the cyber-democrats' claims for the democratizing potential of the Internet. The last two types are most relevant for explaining why so much of that potential remains unrealized.

Online communities in the early days of the Internet, each with its own intra-Net politics, looked like a reincarnation of the Counterculture. Freedom could be achieved in this new type of space, a virtual state of nature in which people could form their own communities independent of the values, traditions and legal constraints of the ordinary world. Each community would exercise authority over its own domain without need for outsiders to regulate their members' behavior or even to assist them in enforcing the community's rules. In contrast to the corrupt politics of organized special interests of the real world, Intra-Net politics was humanistic, egalitarian, and voluntary. Enthusiasts proclaimed that terrestrial governments should not attempt to extend their jurisdiction into cyberspace. Indeed, some argued that the very structure of the Internet itself made the attempt to impose outside regulation futile.[4]

What the Counterculture had promised, cyberspace could deliver. The lonely, the isolated, the oppressed, those suffering from angst, alienation, and anomie: all could find true homes in cyberspace. Possibilities for liberation arose that were beyond the imagination of the most radical counter-cultural theorists. On the Internet people no longer were restricted to their own bodies and the cultural baggage they carried. Anyone could create a new identity, indeed, a multiplicity of identities. The growth of the Internet came at the time when the American Left was deeply involved with issues of multiculturalism and was fascinated by the possibility of postmodern politics. Virtual communities seemed a viable alternative. For some, the familiar trio of race, class, and gender could be transcended in cyberspace—recall the famous *New Yorker* cartoon of a canine at a monitor proclaiming, "On the Internet, no one knows you're a dog" (Steiner 1993). Others saw the possibility of cyberspace deepening and strengthening identities that were devalued in the real world.

Hopes for change did not rely solely on the expectation that powerful identities could be forged in cyberspace. Activists also saw the Internet as a dynamic tool for consciousness-raising and political organizing in the real world. If citizens were passive because media dominated by corporate elites manipulated them, the Internet could furnish alternative sources of information. Conventional news sources no longer could force citizens to swallow the interpretations of reality they fed to them. A few mouse clicks and ordinary citizens could log on to countless alternative news sources.

But why stop there? The Internet could generate a new public space for a true deliberative democracy, one that enabled citizens to fully participate in democratic politics. Documents and databases would be accessible to all. People could make up their own minds without so-called experts to guide them because they could gather and process information on their own. An informed citizenry could engage

4 John Perry Barlow's widely circulated "A Declaration of Independence of Cyberspace" (1996), <http://homes.eff.org/~barlow/Declaration-Final.html> (accessed 5 May 2008), states in part "Governments derive their just powers from the consent of the governed. You have neither solicited nor received ours.... Cyberspace does not lie within your borders. Do not think that you can build it, as though it were a construction project. You cannot. It is an act of nature and it grows itself through our collective action."

in political debate armed with all the information and opinions they could possibly use. Governmental officials could not hide their mistakes, nor could they hide behind the assumption that issues were too complex for the ordinary citizen to grasp. Information, full and free, would empower an invigorated democratic citizenry (Barber 1984; Budge 1996; Margolis 1979).

The political uses of the Net were just beginning. We stood at the frontier of true participatory democracy. Grassroots politics would flourish. Not only would citizens access information with a speed and ease never before available, they would also use electronic networks to communicate and exchange ideas. Those who had been left out of the ordinary political process would find a new voice (Gore 2001).

Cyberspace seemed an endless vista. The Internet provided the means for citizens to communicate with each other or with their elected representatives and governmental officials. It afforded sources of untainted information and created electronic forums to deepen democratic discussions and debates. It held out the possibility of citizens realizing both the new Left's vision of participatory democracy and the Counterculture's vision of personal liberation.

Soaring Hope and Failing Promise

E-democrats focus on the potential of politics on the Net to affect both the formation of public opinion and the conduct of real world politics. Communication in cyberspace differs from broadcasting in that no central cluster of studios is required to distribute information over the network. Each person's connection to the Internet can function as an originating and a receiving node. For populists of both the left and the right, political participation on the Internet can approximate an ideal type of communitarian democracy emphasizing mutuality.[5] Not only do netizens share equal powers of sending and receiving, they also share equal access to vast stores of information, including information relevant to pending problems of public policy. Whether democratic policy making involves resolution of differences among competing interests, cooperative action for building consensus, or some combination of the two, the Internet provides the means for realizing it.

Civic life, of course, extends beyond formal issues of public policy. People interact over a variety of matters, and a sense of community often grows among those who share mutual interests. Thousands of virtual interest groups maintain Usenet newsgroups, listserv mailing lists, web-based chat rooms, wikis, interactive blogs, podcasts and the like as well as Role Playing Games (RPGs) that run the gamut from Massively Multi-player Online (MMORPGs) to restricted islands in

5 See Wall (2003), Wall addresses, *inter alia*, how the Internet's characteristics of mutuality and equality have affected the popular music industry and culture. This issue is contextualized within Wall's larger treatment of Counterculture's influence upon popular culture.

Second Life. Besides these virtual interest groups, traditional communities have established online networks, such as Lily Pad (Cincinnati, OH and Northern KY), wifi-frankfurt.de (Frankfurt, Germany), or Z-Net Wireless (Zagreb, Croatia) that provide easy (often free) access to the Internet.[6] Some of these virtual interest groups, such as The WELL, act as cooperative societies in which due-paying members participate in conferences or exchange information without the expectation of a quid pro quo for each particular service they provide (WELL). Others like Wikipedia dedicate themselves to collaborative projects (often called Wikis) that produce freely accessible databases, most notably the popular international encyclopedia (Wiki About). At its best civic life online resembles the mutuality of a barn raising or a potluck supper.

Nevertheless, nothing compels virtual communities to function as mutual benefit societies. Traditional democratic politics involves the resolution of group conflict through complex exchanges that involve pressuring, bargaining and finding a middle course. In cyberspace, however, like-minded e-citizens can form online communities that insulate members from exchanges with those who may hold different opinions. While hate groups like the Aryan National Alliance are notorious for countenancing only those who espouse the groups' particular views, researchers have uncovered many other virtual communities that exist largely to promote their own interests, whether political or non-political, and to reinforce their own like-mindedness. These communities also make those who disagree unwelcome if they wish to join, and uncomfortable if they decide to participate (Aryan Nations 2002; Bimber 1998; Hill and Hughes 1998; *Online Journalism Review* September 2002; Sunstein 2007).[7]

Regardless of whether specialized blogs, forums or communities in cyberspace tend to be open-minded and welcoming or hostile and close-minded, we question whether they will replace mainstream mass media, political parties and interest groups. Even though the online audience for political affairs continues to grow—a December 2007 Pew Center survey found that 24 percent of Americans reported following the 2008 presidential nominating campaign on the Internet, up from 13 percent at a comparable point in the 2004 campaign—the top three online sources were decidedly mainstream: MSNBC (26 percent), CNN (23 percent) and Yahoo! News (22 percent). Moreover, only 15 percent named the Internet as their dominant source for campaign news. In contrast, 60 percent (down from 68 percent in 2000 and 2004) named television news (local, network or cable) as their dominant source for campaign news. While adults under 30 reported the most Internet news usage (42 percent), they too reported regular reliance on local TV news (25 percent), national network news (24 percent) and cable TV news (35 percent). Twenty-five

6 See FreeNetworks .org <www.freenetworks.org> for a listing of networks and for information about mutual peering agreements.

7 See Chapter 4 for a detailed discussion of democracy and tolerance on the Internet.

percent of young adults even reported using daily newspapers regularly. All other age groups reported making heavier use of all these sources offline (Pew 2008).

Pew surveys in 2005 and 2006 found that about 12 million American adults (8 percent of Internet users) kept blogs and 57 million (39 percent) reported having read one. The largest proportion of bloggers (37 percent) described their blogs as personal observations based upon "my life and experiences." Eleven percent cited public affairs as their main topic, an important but rather distant second. The rest of the blogs focused on sports, entertainment, religion, health, hobbies, business, and a multitude of other interests. Moreover, only one-in three bloggers considered their endeavor to be a form of journalism (Lenhart and Fox 2006). The Institute for Politics, Democracy & the Internet (IPDI) surveyed registered voters in California during the summer of 2006 to estimate and characterize the audience for political blogs. The data suggested that fewer that 10 million of the 57 million blog readers look at political blogs "nearly every day." They appear to be disproportionately men with above average educations and incomes as well as more passionate than average issues positions, ideologies and partisan self-identifications. In contrast to bloggers in general, regular political readers are not disproportionately young adults. Rather, they resemble the political activists who dominate American politics offline (Graf 2006).[8]

Until the mid-1990s when the Web took off, the Internet abounded with academics, computer technologists and researchers, mostly educated white males under age 35. An unusually large proportion of them followed politics online and generated information by accessing email, bulletin boards, Usenet newsgroups, or listservs (Fisher, Margolis and Resnick 1996). The demographics and political interests of current online users more closely resemble those of their real world counterparts. Most users, therefore, don't place a high priority on acquiring information about political or civic affairs, and most politically interested users access the Web to consume such information rather than to generate it. Users generally seek information about other matters, or they want to entertain themselves or conduct commercial transactions (Kohut 2000; Norris 2001, 233). If one surveys the 25 most trafficked websites of each member nation of the Organization for Economic Cooperation and Development (OECD), for instance, familiar names like Google, Yahoo!, YouTube, eBay, MySpace, Facebook, Flickr, Friendster, Wikipedia, Msn.com, blogger.com and YouPorn.com consistently appear. By comparison there are relatively few news media sites and hardly any governmental ones (Alexa 2008).

Recent findings of the Pew Internet and American Life Project confirm that Americans still use the Internet most commonly for non-political reasons. In 2007, 92 percent of online Americans used the Internet for email, 83 percent to find hobby-related information, 81 percent to find product or service information,

8 Barack Obama's use of the Internet during his successful election campaign and since his ascension to the American Presidency aims to increase citizen involvement in public affairs. See Chapters 5 and 7.

71 percent for news-related information, 66 percent to buy a product, 66 percent to visit a government website, 64 percent to make a travel-related reservation, 53 percent for online banking, 51 percent for job-related research, 48 percent to watch videos from such sites as YouTube, and 47 percent for information regarding politics or the upcoming political campaigns (Pew 2008a).[9]

The movement from text-based forums to multimedia Web sites, coupled with the advent of search engines that popularized the Internet encouraged another development: the rise of a formidable presence of mainstream media in cyberspace. Internet users generally list these media as their most frequently visited online sources for campaign news. News media on the Web are not much different from those that exist in the real world. Unorthodox Web news providers may have started first, but the established news media tend to predominate. Major newspapers, magazines, radio and television networks have the expertise and resources to gather, organize, and display more information more expeditiously than their upstart rivals. They generally have better name recognition and more good will to draw upon than do their challengers. Most users, who are not much interested in public affairs to begin with, are likely to turn to familiar names for the headline news they desire.

Both mainstream and new online media, however, face the problem of maintaining advertising revenue in order to support their online journalistic endeavors. Even relatively deep-pocketed online magazines such as *Slate* and *Salon* are finding it impossible to survive without supplementing their income through offline services like special print, audio or wireless cellular editions (Blair 2001). While the expansion of broadband capacity to individual users has opened greater possibilities for innovative online advertising, measuring the effectiveness of such advertising remains problematic. Many potential clients, therefore, have been reluctant to shift major portions of their advertising budgets to online versions of established newspapers, let alone new online media (Taylor 2003; McMains 2007). Circulation of print editions of newspapers has been falling, and competition from local online services like Craig's list has cut into revenue from classified advertising.[10]

Independent political blogs have not displaced the established media's online dominance. To begin with, notwithstanding the enormous choice available, over half (52 percent) of regular readers of political blogs in the United States devote most of their time to one (or more) of the 11 most popular. An additional 25 percent of these regular readers consult these same political blogs at least "once in a while" (Lenhart and Fox 2006, 7; Graf 2006, 3-4, 7). Lastly, the mainstream

9 The figures refer to American adults who use the Internet. They exclude 15 percent who have no access—"off the Network"—plus another 11 percent who use the Internet only intermittently—"indifferent"—because they claim to find using it inconvenient or annoying (Horrigan 2007, ii). Multiply the figures by .75 to estimate percentages of the adult population.

10 See Chapter 5 of this volume.

media have begun political blogs hosted by their better known reporters, news anchors or columnists, and they usually are better positioned to advertise online and offline to direct traffic to their sites.

The news media in the real world devote much more coverage to the major parties and their candidates than to the minor parties and their candidates. As the established news media that dominate coverage of public affairs online present essentially the same types of information as they do in their offline publications, the Democratic and Republican parties and the established political interest groups also receive more coverage online than do their less orthodox rivals. Even Usenet newsgroups and non-elite political blogs generally have more messages posted about the same mainline parties and events that traditional media cover (Margolis, Resnick and Levy 2003; Kim 2007).

The major parties and their candidates have also established a stronger presence in cyberspace than have their rivals. Since 1996 we have periodically browsed the U.S. political party list on Yahoo! The Democratic and Republican parties' websites have consistently outnumbered those of all other parties combined for this entire period (Yahoo! 1996-2008). They and their candidates have more links to bring in visitors from other websites, and they normally succeed in drawing many more visitors than do those of the minor parties. As we discuss in Chapter 7, we find similar patterns for Web presence and news coverage of parties and candidates in European Union nations, the United Kingdom, France, and Germany.[11]

Even though we can cite exceptional cases, political uses of the Net have not altered the pattern of established political outcomes. This should not surprise us. Political science has demonstrated time and again that except when cataclysmic events like war, social upheaval or economic depression impinge on their daily lives, most people don't participate in politics, and most neither know nor care very much about it. Researchers have noted the difficulty of mobilizing citizens to challenge the electoral domination of the two major parties and the interest groups that support them, especially when they view social and economic conditions as mostly stable and relatively benign. Why should we expect access to the Internet to change these habits?[12]

---

11 Even though minor parties and candidates have a relatively stronger presence on the Web than they do in traditional mass media, that presence still pales in comparison to the Web presence of the major parties. Margolis, Resnick and Wolfe (1999); Gibson et al. (2003).

12 Except for the growth in monetary donations to candidates or parties via the Internet, we have not seen a general rise in the proportions of adults who actively participate in political campaigns or turnout regularly to vote. Even before user-friendly Web forums or social networks like MySpace or Facebook offered opportunities to discuss politics, Internet users seemed more interested in viewing information on websites than posting comments about the information or its presentation. "Third Voice," a browser companion program introduced with fanfare in the late 1990s, provided an opportunity pin such comments directly onto websites, much like little "post-it" notes. The comments, visible only other Third Voice users, initially drew protests from Webmasters and generated great

Hopes that political uses of the Net will transform modern politics into participatory democracy remain unrealized because they rest on two dubious premises. The first presumes that entrepreneurial citizens will provide the wherewithal for independent online sources of information to attract audiences comparable to those of the established parties, interest groups and news media. The second presumes that the great bulk of citizens who engage in little of no political activity will become more active merely because the Internet provides them means that will facilitate democratic political participation.

Democracy and the Internet: A Realistic Assessment?

We think of democracy as self-rule, the rule of the people, the demos, either directly or through elected representatives. Most of the suggestions for using the Internet to perfect democracy rely upon the people to form the collective will that ought to initiate laws and policies. Academic literature often employs the term "Computer Mediated Communication" (CMC) to describe using the Internet for this purpose. At the very least, few would deny the Internet's potential to provide citizens with alternative sources of news they can use to curb the influence of the established sources—governmental executives and bureaucrats, technical experts, and their powerful private sector allies—who supply most of the information the traditional media report about political and civic affairs. Yet this focus on communication neglects an important observation. Executives and bureaucrats, most of whom neither the citizens nor their elected representatives select, run modern governments. Regardless of the extent to which they claim to operate democratically, most rules, regulations and services that affect citizens—indeed most encounters citizens have with government—emanate from these officials exercising their discretion regarding how the laws and policies should be implemented.[13] Among other things, the executive largely determines not only how citizens or their representatives can access governmental information online, but also the extent to which secret or "privileged" information will be accessible at all. While some information and executive deliberations must remain secret, executives have proven to be quite adept at classifying embarrassing or even criminal information as secret or privileged. Communication via the Internet facilitates democratic deliberation for citizens, but it is insufficient if the executive can deny to citizens and their representatives access to information that is vital for rational decision-making. In short, even if increased numbers of citizens decided not only to become active in public affairs but also to underwrite ways to generate

---

controversy. Interest soon flagged, however, and Third Voice went out of business early in 2001. See Margolis and Resnick (1999).

13 An independent judiciary may also determine whether or not the executive implements laws correctly, but once again, it is largely the executive's prerogative to implement the judiciary's decisions.

reliable information from public sources independent of the established parties, interest groups and news media, the information would still be unlikely to contain anything that the executive (and its major allies in the private sector) wanted to suppress.[14]

The United States Congress possesses stronger powers than the legislative bodies of most nations. If it must sue the executive branch to obtain information it deems necessary to carry out its constitutionally mandated oversight duties, how much more difficult is it for the parliaments and assemblies of most European democracies, let alone those of less democratic nations like China or Russia, to pry comparable information from their executives? The closest solution to this problem has been to encourage responsible "whistleblowers," people of conscience who work inside of public executive agencies or major private enterprises that contract with government, to bring forward information they believe should come to the attention of the citizens' elected representatives. Beginning with the *Williams-Steiger Occupational Safety and Health Act of 1970* the Congress of the United States has passed numerous acts with whistleblower protections for workers in the private sector. It also passed the *Whistleblower Protection Act of 1989* and subsequent amendments in 1994 to provide protection for federal employees in the executive branch. Nevertheless, the executive and it private sector allies have succeeded through court and administrative appointments to obtain cases and interpretations that undercut many of the protections in these acts (Margolis 1979,167-75; GAP 2008; OSHA 2008).

While we may be mistaken to expect that the Internet will continue to replicate the dominance of traditional media and party elites, the evidence that increased availability of information via the Internet has increased most citizens' political participation remains sparse. Studies have shown that regular use of electronic media for political and civic information correlates positively with higher rates of participation in political and civic affairs, but most people still don't make regular use electronic media for that purpose (Bimber 2003; Kohut 2000; Verba and Nie 1972; Verba, Schlozman and Brady 1995).[15] Nevertheless, some recent studies offer encouraging evidence that young people who use the Internet as a regular source of news show greater participation in political and civic affairs than others in their age group, and it is possible that young adults' online political activities for

14 For background and contemporary controversies about the implementation of executive privilege in the USA, see Lichtbau (2008). See also UNITED STATES v. NIXON, 418 U.S. 683 (1974) <http://caselaw.lp.findlaw.com/scripts/getcase.pl?court=US&vol=418&invol=683> accessed on 12 May 2008 and *Committee on the Judiciary v. Harriet Miers and Joshua Bolten* (2008) at: <http://judiciary.house.gov/Media/PDFS/ContemptComplaint080310.pdf> accessed on 7 May 2008.

15 Philip Converse has even suggested that there can be an inverse relationship between information and voting turnout. The historically high turnout rates of the late 19th century in the USA may have resulted from relatively low levels of information that made voters susceptible to emotional appeals (Converse 1972).

individual candidates through social networks like Facebook and MySpace as well as President Obama's efforts to keep his youthful supporters organized online may develop into a broader wave of political activism the likes of which we haven't seen since the 1960s (Pasek et al. 2006; Zukin et al. 2006).

Email, viral videos, and Web pages have enhanced traditional pressure group politics by making it faster and cheaper to mobilize like-minded citizens. The Internet reduces transaction costs and thus facilitates political organization and mobilization (Boyd 2003). It also makes it easier for citizens to contact their legislators and government officials to demand policies to their liking, but the evidence is mixed regarding the extent to which initiatives organized online have been successful (Anderson and Cornfield 2003, 47-156; Bimber 2003). Since 1996 American parties, candidates and interest groups have made increasing use of the Internet to influence public affairs, and they have induced millions of otherwise inactive citizens to support their causes, especially to contribute monetarily to political campaigns or causes (Cornfield 2004).

The great number of websites advocating social change online, however, has not led to great numbers of people advocating social change offline. We should not confuse the flowering of websites touting all sorts of worthy causes, movements, and interests with a shift in social power in the real world. Organizing sporadic demonstrations for candidates or causes is one thing; sustaining a viable movement over time requires an ongoing organization offline.[16] Demonstrations against the World Trade Organization in Seattle and subsequent venues were organized largely on the Net, as were other demonstrations against international economic organizations and against the 2003-2009 war in Iraq. The events surrounding the Florida vote recounts that led to election of George W. Bush in 2000 also served as an opportunity for political agitation by protestors who used the Internet to further their activities (Boyd 2003; Van Aelst 2002). While such uses of the Net seem impressive, we should remember that the high water mark of 20th century post-World War II protest occurred in the late 1960s and early 1970s, many years before the Internet.

Although men like Ross Perot and Dick Morris who advocate of direct democracy via the Internet have held powerful positions within the mainstream of American political and civic affairs, we see little chance that their suggestions to radically alter the established processes of governmental decision-making in the United States and comparable advanced industrial and post-industrial nations will be adopted anytime soon (Morris 1999; Schudson 2000).[17]

To our minds, replacing representative institutions with direct democracy remains a dubious idea. As we pointed out in Chapter 1, representative institutions were not

---

16 In Chapter 7 and 8 we discuss enterprises like Meetup that facilitate using the Internet to develop community organizations offline.

17 As of May 2008, Morris still forwards results from his Vote.com home page to relevant parties, candidates, executive agencies, members of Congress or the President. See <http://www.vote.com>.

second best systems of self-rule created because of the impossibility of assembling the citizenry to carry out true direct democracy. While we have placed a greater reliance on public opinion polls of late, do we really believe that government by public opinion polls would improve public policy? Constitutionally defined institutions like Congress, the President and the Courts often do not produce wise policies, but do we really think that assembling millions of netizens at digitized networked devices to study and vote on public policies would be preferable? As we will elaborate in the next chapter, Madisonian arguments for the superiority of representative institutions over direct democracy still have much to commend them.

In contrast to the Internet achieving direct democracy, using it as an alternative or supplement to traditional methods of voting is a more realistic reform. Internet voting has emerged as a live option in part because it does not entail a radical transformation of the way citizens cast ballots or answer opinion polls in many advanced nations. Estonia already uses it for national parliamentary elections, a Swiss canton (Geneva) has used it for referenda, the Danes had a city experiment with it for the 2004 European Parliament Election, and USA has used it for members of military stationed abroad. Several other EU nations, Canada, Australia and at least a dozen state legislatures in the USA are also looking into Internet voting.[18]

If the security and integrity of online ballots could be guaranteed, the convenience of receiving information on demand and the ease of voting at home, the office, the mall or elsewhere could decrease voters' ignorance and increase voters' turnout. The USA in particular would no longer suffer the indignity of conducting national elections, the centerpiece of its democratic system, with barely half the eligible voters participating. The voting irregularities of the 2000 presidential election added momentum to proposals to enact reform, and eventually led to passage of the Help America Vote Act (HAVA) of 2002, which encouraged replacing systems using punch cards and mechanical lever machines with (among other things) direct recording electronic (DRE) voting systems. These machines can be programmed to present the ballot and to record and count votes, and to anonymously retrieve hard copies of individually cast ballots. They also can prevent voters from making common errors, such as casting more votes than allowed in multiple candidate races. In addition, they are capable both of receiving ballots and of transmitting counts via the Internet. Despite its advantages, however, safeguarding electronic balloting turns out to be no mean task.

A National Science Foundation report, released in March 2001, argued that the time was not yet ripe for using the Internet to vote from either home or office "Remote Internet voting technology will not be able to meet this standard for years to come," the report concluded. It urged (to no avail) that local, state, and federal officials resist the pressure to implement Internet voting in general elections (NSF News 2001). Indeed, the use of direct recording electronic voting equipment in Florida and Georgia in November 2002 revealed significant problems (Pibel 2003).

18 ePractice.eu (2009) compiles information and studies on Internet voting as well as on other aspects of e-government that extend beyond the European Union.

Moreover, researchers discovered that several of the electronic systems adopted to meet HAVA deadlines for the 2006 US congressional elections still had serious security flaws (Feldman, Halderman and Felten 2006; ePractice.eu 2009).

There is another way to make government more responsive to the people, which does not evoke the enthusiasm of radicals and visionaries, but has more chance to actually change the way government does business. This chapter has focused mainly on the input side of government, the process of translating will into law and policy, but citizens also must deal with the outputs of government. Citizens are not only shareholders of government, they are also customers (Digital 4sight 2001). Governments collect information and taxes, and they distribute permissions and benefits. Laws must be enforced and public policies implemented. Citizens want easy access to government information, and they want government to simplify filling out forms, filing reports and doing whatever the government requires of them in their everyday lives.

Assuredly, one classical democratic ideal is to make government more responsive to citizens. Though we don't expect that the Internet will make government much more responsive to citizens on the input side, we are more optimistic about its long-term effect on the output side. To sum up, we believe the Internet's greatest impact on how citizens interact with government will be to improve routine transactions between government and its citizens, but we doubt that most citizens will use it to participate directly in the formulation of public policy. Like Didi and Gogo, the absurd heroes of *Waiting for Godot,* e-democrats who expect citizens to run government via the Internet will have to wait a very long time.[19]

---

19 We elaborate upon this argument in Chapters 8 and 9.

Chapter 3
Tempering the Dreams: Revised Theories of Cyber-Democracy

Question: How many Microsoft engineers does it take to change a light bulb?
Answer: None. They just declare darkness the new standard.

Toward the end of Chapter 2 we argued that political participation via the Internet seemed likely to have limited impact on the policy process. We expect to see increased responsiveness from public officials[1] regarding the efficiency and quality of public services and the ease of transacting business with government, but we don't expect such participation to completely alter the patterns by which most public policies are proposed and promulgated. Although we juxtaposed these modest expectations against what we termed the "impossible dreams" of radicals and visionaries, we must acknowledge that the dreamers' underlying concerns for increasing citizens' influence over the development of public policy hark back to traditional concerns of classical democratic theory.

We divide this chapter into four major sections. The first reviews mid-century restatements of elite democracy that attempted to integrate the findings of scientific studies of political behavior with elitists' longstanding interest in curbing the excesses of classical forms of democracy. Although these restatements avoided utopian assumptions about the attentiveness and capacity of average citizens regarding governance, they tended to reify American patterns of governance as the essence of modern democracy. This led to a rather conservative and complacent elitism that failed to anticipate the political unrest of the 1960s and 1970s. The highly circumscribed participatory roles that elitist democrats assigned to ordinary citizens also elicited strong reactions from theorists who sought to reinvigorate classical models of democracy. When the Internet connected various computer networks, it provided impetus for both the radical democratic theories discussed in Chapter 2 and the more temperate ones we discuss in this chapter.

In the second section we critique the arguments of those who claim to have developed temperate and realistic theories for utilizing the Internet to increase

1 It may be the case that not all public officials will be responsive. For example, Mitt Romney's rejection of participating in the CNN and YouTube presidential debates on the grounds that these potentially trivialize such debates suggests that responsiveness may be a function of party membership, public function, public role and perhaps even personality and psychological factors.

citizen influence over policy development. The theories are more temperate in that they don't encourage the majority of adults to participate in every significant public policy decision. They are more realistic in that they avoid placing undue participatory burdens upon the general citizenry, while at the same time they utilize the Internet's potential to inform and mobilize broad elements of the population before—not after—political decision-makers have acted. Even though we sympathize with these theories, we remain skeptical of the Internet's ability to mobilize sufficient numbers of citizens to revolutionize policy-making in the real world. Despite the advent of the Internet, most citizens still neither know nor care very much about most political issues. More importantly, however, the theories underestimate the ability of political as well as socioeconomic and cultural forces in the real world to replicate familiar patterns of political activity on the Internet. The evidence suggests that real world politics that affect the Net generally trump political uses of the Net to influence real world politics.

In the third section we address a problem implicit in the riddle with which we began this chapter: the transmogrification of cyberspace from a largely unregulated but publicly supported communications medium to an increasingly well-regulated but privately supported vehicle for commerce. Where Internet pioneers were mostly skilled programmers associated with governmental agencies or with educational or research institutes, today's Internet users are mostly information consumers. They lack significant programming skills, and relatively few are affiliated with educational or research institutes within or outside government. The great majority rely on commercial enterprises like Microsoft to supply them with the software necessary to pursue their interests in cyberspace. Commercial transactions require structure, and commercial enterprises need government to help them establish and enforce standards, rules, and regulations that facilitate conducting business online. While establishing such structure increases the efficiency and convenience of transactions between business enterprises and their customers, it also raises the stakes in the inexorable struggle among capitalist enterprises to have the rules and regulations advantage their products and services. Simply put, if Microsoft can set the standards, Microsoft stands to profit most.

As an unintended by-product, standardization also makes it easier for governmental agencies or other powerful groups to monitor, collect, store and analyze data about citizens' behavior and to regulate and possibly manipulate that behavior. Finally, the movement from open source to proprietary code that has accompanied popular expansion and privatization of the Internet raises additional questions about the propriety of secrecy and the potential for control.

In the last section we address the predominant contemporary trend toward commodification and its impact on e-democracy and Internet politics. Even if the idea of an e-Agora were possible, it still might not provide the type of democratic politics that deliberative democrats advocate. The trend toward commodification also raises the troubling issue that the concept of consumer is becoming the prevalent self-understanding of 21st century netizens and citizens alike. Such commodification suggests that civic affairs and public policies are largely products that citizens can participate in or decide upon according to their whims, passions, and desires. The commodification of politics encourages citizens to view public policy-making as trivial at best or unnecessary at worst, particularly if citizens believe they can acquire more personally satisfying products on the market. This tends to make conducting bureaucratic transactions via e-government—citizens as customers—the most popular political use of the Net.

Restatements of Elite Democracy

As we mentioned above, the typical citizen of modern democratic societies neither knows nor cares very much about most current public issues or policies. Indeed, most citizens understand little about the complexity of their governmental institutions. Were questions of public policy put directly before the people instead of before their representatives, most people's honest response would be "no opinion." Personal concerns normally demand far more attention than do those of politics. Most citizens become actively involved in politics only when they perceive that the consequences of public policies have impinged upon their personal concerns or when they conclude that governmental action is necessary to relieve or remedy problems that have hurt (or threaten to hurt) the people, values or causes they hold dear.

While these observations are common knowledge among students of politics, the average citizen they picture does not comport with the popular image of American democracy. The average citizen, according to this popular image, is the modern equivalent of the 18th-century yeoman: a hard-working individual of modest means and independent mind, attentive to public affairs, protective of his own interests, but fair in balancing those interests against the interests of others and of the polity in general. This image of a mythical rational citizen, traceable to the writings of western democratic theorists, such as John Locke, Jeremy Bentham or Thomas Jefferson, highlights the virtues of individualism and contrasts with values like deference, obedience or collectivism (Hartz 1962).

Needless to say, citizens of modern democracies—particularly Americans—happily accept this inflated estimate of their virtues. It complements the chauvinistic view most Americans hold regarding the United States' place in the world. The land of opportunity, the fount of scientific discovery, the world's only "superpower," America is the exemplar of democracy—Watergate, Enron, and other warts upon the body politic notwithstanding. Indeed, we Americans are rather arrogant about our right and competence to participate. Consider the following satiric dialogue from Scott Adams' "Dilbert" comic strip:[2]

2 'Dilbert', *Dilbert Comic* <http://www.dilbert.com/comics/dilbert/archive/dilbert-20030731.html> accessed 1 August 2003.

> **Dogbert:** I've decided to spend more time criticizing things I don't understand. I say we should flat-tax the Kyoto Treaty all the way back to the Security Council.
>
> **Dilbert:** Wouldn't that be unfair to stem cells?
>
> **Dogbert:** Bah!

Despite their sophistication, this popular image of American democracy often beguiles even political scientists, journalists, pundits, and politicians. How can they remain untouched when most grew up in the United States, exposed to beliefs in the wisdom of American political institutions and the goodness of the people? The political history of the USA was presented to them in school as the epitome of progressive democratization. The expansion of the franchise, the direct election of the Senate, the introduction of primary elections, and the institution of initiatives, referenda and recalls—to name just a few progressive developments—postulated a citizenry capable of deciding in some detail upon questions of public policy. Americans are predisposed to believe Al Smith's famous dictum: "All the ills of democracy can be cured by more democracy" (Smith 1933).

To be sure, critics have questioned this unbounded faith in the people. The nation's founders were by no means enamored with classical democracy, and they designed institutional checks and balances, indirect elections of the President and the Senate, and virtual lifetime tenure for federally appointed judges in order to curb citizens' tendencies toward democratic excess. Foreign observers, such as Alexis de Tocqueville and John Stuart Mill, worried about the dangers of conformity and suppression of minority opinion as the franchise expanded during the 19th century, and domestic critics, such as H.L. Mencken and Walter Lippmann, argued that most citizens lacked the information or the capacity to decide rationally about complex questions of 20th century politics (Lippmann 1922; Mencken 1926; Mill 1991; Tocqueville 1953). Nevertheless, defenders of the popular image could match the instances of irrational or suppressive behavior the critics cited with counterexamples of rational democratic behavior (Page and Shapiro 1992).

The advent of systematic polling based upon probability sampling, coupled with the general adaptation of empirical methods of the natural sciences to political science, however, produced incontrovertible evidence that relatively few individuals fulfilled the popular image of a democratic citizen. In truth, relatively few possessed even the modest levels of information necessary to distinguish substantive policy differences among candidates in most elections. By the early 1950s, democratic theorists who professed faith in both scientific methods of social research and in democracy in the United States faced a dilemma. They had to admit that despite widespread civic education, most Americans did not—and perhaps could not—satisfy the fundamental democratic requirement of *enlightened understanding*; or else they had to declare that, notwithstanding claims to the contrary, the United States simply was not a true democracy.

To escape this dilemma, American political scientists needed to develop new alternatives. Democracy literally means rule by the *demos,* the common people. Dahl's description of democracy captures this meaning by requiring the *inclusion of all adults* in the political decision-making process. But how does a modern mass society achieve democratic rule when people cannot possibly meet face to face to debate and resolve public issues? The common solution had been for the people's elected representatives to meet face to face in lieu of the people themselves. Through regularly scheduled elections and limited terms of office the common people would maintain direct control of their representatives and indirect control of public policy.[3]

What happens, however, when many citizens appear to lack the basic knowledge of political issues, public policies or political institutions necessary to provide guidance for their representatives?[4] Classical statements of democracy, however exaggerated their popular image, had nonetheless taken for granted the general capability and rationality of individual citizens. Yet for many behavioral political scientists, particularly in the USA, the survey evidence indicated that these classical presumptions were overly optimistic. They proposed alternative theories based upon three models of plural-elite democracy that fit the evidence: the first emphasized interest groups; the second emphasized political parties; and the third leadership elites.

Group theories of politics have a long pedigree. The idea that democratic forms of government can be achieved through an appropriate balance of power among contending groups is discussed in works as ancient as those of Aristotle and Polybius. The 20th century impetus for group theories, however, can be found in Arthur Bentley's landmark study, *The Process of Government*, first published in 1908 (Bentley 1908). Bentley's work suited the needs of plural-elite democratic theorists not only because it emphasized the active roles of groups in politics, but also because it attempted to measure activity in a scientific manner:

> If a statement of social facts which lends itself better to measurement is offered, that characteristic entitles it to attention. Providing the statement does not otherwise distort the social facts, the capacity to measurement will be decisive in its favor. The statement that takes us farthest along the road toward quantitative estimates will inevitably be the best statement (Bentley 1908, 201).

Of Bentley's intellectual disciples, David B. Truman had the greatest direct impact on group based models of plural-elite democracy. In his *The Governmental Process*, first published in 1951, Truman raised open competition among interest

3 It is of course presumed that *each adult's vote counts equally.*

4 It is possible to suggest that another contributing factor may be individual-based. Even if knowledge and time are present, individuals still may choose not to become involved given a changing understanding of the self and of politics. This observation is addressed in more detail below.

groups to a normative principle of government (Truman 1951). In his view modern democracy consisted of a pluralistic struggle among diverse interest groups. The United States was a democracy because no small set of interest groups controlled the dominant share of public policy decisions. The behavior of individual citizens *per se* mattered little. The virtues of groups would make up for the failures of individuals to conform to the popular democratic image.

If citizens were ignorant of the political issues that affected them, the relevant interest groups would protect them. If individuals lacked the wherewithal to make their wishes known, the relevant groups would pool their resources, aggregate their separate concerns, and articulate them to appropriate decision-makers. Groups would also discourage extremism and intolerance by moderating their members' demands in order to achieve a common front and by negotiating with opposing groups in order to achieve mutual accommodations of interest.

Truman's work inspired a slew of studies that used interactions among multifarious interest groups to orient their analyses both empirically and normatively.[5] While these works differed in detail, they all emphasized that democratic politics required that no single group or minority coalition dominate all the important political decisions. Indeed, one of Robert Dahl's early theoretical works defined democracy as a system of governance in which minorities—plural—rule (Dahl 1956). In order to effect such rule the theorists postulated an open political system, in which all citizens had the legal opportunity and the economic resources to organize and to pursue their interests in the political arena. (This resembles what Dahl later came to call *effective participation.*) Democratic politics normally consisted of the resolution of conflict among groups, preferably using stable channels of communication that groups provided between citizens and public officials. Even if it were practical, most citizens lacked the interest or the competence to govern directly. Democracy worked better, therefore, when citizen governed indirectly through membership in or identification with groups that supported their interests.

In order to assure the quality of group-based politics, theorists cited the greater commitment to democratic principles that studies had found among interest group leaders and activists in comparison to the general public (Stouffer 1955). Democratic governance consisted of little more than taking account of differing demands and facilitating their resolution through bargaining and compromise. That some higher collective or public interest might exist was largely discounted. The closest thing to public interest was a consensus regarding the rules of the political game. If decision-makers were to violate this consensus, group theorists expected "potential interest groups" to organize and to mobilize available resources to defend or restore the democratic status quo (Truman 1951, 501-536).

Friendly critics of interest group theories of democracy focused mainly on two shortcomings. First, the theories characterized governments in unrealistically neutral roles. Surely political institutions did more than mediate group conflicts and

5 See Margolis (1983, 119) for citations.

then register the results as laws and regulations. At the very least public officials tended to support and defend the interests of those groups with whom they routinely conducted governmental business. Secondly, the critics pointed out that just as studies had revealed the inadequate democratic characteristics of average citizens, so too had they revealed the inadequate democratic characteristics of interest groups. Significant portions of the citizenry—by some estimates a majority—belonged to no voluntary associations. Moreover, most of the associations to which citizens did belong had little or nothing to do with politics. And to make matters worse, disproportionately large numbers of those who participated in political associations came from higher than average socio-economic strata (Verba and Nie 1972; Schattschneider 1960; Simon, Smithburg and Thompson 1959, 296-311).

An alternative plural-elite model that rectified these problems placed emphasis on political parties rather than interest groups. In contrast to interest groups, political parties nominated candidates for office, who, if elected, took responsibility in the names of their parties for running the government. Voters could identify whom to praise or to blame for the successes or failures of public policies more easily than they could if interest groups decided most policies. Better yet, where a majority of citizens had little or nothing to do with political interest groups, nine out of ten Americans readily identified themselves as Democrats or Republicans. Instead of relying upon potential interest groups to uphold democratic principles and procedures, party theorists argued that democracy could be preserved and defended by responsible parties whose leaders respected the constitutionally defined rules of the political game and whose followers comprised the great majority of the electorate.

Responsible parties acted like supereminences, aggregating various interests into party platforms and articulating those platforms to the electorate and to the appropriate governmental authorities. As successful party candidates assumed positions of authority, they could be expected to use their powers of office to implement their parties' platforms. At the same time studies had found that party leaders and public officials, much like interest group leaders, showed greater commitment to democratic principles associated with their governmental positions than did the general public. A good Democrat like Harry Truman might prove to be a good democratic statesman.

American political scientists pointed to the British party system as the principal example of the "responsible parties" theory of democracy. Samuel Beer suggested that the British system of "collectivist democracy," rested upon responsible parties that represented broad but differing class interests. This was "as practicable a solution as one is like to find" to the problem of how "to combine a substantial degree of popular participation with a system of power cable of governing *effectively* and *coherently*" (Beer 1962, 46). Beer's interpretation of British democracy paralleled that of the American Political Science Association's Committee on Political Parties, whose *Toward a More Responsible Two-Party System* had argued the necessity of responsible parties for democratic governance. The Committee's position in turn bore the stamp of its chairman, E.E. Schattschneider, who had previously defined competition among political parties as the essence of democracy (Committee 1950; Schattschneider 1942).

Even though the responsible parties model of democracy claimed to foster greater involvement of the general public and greater consideration of broad public concerns than did the interest group model, it did not gain much acceptance. It went against the individualistic ideology that associated American democracy with the independence of elected officials from their parties. Indeed, sober analysis of the Constitution and the *Federalist Papers* left no doubt that federalism, checks and balances, and separation of powers among political institutions were designed to discourage the formation of "majority factions," which, in contemporary terms, translated into "broad-based disciplined political parties." Nor was it necessary to rely upon historical arguments. Political scientists like E. Pendelton Herring argued that lack of discipline among legislators and party leaders was a highly functional response to the demands of the great diversity of American interest groups. In contrast to building unity within British political parties, imposing strict discipline upon the Democratic and Republican parties most likely would splinter them into a confusing array of small parties. Each would have a relatively narrow focus, and none would have a serious chance of governing responsibly in its own name (Downs 1957; Herring 1940).

In place of the interest group or responsible parties models, therefore, plural-elite theorists developed a third variation that stressed competition among leaders who were socialized to uphold democratic electoral process. As we noted in Chapter 1, theorists who stressed the importance of this leadership elite averred that the essence of modern democracy was the "institutional arrangement for arriving at political decisions in which individuals acquire the power to decide by means of competitive struggle for people's vote" (Schumpeter 1962, 269). The success of this system of governance depended primarily upon the quality of the competitively elected leaders, not upon the coherence or the rationality of interest groups, political parties or ordinary citizens.

Implicit in this theory was a strong faith in the democratic commitment of the leaders whom the voters elected. Scientific studies in the burgeoning field of political socialization vindicated this faith. The studies uncovered ample evidence of the benign influence that major social institutions exerted to instill American political leaders with democratic values. Lastly, plural-elite theorists noted that the socialization process helped create a general feeling of support for American political institutions among the populace (Almond and Verba 1963; Greenstein 1965; Hess and Torney 1967).

The USA was blessed with a civic culture, a bundle of attitudes that allowed democracy, as defined by leadership elite theorists, to flourish. Gabriel Almond and Sidney Verba dubbed this an "allegiant-participant" civic culture. Even though most citizens failed to fulfill the expectations of the popular image of democratic participation, they nonetheless supported the political and social institutions and processes that encouraged proper democratic behavior among political leaders. And even if most American adults normally did not participate directly in politics, they believed their votes could express their approval or disapproval of public policies, and most expressed confidence in their gaining sympathetic hearings and desired actions from public officials if they chose to exert themselves. By and large, the inactive citizen was a happy citizen, apathy a tacit expression of satisfaction (Almond and Verba 1963; Milbrath 1965).

This view accorded with the influential postwar statement of the leadership elite thesis Bernard Berelson and his collaborators developed in the concluding chapter of their classic study, *Voting*. Having demonstrated that most citizens they surveyed did not satisfy the requirements for informed political participation, Berelson et al. went on to argue that even if citizens were to participate with all the zeal they were supposed to show, the results would be unsatisfactory. Persistently high levels of political participation would produce deadlock at best and social breakdown at worst, for such participation inevitably centered about emotionally charged issues that polarized the large blocs of citizens. Better to strive for a balance—a few highly motivated citizens and a few apoliticals. The rest should form an Aristotelian middle class, a moderate center whose members concerned themselves only sporadically with special issues, but who supported the institutions and processes of the polity (Berelson, Lazarsfeld and McPhee 1954, 305-326).

V.O. Key, after a thoroughgoing analysis of the empirical political literature of the 1950s, concluded:

> The longer one frets with the puzzle of how democratic regimes manage to function, the more plausible it appears that a substantial part of the explanation is to be found in the motives that actuate the leadership echelon, the values that it holds, the rules of the political game to which it adheres...and perhaps, in some objective circumstances, both material and institutional, in which it functions (Key 1961, 537).

Better to place faith in the democratic predilections of the leaders than in the whims of the people.

Regardless of their specific emphases plural-elite theorists viewed democracy as open competition among interest groups, political parties, or freely chosen political leaders actualized through appropriate arrangement of political institutions. If Americans failed to fulfill the expectations of classical theories of democracy, then the classical theorists, who lacked modern scientific methods of observing political behavior, were mistaken in those expectations. Empirical methods adapted from the natural sciences became the dominant research paradigm in American political science and the plural-elite models of democracy that derived from them were carried along like smart-looking baggage. By the mid-1960s these models, broadly labeled "pluralism," had become the dominant representations of American democracy presented in major textbooks (Margolis 1973).

By the mid-1960s, however, people also began to pay greater attention to theorists like C. Wright Mills, who questioned the empirical adequacy of these interpretations. If interests really had fair chances to participate in politics, then why did people with low incomes, minority racial groups and women generally have poorer housing, health care, educational, employment and investment opportunities than those of comparable white males? If the political system was sensitive to each group's needs, then what led blacks in the ghettoes to riot? If organized political protest was essential for plural-elite democracy, then why did both the Johnson and Nixon administrations treat much of the organized opposition to the increasingly unpopular war in Vietnam as though it were illegitimate? If the faith and trust in political institutions and policies bred through political socialization were necessary to sustain democracy, then did the precipitous decline of trust in these institutions that followed the 1964 presidential election signal a crisis? (Mills 1957; Miller 1974; Walker 1966).

Prominent behavioral political scientists began to realize that looking mainly for explainable regularities in the present political system tended toward conservatism. Their search for regularities within a presumably democratic system could fail to recognize—let alone analyze—those problems which governments ignore, and they, along with the political parties and interest groups favored by government, might view with suspicion any social movement that threatened to disrupt the established patterns of behavior. It appeared that the scientific study of political behavior contained its own biases after all (Bachrach 1967; Connolly 1969; Gamson 1968; Kariel 1970).

There were philosophical difficulties with plural-elite theories as well. They lacked the traditional liberal democratic concern for ordinary citizens to achieve self-improvement through political participation. Instead the theories asserted that with proper institutional arrangements the virtues of political leaders could substitute for the virtues of the people.[6] Plural-elite theories postulated an empty political and civic life that bore little resemblance to the rich one envisioned by democrats such as Thomas Jefferson, Jean Jacques Rousseau or John Stuart Mill. This impoverished conception of citizenship stemmed from an emasculated conception of democracy itself.

Plural-elite theories presumed that the United States and most other Western nations already functioned as modern mass democracies. Their central focus, therefore, concerned how to *preserve* democracy rather than how to *achieve* it. Yet a traditional concern of liberal democratic governance was to make available the widest possible range of options consistent with democratic values. Change, not preservation, was the watchword of liberal democracy. Any set of public policies should be viewed as impermanent, constantly open to challenge. Nor did liberal democracy require that all changes be incremental. Policy changes could be radical or incremental. Solutions depend upon the nature of the problems faced, the values involved and the preferences of the citizens.

Classical democracy valued substantial participation by citizens in the formulation, adoption and implementation of public policy, and it measured

6 We will discuss the implications of this type of thinking for higher education in Chapter 6.

democracy's success by citizens' satisfaction with the results as well as the processes of politics. Classical liberal democracy had faith in the ultimate rationality of the citizenry, and it presumed that participation in politics would improve citizens' political knowledge and abilities. If the plural-elitists' research found insufficient empirical basis for this faith in the American people, this sad fact indicated that the United States simply was not a liberal democracy. Reconstructing democratic theory to accommodate the American situation did not resolve the dilemma.

But did American citizens really lack sufficient rationality to provide a base for a democratic politics that involved classical participatory values? If, as scientific studies also showed, the most powerful organized interests generally consisted of large manufacturers, marketers, utilities, bankers, investors, defense contractors, organized labor, and large farm producers—groups that excluded most citizens of lower socio-economic status—then was it irrational for such citizens to remain apathetic? If similar studies revealed that substantial numbers of citizens (e.g., four out of ten in the national election of 1972) could not distinguish differences between Democrats and Republicans on issues they thought government should act upon, then apathy also would be a perfectly rational response. Similarly, public distrust and disaffection for political leaders and institutions seemed like a perfectly rational response to the bitter experience of the Johnson and Nixon years. Too many leaders, in whom Americans had placed their faith, not only had lied, cheated or stolen, but had also tried to suppress those who had found them out.

The upshot of the new critiques cast considerable doubt upon plural-elite theories of democracy. By the early 1970s unexamined acceptance of plural-elite assertions of the openness and evenhandedness of the American political system had disappeared from most mainstream textbooks, and a new wave of textbooks skeptical or highly critical of the democratic quality of American politics had appeared (Margolis 1973). Within the American Political Science Association critics of plural-elite interpretations of scientific research formed the Caucus for a New Political Science. The Caucus avowed to return the discipline's attention toward research about fundamental questions of liberty and justice, but unlike earlier critics of scientific method, the Caucus avoided prejudging how such research should be conducted.

By the mid-1970s American political thought had come full circle regarding modern democracy. The critics had demonstrated the inadequacy of the plural-elite theorists' attempt to reconcile democratic theory with scientific findings about democratic practice. Not only did it misinterpret some of the scientific findings, but more importantly, its reliance on the virtues of interest groups, political parties and leadership elites compromised utterly the traditional democratic concern for the benefits that citizens were supposed to derive from political participation. Unfortunately, after having exposed the inadequacies of plural-elite theories of democracy, the critics seemed to have run out of steam. They offered no realistic statement about how to arrange political institutions and processes to enable citizens to cope democratically with the responsibilities of modern governance.

This state of affairs began to change with the advent of a forceful participatory theory of democracy known as deliberative democracy.[7] Deliberative democracy was heralded as the antidote to an entrenched political pessimism in regards to the actual practice of democracy. For deliberative theorists, democracy should not be understood solely as adversarial in nature. Rather, it could be based on a friendlier and communally oriented outlook where self-interest could be laid aside for other-interest (Miller 1993). As such, a democracy that is regulated by other-interest is an "association whose affairs are governed by the public deliberation of its members" (Cohen 1997, 67).

Deliberative democracy did not arise *ex nihilo*. It was part of a broader theoretical movement known as participatory democracy.[8] As Bohman and Regh (1997) suggest, the concept of deliberative democracy did not take shape until the 1980s. As a concept, participatory democracy is much older than its deliberative counterpart and can be traced as far back as Jean-Jacques Rousseau, John Stuart Mill and Alexis de Tocqueville with strong 20th century versions found in Dewey (1927), Habermas (1962; 1989), Bachrach (1967), Pateman (1970), Mansbridge (1980), Barber (1984; 2004), and Dahl (1989). Deliberative democracy's uniqueness arises as:

> A form of government in which free and equal citizens (and their representatives), justify decisions in a process in which they give one another reasons that are mutually acceptable and generally accessible, with the aim of reaching conclusions that are binding in the present on all citizens but open to challenge in the future (Gutmann and Thompson 2004, 7).

Deliberative democracy acknowledges three important facts of civic life. First, citizens need the contributions of others to realize a variety of public goods. Besides cooperation, deliberative democracy recognizes that moral disagreement is an intrinsic part of life. Reasonable people often have good reasons for disagreeing with each other, reasons they ought to consider and discuss, not merely gloss over. Lastly, deliberative democracy emphasizes that governmental legitimacy and trust requires open flows of information. Citizens' access to information is essential for civil and political discourse to result in sound governmental policies. Deliberative

7 For a short survey of the history of deliberative democracy, see Bohman and Rehg (1997).

8 Sartori (1987a) suggests that the "notion of participatory democracy remains fuzzy" (Sartori 1987, 111). However, there are some characteristic trademarks. Dryzek (1990) contends that participatory democracy models advance a politics that is "increasingly discursive, educational, oriented to truly public interests, and needful of active citizenship," (Dryzek 1990, 13). Thus, models such as contestatory democracy (Parijs 1999), discursive democracy (Dryzek 1990), and strong democracy (Barber 1984; 2004) all advance an ethic of substantive democratic political engagement predicated upon a thick account of deliberation.

democracy, then, is a cooperative process of collective decision-making that is dynamic, inclusive, information-based, and, as some argue, vital for invigorating the waning democracies of the 21st century.[9]

That citizen deliberation is essential for democratic government can be traced back to ancient Athens in western political thought. Even though the Athenians restricted citizenship to a narrow band of males relative to modern standards, their idea that substantive deliberation fostered cooperation, tolerance, and mutual respect that strengthened social and political bonds provides the basis for modern democratic theory. We generally take for granted that the strength of a democratic society depends upon the quality of social trust and cooperation exhibited in the deliberative practices of its citizens. If democratic citizenship is the "aptitude of ordinary people to take part in political life and to exert influence upon it" (Hadenius 2001, 12), then deliberative democracy seems to be one of the strongest candidates for the robust political engagement of ordinary citizens.

In the contemporary era, Jürgen Habermas has done more than any other theorist to connect the notion of deliberation with democratic government.[10] Habermas' theory of communicative rationality argues that democratic legitimacy arises out of a communicative inclusiveness of all of the "lifeworlds" within modern society. For Habermas, communicative inclusiveness provides a structure that enables actors to reach consensus through rational justifications for their moral claims. It is not an "immediate source of prescriptions" (Habermas 1998, 4). Rather, this structure facilitates social discourses from which "the matrix" of "democratic authority emerges." Habermas argues:

> From this perspective, the forms of communication that confer legitimacy on political will-formation, legislation, and the administration of justice appear as part of a more encompassing process in which the lifeworlds of modern societies are rationalized under the pressure of systemic imperatives (Habermas 1998, 5).

Habermas' theory of communicative rationality is reminiscent of the ancient legal principle *quod omnes tangit debet ab omnibus approbari* (what touches all should

9 Deliberative democracy is a highly debated concept and not all agree that it represents the solution to democracy's ills. For example, Mill (2006) argues that deliberation cannot overcome the problem of cyclical majorities and should thus be rejected. Social choice theorists (e.g., Riker 1982) consider more participatory notions of democracy not only as ill conceived but also "inconsistent and absurd" (Riker 1982, 241). Mackie (2003) provides a vigorous critique of Riker and social choice theory and ardently defends representative democracy.

10 While Habermas is one of the chief advocates of a deliberative conception of democracy, he is by no means the only one. Other important statements are found in the works of Joshua Cohen, Jon Elster, Amy Guttman, John Rawls, and Dennis Thompson.

be approved by all) and is firmly rooted in the doctrine of popular sovereignty and belief in the collective wisdom of the citizenry.[11]

Beyond his theory of communicative rationality, Habermas' other important contribution to participatory and deliberative theories of democracy has been that of the public sphere. For Habermas, the public sphere emerged and developed in Western Europe from the late 18th through the early 20th century. It was a public space that grew without state initiative or control, and it fostered rational discussion and deliberation on questions of politics. While Habermas considers the public sphere a thing of the past, he believes that the communicative features of such a public sphere can be replicated today along with their transformative democratizing power (Habermas 1997).

Habermas' ideas have been tremendously influential in shaping models of e-democracy as well as their assessments and critiques. For e-democrats of the classical persuasion, the Internet provided the perfect raw materials for the creation of a public sphere whose communicative power would transform an apathetic and adversarial democracy into one characterized by deliberation and participation among friendly citizens. As the revolutionary computer technology developed in the 1960s and 1970s replaced mainframes that processed jobs serially with decentralized distributed computing and time-sharing, political theorists, information specialists, and others saw the potential for computer networks to effect viable democracy in modern mass societies. If deliberative democracy was just too good to be true in the real world, as some of its critics argued, perhaps it could come into being virtually and then spill out into mass society.

Computers, the Internet and the Promise of Democracy

Although critics of plural-elite and adversarial models of democracy found multifaceted empirical and philosophical flaws, two objections formed the core. Critics rejected the models' assertions of the average citizen's inability to achieve *enlightened understanding* of political issues and their consequent handing over *control of the public agenda* to leaders of political interest groups, political parties or other ostensibly civic-minded political elites. Pluralists and adversarial theorists tended to ignore that the key element of democratic politics is its transformative effect on the participants:

> [O]ver time private and unreflect[ive] prejudices are transformed by education, exposure to other views, and political experience into civic judgments; ...privatized

11 This dictum appeared first as a Roman legal principle and was later incorporated into medieval canon law. In its essence, the principle suggested how a body of individuals should operate and was at the center of debate concerning where legislative power was rooted—in the sovereign or in the people.

> views give way to views reflecting membership in a community that evokes an obligation to consider the needs and interests of others (Barber 1994, 69).

CMC via the Internet, had the potential to overcome barriers to enlightened understanding and to achieve control of the public agenda.

CMC drastically reduces the citizen's information costs. Enormous stores of information can be accessed at a touch of a screen, the click of a mouse, the push of a button or a key or even the statement of a command. Combined with the ease of communication this information makes it feasible to create political agendas and to form political organizations to carry them out. Most—possibly all—of this can be accomplished without requiring the members to meet face to face. The Internet is a worldwide network, accessible from myriad computerized devices with appropriate hardware, software and access to wired or wireless connections: terminals, PCs, cellular telephones, cable televisions, almost anything with a keyboard and a screen.

J.C.R. Licklider, who became Director of the Command and Control Research Division of the U.S. Defense Department's Advanced Research Projects Agency (ARPA) in 1962, was among the first to see these possibilities. Indeed, he envisioned citizens using "home computer consoles" to keep themselves,

> ...informed about and interested in, and involved in, the process of government.... The key is the self-motivating exhilaration that accompanies truly effective interaction with information through a good console and a good network to a good [central] computer (Hafner and Lyon 1996, 34).

Licklider changed the Division's focus from playing out war-game scenarios to developing time sharing systems and common languages among computers. To this end, he distributed research contracts to the USA's leading computer centers, including Stanford, MIT, UCLA and UC-Berkeley. In 1967 the Division, having changed its name to the Information Processing Technology Office, produced the design for what became ARPANET, a major forerunner of today's Internet.

Inspired by his wartime experience at Los Alamos and by Licklider's vision, John G. Kemeny, the great mathematician (and President of Dartmouth College 1971-80), co-invented and developed the Dartmouth Time Sharing System and the BASIC computer language suitable to such systems. He popularized the social possibilities of computer networks in *Man and the Computer*, published in 1972. He predicted a national computer network with terminals in millions of homes, a National Automated Reference Library, computer that provided personalized news and greatly enhanced education via time sharing and simple programming languages (Hauben n.d; Kemeny 1972).

Even though democratic theorists had long been concerned about citizens' access to relevant information, until the advent of Internet and related ICTs most had focused upon the importance of free and independent mass media. For mass publics and for most organizations, communication patterns were assumed to be predominantly hierarchical or else aligned in a series of spokes and wheels. Information was distributed to citizens or to members from the top down or from the center outward, that is, from the few to the many. Feedback from citizens or members to those at the top or the center, however, was largely restricted to established channels, that is, limited from the many to the few.

Ithiel de Sola Pool's exploration of the implications of cable technology for political participation represented one of the first efforts to integrate CMC with traditional concerns about active democratic citizenship. In his edited volume, *Talking Back: Citizen Feedback and Cable Technology*, Pool and his contributors pondered problems that foreshadowed those raised about the Internet (Pool 1973). To what degree should local communities exercise control over cable television? How could people of modest means, let alone the poor, be assured access to broadband cable and other advanced technologies that promise to enhance citizen feedback to elected representatives and other public officials? What were the prospects for using cable technology for group dialogue and social choice? To what extent would cable television technology allow citizens to access other media? And finally, how would commercial users of cable technology affect CMC?

The above works made clear that citizens could employ publicly accessible interactive computer networks to learn about issues of public concern and to communicate their ideas to fellow citizens, elected representatives and other public officials, but they could not assure that CMC would be used for public purposes. Feasibility did not guarantee inevitability. Public or private resources, for which there were many competing purposes, had to be allocated to the task. And in the late 1960s and early 1970s governments did not give a high priority to developing computer networks that enhanced political participation.

In fact, the late 1960s and early 1970s were punctuated with periods of domestic turmoil in the United States and Western Europe. As the Vietnam War dragged on and as big corporations merged and became multinational, many feared that the balance of power was tipping away from the people and their representatives and toward the interests of the few. The few were mostly those who controlled the vast military-industrial complex that President Eisenhower had warned against in his Farewell Address (Eisenhower 1961; Zinn 1999, 541-562). Far from viewing the expansion and consolidation of the economic power of multinational corporations—globalization in today's parlance—as largely benign, critics alleged that uncontrolled economic expansion was itself an impossible dream. They saw too few acres of land, even too few fish in the sea, to provide everyone with meaty diets of the sort consumed by citizens of advanced industrial nations. Moreover, the world lacked sufficient mineral resources and fossil fuels to replicate the industrial growth in developing nations that advanced nations had experienced. And to top things off, they feared that the environmental pollution caused by current patterns of production and consumption portended ecological disaster. The French political scientist, Maurice Duverger, summarized this discontent:

> Cities are becoming uninhabitable just when almost everyone is compelled to live in them; nature is polluted and destroyed just when people feel a growing need to enjoy it; all modes of travel are intolerable just when journeys are increasing in number and length; old age takes on the proportions of a curse just when the ratio of old to young is rising; the grip of bigness is tightening just when everyone is acquiring the material and cultural means to enhance his own individuality; and so on (Duverger 1974,191).

These objections were difficult to dismiss out of hand, for they emanated from mainstream journalists and social scientists, not just from the favorites of the radical left. Books that expounded remedies to limit corporate influence over governmental policies and to stem environmental degradation gained wide readership (Dahl 1970; Galbraith 1973; Mintz and Cohen 1971; Vernon 1971). E.F. Schumacher's *Small is Beautiful: Economics as if People Mattered*, first published in 1973, became an international bestseller and inspired a number of organizations devoted to implementing sustainable economic plans for decentralized units of limited scale (Schumacher 1975).[12] Even though these critics recognized control of information as a critical resource, none placed networked CMC in the central roles that Licklider, Kemeny, or Pool had foreseen (cf. Bimber 2003, 1-33).

In *Viable Democracy*, published in 1979, Margolis developed a model that attempted to combine the advantages of decentralized autonomy and control of information with networked CMC's capacity to overcome problems of distance by providing access for citizens or their elected representatives to obtain otherwise costly information:

> Such a computer-based network can be operated in interactive mode. That is…the citizen users can converse with the system, inquire about information available, delve as superficially or as deeply in subjects as they desire. …Any user of a properly programmed network should be able to send messages to any other user (or classes of users). In practical terms this means that a citizen could easily send a message to any of his representatives, indicating his opinions about some subjects, his ability or desire to present new information, or any other suggestions he thought appropriate. And members of organized groups could easily communicate with one another and exchange information (Margolis 1979, 161).

The model aimed to provide citizens with equal opportunity to gather information and to express their thought. While no artificial barriers would preclude a citizen from becoming involved in any given policy question, it presumed that different

12 See, for instance, the E.F. Schumacher Society <http://www.schumachersociety.org/> and the Community Economic Development Center <http://www.sfu.ca/cedc/ > accessed 15 August 2003.

groups of citizens would concern themselves with different issues and that most would choose not to participate. The model encouraged a broader—though still elite—type of political participation, a more democratic form of pluralism.

The scope of this pluralism, however, extended beyond what we ordinarily think is the public's business. Recognizing that large privately capitalized corporations used proprietary information to affect public policy Margolis argued that the network should allow access to "all computerized files of appropriately designated organizations, whether public or private" (Margolis 1979, 164). Nevertheless, a good deal of proprietary information seemed *prima facie* to be none of the public's business. Consider military and trade secrets, ongoing investigative reports, manufacturing formulas; lists of purchases and inventories; or employee and clientele records. And what about medical, credit and insurance files? Margolis conceded the necessity of restricting the general public's access to some sensitive data, but "in no case should any computerized information be excluded from the purview of elected members of the central legislature" (Margolis 1979, 164). Data could be shielded from public access in accordance with general principles laid down by legislation or through exclusions granted by special legislation. The burden of demonstrating the necessity of restricting access would fall upon those who wished to restrict it. They would have to convince the people's elected representatives that such restrictions were required. Otherwise, citizens and their representatives would find themselves saddled with the same burdens they already had when they needed access to proprietary information in order to decide questions of public policy.[13]

But could citizens trust such information to their representatives? Some unscrupulous legislators would undoubtedly attempt to exploit their privileged access for private advantage. It was here that democrats had to make a leap of faith. Democracy presumed that the overwhelming majority of legislators would use their own equal access to networked information to expose for public scrutiny the demagogues' false or distorted claims, and that faced with such evidence, a reasonable citizenry would reject their demagogic appeals. In the end, to whom could people trust sensitive information, if not to their elected representatives? Should the information be left in the hands of unelected bureaucrats and technological elites? At least the legislators must answer directly to the citizenry; the others need not.

The information network was a necessary but not sufficient condition for rational citizen participation. It had to be overlaid with the institutional reforms that concentrated decision-making in smaller units of government and industry insofar as possible. This did not mean that large units of government or industry were inherently bad. But it did imply that their decision-making should be limited to those problems that smaller units could not handle well, such as environmental

13 Enron's "private entity" partnerships provide a good example of a corporation's using proprietary information to obscure violations of accounting standards and to hide evidence that would subject it legal penalties. See Emshwiller (2001).

pollution, exploration of the ocean floor and outer-space, and the underwriting of national defense and national infrastructure projects that required heavy capital investment. Other reforms such as the following were also proposed:

> protection for whistleblowers who came forward with responsible criticism of their organizations; placement of public representatives on policy-making boards of large corporate enterprises; and new methods of accounting that included the costs of environmental damage, depletion of natural resources, or displacement of population (Margolis 1979, 170-179).

Benjamin Barber also placed a publicly accessible information network at the heart of his *Strong Democracy* (Barber 1984). He too favored community based political decision-making, particularly because it tended to involve and enlighten a larger portion of the citizenry than did the "thin democracy" that elitists like Berelson had advocated. More than Margolis, however, Barber stressed the importance of politics as a group activity involving dynamic interaction. He advocated placing interactive nodes at community centers where citizens would meet to deliberate matters of public policy and to communicate the results of their deliberations to their representatives. To encourage direct responsible participation Citizens would gather at the community centers at the same times that their local Councils met.

Jeffrey Abramson, F. Christopher Arterton, and Garry R. Orren, in accord with Barber and Margolis, advanced a strong argument on behalf of what they called The Electronic Commonwealth, a new vision for how the new media of computers, two-way television, satellites, videos and telephones could remedy "lost citizen power" in democratic polities (Abramson et al. 1988, 277). For Abramson and his colleagues, an electronic commonwealth would harness computer power and other ICTs to end the isolation and parochialism of democracy. The new media's power could be used civically to create an electronic and borderless town hall meeting where citizens could substantively deliberate local, regional, and national issues. By the mid 1980s various communities had set up cable networks that allowed for interactive feedback. Some covered city councils or commissions; others involved neighborhood housing groups or community boards. Some were underwritten experimentally with one-time grants; others were intended to become more permanent. Christopher Arterton and his associates were in the forefront of political scientists observing and assessing the success of these networks for increasing responsible and effective citizen participation (Arterton 1987; Abramson, Arterton and Orren 1988).

The resultant impacts of new ICTs upon democracy have been decidedly mixed. Even though the technologies worked, attendance dropped and participation generally lessened after the initial novelty wore off. As Max Weber had famously observed, "Politics is a strong and slow boring of hard boards."[14] The general public

---

14 Weber's 1919 lecture, 'Politics as Vocation', Harper's Magazine Archive <http://www.harpers.org/archive/2008/06/hbc-90003050> accessed 9 February 2008.

ordinarily seems unwilling to expend great efforts on politics. And notwithstanding CMC's ability to cut citizens' information and communication costs, the process of building coalitions to resolve problems democratically remains slow, difficult and tedious. In the end, it seems as if most people would rather get on with their lives and leave public policy decisions to their representatives. As Coglianese (2007) argues, "most citizens are disengaged from politics and public policy to such a degree and for reasons that no amount of computer programs or technological innovations are likely to change" (Coglianese 2007, 119). Those who used the new technologies to participate tended to be those who participated using the old ones. Even as the World Wide Web, combined with the emergence of graphic browsers, turned the Internet into a mass phenomenon, the dominant political participants remained largely those individuals, elites, political parties, and interest groups who dominated politics in the real world (Hindman 2007, Margolis and Resnick 2000).

E-democracy initiatives have not fared much better. As Andrew Chadwick has pointed out, "the road to e-democracy is littered with the burnt-out hulks of failed projects" and has very few success stories (Chadwick 2006, 102). The theoretical impetus for e-democracy initiatives stems from newer versions of participatory democracy, especially the ideas of deliberative democracy and the public sphere. As suggested earlier, deliberative democracy provided a viable alternative to adversarial versions of democracy. The Internet and related ICTs imbued participatory democrats of the deliberative strand with much optimism for bringing about what Al Gore called a "new Athenian Age of democracy" (quoted in Brook and Boal 1995).

Three new models heralded this new age of democracy: communitarian Internet democracy, liberal individualist Internet democracy, and deliberative Internet democracy (Dahlberg 2001a; 2001b). The first two models offered little in the vein of participatory and deliberative democracy. Communitarian models are exemplified by virtual communities where members can isolate themselves from the realities of life and focus upon their common interests, interests which ordinarily are not perceived to be political in any sense. Liberal individualist models of Internet democracy are the virtual representations of adversary democracy. These models presuppose the sanctity of individual self-interest and frame politics as a market of sellers and consumers where citizens are provided political information to make them savvy political shoppers. Both of these models provide forms of democratic politics within the Net, but with weak or thin participatory elements.

Using Habermas' communicative theory and public sphere arguments as criteria for evaluating how well deliberative e-democracy models perform in practice has proved difficult. To begin with, examples of e-democracy initiatives of the deliberative kind are few in number. Dahlberg (2001a) has established a set of six requirements of public sphere discourse to determine whether or not attempts to realize e-democracy create an online deliberative public sphere of the Habermasian kind. Chadwick (2006) has argued that only a handful of these initiatives e.g., E-democracy.org and Commbill.net, are sufficiently plugged into the policy-making process to provide opportunities for substantive citizen participation. Dahlberg himself has remained skeptical concerning the prospects of substantive participatory e-democracy. Arguing in concert with Benjamin Barber, he suggests that the failure of even the most deliberative models to create a meaningful public sphere stems more from a misguided political culture of commercialism and individualism than from a lack of proper technology.

As early as 1997, scholars expressed doubt about the Net's ability to foster a truly deliberative democracy Buchstein (1997); Shapiro (1999) and Sunstein (2001) cited the narrowness of individualistic concerns as hampering the Internet's ability to foster a flourishing public sphere with a healthy dose of deliberation. Papacharissi (2002) suggested that while the Internet had indeed created a public space for political deliberation it had done little to transform this space into an actual public sphere. Like Dahlberg, Papacharissi was concerned that politics on the Net would replicate the "bricks and mortar" political culture rather than foster a new and more open one. Other scholars began to advance alternative perspectives to address what they considered to be the shortcomings of Habermas' public sphere theory as applied to Net politics. Dahlgren (2005) contended that even though deliberative democracy and public sphere theorists claimed to recognize a multiplicity of values in politics, they prized rationality in politics above all else. It followed that e-democracy initiatives that incorporated these values were unlikely to succeed because they ignored irrational aspects of "civic cultures" and the "many ways in which citizenship and democracy can be enacted" (Dahlgren 2005, 158). Still, scholars and practitioners have continued to advance e-democracy on the shoulders of deliberative and public sphere theorists with calls for transnational e-democracy and a more participatory e-government (Bohman 2004; Wiklund 2005).

The difficulties of implementing strong democratic politics on the Net do not mean that ordinary citizens are incapable of intelligent democratic practice. James Fishkin and his associates conducted experiments throughout the 1990s that demonstrated the sophistication of ordinary citizens when they were placed in an environment conducive to democratic deliberation (Fishkin 1991; Fishkin and Laslett 2003). The experiments worked well for those who participated, but how much would (or could) society pay to support an infrastructure that allowed any citizen to join in virtually any political deliberation? Even the idea of deliberative polling, where citizens receive background information for any given question, together with arguments pro and con, is costly to implement. Deliberative democracy on a face-to-face basis is possible but impractical for governing entities with populations larger than a few thousand people. Deliberation via ICTs is possible, but practical only if there were a political culture in place that prized such deliberation, and a society willing to maintain a publicly accessible infrastructure stocked with accurate up-to-date information.

Even though networked CMC makes it possible for citizens to participate more fully in public policy decisions, at least three major problems remain unresolved. 1) Who determines the standards for the network and how are they enforced?

Ultimately, who is responsible for running the network? 2) Who pays the costs not only for running the network, but also for supplying information, maintaining security, and providing citizens access? 3) Finally, what are the socio-political consequences of a worldwide network that allows users a wide latitude of choice but also has the power to record every exchange of information—commercial transactions, emails, website visits, page views, downloads etc.—that takes place on it?

Whose Cyberspace?

The "realistic" remedies discussed in the previous section rely upon the Internet to reestablish a modern equivalent of the Agora, a public sphere online where citizens can conduct informed deliberations and achieve agreement on public policy. To make such a space functional, however, those who operate the network must (as J.C.R. Licklider observed) "agree upon some language or, at least upon some conventions for asking such questions as 'What language do you speak?'" (Hafner and Lyon 1996, 38). Most importantly, from the standpoint of democratic theory, someone must write the code that implements the agreement. Who will do this, and how will it be paid for? (Lessig 1999).

In the beginning, what we call the Internet was occupied mostly by researchers and academics who worked in the public and non-profit sectors and were fairly sophisticated computer users. Altruism and mutual aid were dominant ethics among these individuals. Although some were more skilled than others, no strict division of labor prevailed. Each could freely produce, share and consume information. The U.S. government and other public and non-profit organizations underwrote most of the costs, and commercial activity was generally forbidden. Politics within the Net resembled something like a free market of ideas, although when it came to determining standards, the most technologically skilled usually held sway. (Margolis and Resnick 2000, 1-52).

All this changed when the World Wide Web and graphic browsers drew millions of users into cyberspace. The great majority came to cyberspace as consumers rather than creators of information. They could be guided into a political economy that yielded a profit. They brought with them the same interests they had in the real world, and political participation hardly ever ranked among the "top ten." Most of the infrastructure was privatized, and commercial activity became the norm. Professionals were hired to design and develop the content of websites and to attract potential customers through advertising both online and through established media in the real world. Today, most users find that their online activities—whether economic, social, political, recreational or otherwise informational—are structured by Web professionals.

Even though we shall see that the Web has increased the visibility of some political parties and interest groups that the established mass media generally have ignored, their impact on public policy thus far has not grown significantly. Nor has there been a great surge of new interest in politics: why would citizens necessarily change their habits once they hopped onto the Web? By and large the dominant political, social and business groups of the real world have succeeded in replicating their dominance in cyberspace. Contrary to the hopes of classical democratic theorists, established political parties and interest groups have used the Web with better effect to mobilize their supporters than have grassroots organizations used it to increase deliberative participation in public policymaking.[15] As we have pointed out, citizens use the Web more frequently to conduct routine business with government—the implementation of public policies—than to participate in deliberative political discussions—the formulation of those policies.

To conduct business online with government agencies or commercial firms, however, requires a far more structured and bureaucratic environment than did the free-wheeling interchanges of early Internet. And it has been the conduct of e-government—the routine business between citizens, agencies, corporations, and government—that has characterized most e-democracy efforts. Part of this trend had already been suggested in scholars' observations regarding the expansion of commercial and consumer interests and interaction models on the Internet, that is, e-commerce). Papacharissi (2002) had already warned that global capitalism could force the Internet to adapt to the existing political culture rather than forge new ground. And Chadwick (2006) has rightly pointed out that even within deliberative online communities, the principles of operation and mission have been organized largely around business and pecuniary interests. This commodification of the Net has had a profound effect on how citizens conceive Internet politics and democracy. E-government models, largely formed on the basis of e-commerce principles, now dominate the concepts of politics and democracy on the Net.

The commodification of Internet politics was no surprise. Deliberative theorists Amy Gutmann and Dennis Thompson had already suggested that adversary models of democracy (what they termed "aggregative democracy") were not only far removed from substantive deliberation but also resembled a consumer market. In such democracies:

> Politicians and parties, [like producers], formulate their positions and devise their strategies in response to the demands of voters who, like consumers, express their preferences by choosing among competing products (the candidates and their parties). Whatever debate takes place in the campaign serves a function more like that of advertising (informing the voters about the comparative advantages of the candidates) than like that of argument (seeking to change minds by giving reasons) (Gutmann and Thompson 2004, 14).

Aggregative democracy, by its very nature, furthers a non-deliberative spirit and a weak democratic citizenship. It enshrines a democratic politics where citizens are socialized as political consumers. In such market style politics, information and

15 See Chapters 5 and 7.

deliberation are also important but for different reasons. Whereas in a deliberative democracy open information and discourse are essential pieces of collective judgment and do not presuppose any normative closure, in aggregative politics they are pre-fabricated centrally and designed to elicit wide acceptance and rapid closure.[16] Transforming citizens into consumers is part of a larger cultural shift from a market economy to a market society. This shift nurtures a perilous propensity to reduce civil society's human goods and desires to simple economic goods and desires.[17]

"The commodification of everything" or what Habermas termed "the colonization of the lifeworld" is the rapid and seemingly unending transition from a market economy to a market society.[18] In such a scenario, "the market and its categories of thought…dominate ever more areas of our lives," areas such as "our most intimate relationships…[and]…our understanding of what it means to be human."[19] In a similar vein, Zygmunt Bauman has called our current era a "society of consumers" by which he means a "society that 'interpellates' its members primarily…as consumers; and a society that judges and evaluates its members mostly by their consumption-related capacities and products" (Bauman 2001, 83). Such a phenomenon, he argues, leads to the:

> …perception and treatment of virtually all the parts of the social setting and of the actions they evoke…by the 'consumerist syndrome' of cognitive and evaluating predispositions. 'Life politics,' containing Politics with a capital 'P' as much as the nature of interpersonal relations, tends to be reshaped in the likeness of the means and objects of consumption and along the lines implied by the *consumerist syndrome* [italics original] (Bauman 2001, 83-84).

Call them what you will: "The commodification of everything," "the colonization of the life-world" or "the society of consumers": all of them transmogrify political life into a state of affairs where "citizens are consumers, and politics are economics by other means" (Sandel 2003, 96).

The citizen as consumer syndrome represents a broader cultural shift toward a market society. Such a society and its accompanying politics are antithetical to

16 Although neither Senator Clinton nor Obama was likely to have a sufficient number of popularly elected delegates to secure the Democratic Party's nomination prior to the 2008 national convention, witness the prominent party officials, contributors, and commentators who urged Senator Clinton to withdraw from the presidential nominating contest even before the Pennsylvania primary took place. All for the good of the party, of course.

17 *The Hedgehog Review*, an influential contemporary journal of culture and ideas, devoted an entire issue to this serious problem. See "The Commodification of Everything," *The Hedgehog Review*.

18 For an excellent discussion of this concept see P.H. Sedgwick (1999). Also consider S.K. White (1988).

19 See 'The Commodification of Everything: Editorial Introduction' (2003, 5).

the classical democratic view of the citizen as policy-making participant and to the deliberative conception of democracy. As things stand, therefore, the dynamics of a market society reinforce the habits of an aggregative democracy to produce the citizen as consumer syndrome that characterizes much of today's democratic politics.

The commodification of politics on the Net reflects the commodification of politics and society in the real world. While there have been numerous attempts to establish models of e-democracy that are faithful to the classical ideals of participation, recent models tend to consider politics on the Net in terms of e-government where citizens are customers and clients, where government and public officials are sellers, and where politics is a market. The adaptation of market categories and e-government to politics on the Net has perhaps led scholars to argue that the term *information government* best encapsulates

> "the significant changes of governing and governance that occur in part facilitated by new technologies...[that alter]...the flows of information within government as well as between government and citizens" that characterize most accounts of e-government and e-democracy (Mayer-Schönberger and Lazer 2007, 5-6).

These accounts emphasize providing online services to citizen-consumers, increasing efficiency, automation, and storage and retrieval of information within public agencies to a greater extent than bringing democratic participation into the policy making process. Narrow conceptions of e-government focus solely on the provision of online services to citizen-consumers (e.g., West 2005).

Broader understandings of e-government add considerations of information and communication flows that produce an efficient and automated public sector where "the Internet [is used] as an instrument to improve government structures and processes and to foster the culture and values of public administrations" (OECD Observer 2003). The broadest accounts of electronic government add the implementation of some forms of democratic processes to encourage more robust political participation (e.g., Thomas and Streib 2003). Just as all versions of electronic government can be conceptualized through the lens of information flows, so too can they be conceptualized in terms of the citizen as consumer syndrome rather than the citizen as policy-making participant. We believe that for the foreseeable future, e-government will further the citizen consumer model of democratic politics—both in its aggregative sense as well as in its online provision of services—rather than the deliberative citizen model in which the citizen actively participates in policy-making.

Electronic government that treats citizens as consumers represents an outgrowth of CMC, the Internet, and other ICTs to conduct business transactions. In its most generic sense, the definition of e-commerce is readily applicable to any e-activity including politics. Rayport and Jaworski (2002) suggest, it is "a technology-mediated exchange between parties (individuals or organizations) as well as the electronically based intra- or inter-organizational activities that facilitate such exchanges" (Rayport and Jaworski 2002, 4). If one considers e-commerce from a number of different perspectives (e.g., communications, commercial, business processes, services, learning, collaborative, and community), one finds a great deal of similarity and overlap between e-commerce and e-government (Turban et al. 2004). E-government replicates e-commerce practices and procedures. The assumptions are in many ways the same—online transactions about goods and services within businesses (government agencies), between businesses (agency to agency), and between businesses and consumers (government agencies and citizens). Berthon and Williams (2007), for example, propose a re-conceptualization and extension of e-democracy based upon the rapid changes in electronic business and marketing practices (e.g., Linux and open-source software) that govern the interaction between producers and consumers. The authors suggest that political consumers (i.e., citizens) should be characterized as coducers (i.e., co-producers) and no longer simply as consumers. Regardless of their analyses and suggestions, many scholars continue to consider e-democracy, broadly understood, through the categories of commercial society.

This is not to say that employing new ICTs will have no significant effect on governance. As we have pointed out, citizens in a democracy are both rulers and subjects. They hold the ultimate authority to choose and to dismiss those who decide great political issues of the day, but they also have obligations to the authority they wield collectively, that is, to the legitimate rule of the officials they have chosen. Governments enforce laws and implement public policies. Democratic citizens should expect their government to be responsive to them in their everyday transactions with it. Considerations such as these have led theorists to extend the idea of democratic responsiveness to the administration of governmental policies. Citizens are not only franchise holders who ultimately exercise political power; they also are the government's clients and customers.

As we have argued, the idea of citizen as client or customer, combined with burgeoning worldwide access to the Internet and related ICTs, has led many theorists and practitioners to advocate e-government as the modern form of representative democracy. They envision e-governments realizing modern representative democracy by employing ICT features that implement policies expeditiously and provide services efficiently. With transparent organization and user-friendly programming, elected officials and bureaucrats can employ ICTs to exchange relevant information with their peers as well as with their citizen clientele individually or in groups. In addition to reducing duplication of records and services among governmental agencies, these exchanges can provide administrators with better feedback regarding citizens' satisfaction with the policies and services they provide.

Nearly everyone concedes that citizens of a democracy must have the authority to choose and to dismiss those who ultimately decide the great political issues. Theorists who emphasize the importance of preserving classical democratic virtues, however, contend that modern democracies ought to encourage their citizens to employ new ICTs to help determine which policies and services government should offer in the first place. Citizens cannot exercise this authority properly if their roles are merely analogous to those of savvy customers. Customers, after all, concern themselves mostly with the quality of transactions that satisfy private demands. They generally are not expected to consider questions about whether or not certain products or services ought to be offered or about how the collective impact of customers' private transactions might affect the quality of life for the society as a whole.[20]

20 See for example, Clift (2002) and Slevin (2000).

Chapter 4
Democracy, Tolerance and the Internet

Tolerance has long been considered not only one of the key political virtues of the modern era but also one of the core values of a liberal democracy. Indeed, it would be impossible for a modern liberal democracy to function without a significant amount of it. Democratic procedure, which we discussed in Chapter 1, is a peaceful method of resolving disagreements that implies tolerance. Political opposition must be tolerated and incorporated into the process of democratic decision making. Though the conflicts which divide citizens are often intense, citizens in a democracy must be willing to accept the outcomes of a fair democratic process–one that requires a general adherence to constitutional procedure, or "the rules of the game." A commitment to tolerance prevents conflict from degenerating into violence and chaos. Without a commitment to the norms of political tolerance, a democratic regime could not survive.

The modern concept of tolerance was born in a post-Reformation world wracked by religious conflicts and wars.[1] One of the first problems that had to be solved was how to reestablish peaceful relations between state and church. Authoritarian solutions, which relied on political power to impose religious uniformity on a society composed of contending religious factions, raised deep moral and political questions. Using force against those who were simply following the practices they believed would save their souls threatened the civic peace, if not the legitimacy of the state itself. Liberal political thought worked out a framework for handling problems that arose when politics and religion intersected. Peace was to be established on the basis of religious toleration rather than repression, and order was to be preserved by holding religious fanaticism in check. The hope was that a moderate, tolerant state could live in a peaceful harmonious relationship with moderate, reasonable and tolerant religions. This early form of limited tolerance has gradually expanded beyond the sphere of religion. Our contemporary understanding of tolerance encompasses differences in social and political views, cultural practices, and ethnic, racial and gender identities.

Though it is not clear how much tolerance is necessary for a democratic society to function, a certain minimum is required. The democratic political process necessitates that citizens, no matter how unpopular, be allowed to voice their views on public affairs, join political groups, vote and stand for public office. A

1 This is not to suggest that previous historical periods were inherently intolerant and oppressive. Several studies have reasonably established the existence of robust practices of tolerance prior to the modern period. Consider Laursen and Nederman (1998) and Nederman (2000).

liberal democracy, cannot permit the public to use the force of numbers to prevent full political participation of unpopular and disfavored minorities. Even if citizens strongly disagree with other people's religious beliefs or find themselves offended by others' cultural practices, they should not look to the state to enforce social and cultural uniformity. They need not approve of all the life styles, but they must respect the fundamental rights and the equal liberty of other citizens.

Critics of modern American society believe that such formal, legal tolerance by the government is not enough. For them, tolerance is not simply a matter of constitutional restraints. A democratic society should be tolerant of diversity in all aspects of its social and political life. Civil society should recognize diversity, and citizens should be truly tolerant in their personal interactions. For these critics, tolerance is an ideal to be cherished and struggled for. When the Internet was created it seemed to be exactly what was needed to realize the dreams of a free, democratic and tolerant society. In short, the Internet would emancipate individuals to be co-producers or *coducers* of the democratic good life. As Yochai Benkler suggests, "it is in this sense that the Internet democratizes" (Benkler 2006, 272).

Tolerance and Democratic Theory

Classical democratic theory insists that a functioning democracy requires tolerance of the "rules of the game" of democratic politics. Civil liberties must be protected, and dissenting political groups must be permitted to function. We must neither restrict nor suppress ideas and views with which we do not agree, nor use the government to oppress those whose culture, ethnicity, or sexual orientation we find distasteful. This understanding of tolerance which extends the idea of religious toleration to other forms of social and cultural differences in society has been greatly influenced by the liberal ideal of individual autonomy developed in the 19th century.

The ideal of individual autonomy entailed freedom of thought and expression as well as freedom from intolerant social attitudes and prejudices. The autonomous individual was the individual freed from the constraints of repressive political regimes, stultifying authoritarian traditions, and mind numbing ignorance. The autonomous individual required liberty to fully develop his or her humanity, and such development was a basic driving force for further human progress. Individual autonomy must be protected against those political and social forces which would stifle it. Tolerance was seen as a means for permitting fully human development.

J.S. Mill in his great work *On Liberty* supplied a number of liberal arguments for individual autonomy and tolerance. In the realm of freedom of speech and expression he argued that society needs to tolerate dissenting opinions and unpopular views because they are necessary for the emergence of truth and progress in the long run. Similarly, a progressive society must allow for individual experiments in living because only in a society which tolerates social differences can the full potential of each human being be realized. Such liberal arguments helped extend the modern understanding of tolerance beyond the sphere of religion to encompass differences in social and political views, cultural practices, and ethnic, racial and gender identities.

Upper class prejudice against the lower classes was one of the most important social barriers to extending democracy at the time Mill was writing. He was a strong advocate of increased democracy, and confronted those who opposed full citizenship for the lower classes because they feared their lack of education and political sophistication would ruin society. He argued that political participation would widen their social horizon and motivate them to learn about social and political issues. Though somewhat of an elitist himself, Mill still believed in the possibility of mass democratic participation as well as its value for human progress and development.

Elite democratic theory, which we referred to in Chapter 1, shares neither Mill's nor the modern classical democrat's optimism about political participation. The collapse of European democracies in the face of totalitarian challenges in the 20th century made such idealism seem naive. Democratic elitists called for more realistic democratic theories grounded in empirical science not in idealistic fantasies about how citizens in a democracy should act. Unlike the hidebound conservatives of Mill's day, elite democratic theorists accept universal suffrage. Nonetheless, they make many of the same assumptions about the inadequate political capacity of the poorer sectors of society.

According to elite democratic theory the masses are ill equipped to play an active and creative role in the political process. Their political participation ought to be limited to a choice among competing elites. Elite democrats fear that many ordinary citizens harbor intolerant attitudes and views which they would unleash in the right political circumstances. There must be sufficient political participation to legitimate the regime, but excessive participation is dangerous because it will empower those who do not respect the norms of democracy and civil liberties.

While tolerance plays a major role in the description of the citizen in liberal democratic theory, its role is not as significant in elite democratic theory. That the ordinary citizen does not live up to the ideals of tolerance does not worry elitist democrats. In their view, the attempt of liberal political scientists to measure the amount of tolerance in American society has often confused tolerance per se with democratic norms or attitudes. Findings that citizens are not fully tolerant of extremist groups led classical liberal democrats to conclude that American democracy was in danger (Stouffer 1955). Such results raised no serious problems for elitist democrats. Their democratic theory does not require high levels of tolerance among the ordinary citizens. They need not be tolerant of dissent in general or political groups or movements that radically challenge the existing democratic order. It's enough for the operation of a democracy if the masses are willing to tolerate a loyal opposition that can serve as a check on those in power.

Elite democratic theory holds that democracy can be preserved so long as there are competing elites committed to democratic values.[2] The democratic elites

2 One wonders if elite democratic theory could be substantiated in today's political and civic culture. For example, in a recent study conducted by the Intercollegiate Studies

should have the psychological traits of openness, flexibility and tolerance. These traits are correlated with high status occupations, privileged social class position, wealth and higher education (Sullivan et al. 1982, 17-19). Tolerance is a virtue for elite democratic theory just as it is for liberal democratic theory, but it doesn't expect that this virtue will be widely distributed. Nor does elite theory worry much that ordinary citizens are neither terribly tolerant of others nor fully committed to the rules of democratic politics and civil liberties.

Radical democrats also see tolerance as a virtue, but they believe that modern society suffers from an appalling lack of it given its profound lack of real democracy in the first place.[3] Findings that significant sectors of society are intolerant of others must not be accepted simply as a fact that cannot be changed; rather it should serve to spur concerted political action to change social attitudes and institutions. Pointing to constitutional protections of freedoms and the legal tolerance of dissent is not sufficient. Radical democrats envision a society that has a deeper understanding of tolerance, one grounded in the idea that truly liberal autonomy requires more than legal or constitutional tolerance. Just as representative democracy as practiced today does not fulfill the ideal of direct political participation, liberal democracy's limited tolerance of some forms of dissent fails to satisfy the ideal of full tolerance.

In *Tolerance: Between Forbearance and Acceptance*, Oberdiek argues that tolerance encompasses three types of attitudes. He identifies them as follows:

1. Bare toleration, a grudging acknowledgment that we have to live with others though we would prefer not to. The barely tolerant can easily cease being tolerant given the slightest provocation.
2. Mere toleration, an acceptance of the other supported by the judgment that they are inferior in some way. This attitude approaches indifference and complacency, a satisfaction with the status quo.
3. Full tolerance, the recognition that others' attitudes, beliefs and ways of life are of value to them because they have chosen them freely for themselves.

Institute, more than 1,700 people failed a basic test of American political history, cultural institutions, foreign relations and market economics with the average score being 49 percent. Elected officials failed the exam with a lower average score than that of the general public – 44 percent. See Intercollegiate Studies Institute (2008), *Our Fading Heritage: Americans Fail a Basic Test on Their History and Institutions* <http://www.americancivicliteracy.org/> accessed 3 December 2008.

3 Some radicals are opposed to toleration as a virtue arguing that those who want greater tolerance merely want to see the triumph of liberal capitalism. They equate tolerance with a shallow skepticism that undermines commitment to all values and movements other than those which uphold liberalism itself. One who is certain of his or her values and on the right side of history should not be tolerant of those who are committed to deeply mistaken and morally bankrupt values.

Oberdiek equates full tolerance with Mill's idea of individuals being free to devise their own experiments in living and to develop communities according to their own idea of the good life. He points out that this attitude of full acceptance of others moves beyond mere tolerance. Even though we are not tempted to adopt another way of life, we nonetheless acknowledge the value of alternative ways of living (Oberdiek 2001, 28-33).

Radical democrats envisage a true democratic society as one that reflects the ideal of full tolerance or full acceptance, not merely the narrow tolerance necessary for the formal process of democratic decision-making. Indeed, to the extent that they have been influenced by modern multi-culturalism, some insist that tolerance is not the appropriate stance for us to take in a multi-cultural world. We should endorse the moral values of difference and accept other cultures, not simply tolerate them.

Early advocates of the Internet had such high hopes for its transformative effects on society because it seemed a domain of pure tolerance. Those concerned with radical politics hoped that the marginalization which so many dissident groups faced could be overcome by this powerful new communication medium. Those outside the political mainstream could easily and cheaply express themselves, broadcast their message and organize without having to deal with intolerant publics manipulated by organized interests. People who faced discrimination because of their race, religion or sexual orientation could freely join with sympathetic others in truly humane communities. Cyberspace seemed to promise the transcendence of the prejudice and intolerance that infected much of life in the real world.

Alas, many of these hopes have not been realized. Those who looked to the Internet to solve the problem of intolerance failed to consider that, in addition to creating new opportunities to promote tolerance, the Internet itself could also generate new forms of intolerance. Moreover, we must consider the problem of how extensive tolerance should be. Need we tolerate the intolerant, even those who, if they had the chance, would destroy tolerance itself? This has been called the "paradox of tolerance" because it seems to imply that defending tolerance requires a degree of intolerance (Sullivan et al. 1982, 9). Actually, this is not a true paradox. It simply illustrates the complexity of social reality and the limits of our concepts. John Rawls, one of the most influential philosophers of modern liberalism, argued that though an intolerant group cannot complain if we do not tolerate them, their intolerance alone is not a good enough reason to repress them. In order to restrict their freedom, we must show that they pose a significant threat to society. Even though we can hope to persuade an intolerant group living in a free society to give up their intolerant beliefs and accept common principles of justice, it is always possible that the intolerant group will become too strong for such hopes to be realized. Rawls considers this is a practical problem which philosophy alone cannot resolve (Rawls 1971, 216-220). Utopian partisans of Cyberspace believed that the Internet would not be beset by the problems of tolerating the intolerant. This new liberated space would by itself lead to greater tolerance and freedom. Yet as the Internet matured, more and more evidence arose about its ambiguous nature. It had been touted as a place where free expression reigned, but the intolerance that democratic elitists always knew existed was becoming manifest. Hate groups of all sorts made free use of the Internet to propagate their ideas. As a result, the questions arose as to the ultimate impact this new powerful means of communication would have on tolerance. Would it prove so attractive to the alienated and disaffected that they would form new mass movements opposed to the ideals of tolerance and democracy? Would it foster democratic discussion or lead to an increased fragmentation of the population into narrow intolerant groups exchanging ideas only among themselves? What are the challenges the Internet poses for the future of democracy? To answer such questions we turn to a discussion of the complex ways the Internet has impacted tolerance.

Tolerance and the Internet

The Internet was born as a regime of tolerance. Unlike its history in the real world, tolerance was not achieved through long and protracted political struggle. It was written into the Internet code and was a basic norm governing its operation. In no small measure the Internet's development and flourishing as a realm of pure tolerance was because at the time of its creation, it was under the radar screen. It was an elite and "geeky" form of computer mediated communication in which governments in general as well as the public at large, were not interested. As new, easier to use and less expensive technology spread, however, the Internet attracted millions of new users. It also attracted the attention of people who thought that the tolerance of the early Net was too extensive and who had the power to do something about it.

At its dawn the Internet was hailed as a savior of modern civilization. It would remake our social and political world. So-called Netizens would create free, open and tolerant new communities. Not only would the Net empower ordinary persons to become active citizens of Cyberspace, but it would enable them to transcend the narrow, selfish and bigoted perspectives which dominate the institutions and practices of ordinary life. While most pundits held that it would be greatly beneficial, there had always been an undercurrent of doubt, a fear that this new and powerful technology would result in a more repressive and less tolerant society. Early enthusiasts and detractors alike agreed on one point: the Internet would change everything. So far both the utopian celebrants and the technophobes have been proven wrong. Not everything has changed; indeed, it is not clear exactly what has changed other than the Internet itself. It has turned out to be a highly complex and ambivalent phenomenon, and no more so than when we examine its impact on tolerance.

We will frame the discussion of the impact of the Internet on tolerance in terms of tolerance/intolerance, since a particular practice might have both a positive and a negative impact. It is useful to consider the impact of the Internet in terms of three aspects:

1) Tolerance/intolerance within the Net, which refers to the life of cyber-communities and other Net activities which have little or no impact on life off the Net. It considers how Netizens interact with each other online. Further, this aspect also considers how offline groups and individuals use the Internet to advance tolerance/intolerance solely *within* the Internet itself. 2) The impact of the Net on tolerance/intolerance, which refers to the ways that the Internet affects ordinary life in the real world. This has two aspects, the impact of the structure of the Net itself, and specific intentional uses of the Net to spread tolerance or intolerance offline. 3) Tolerance/Intolerance which affects the Net. This refers to the host of attempts by governments and others to make the Internet a more tolerant (or intolerant) medium. Prior to this discussion, however, it is necessary to examine some important research findings that provide insight into related factors that might affect the possible connections between tolerance/intolerance and the Net.

The Etiology of Tolerance/Intolerance on the Net

The causes of tolerance/intolerance offline have been a subject of much debate and research ever since Samuel Stouffer's classic treatise *Communism, Conformity, and Civil Liberties* (1955). Scholars have suggested numerous explanations often focusing on psychological, cultural, social, and demographic variables.[4] Studying the etiology of tolerance/intolerance has also been the subject of research considering the online activities of individuals. In such work, scholars have discovered that some of the same explanatory variables for tolerance/intolerance offline are mirrored in the online environment. Bimber (2003) has argued that the Net only changes how democracy is practiced making no other difference per se. In his view, the engaged democratic citizen will continue to be engaged online and the offline apathetic citizen will remain the same online. Prior (2007) has also demonstrated this mirroring of offline interest (or lack thereof) on the Internet. For Prior, Internet users come online with prefabricated political, ideological, and media preferences and simply map their offline preferences online. Kobayashi, Ikeda, and Miyata had already demonstrated this finding in their work on the relationship between online and offline social capital and social life arguing that the former "is embedded in the social context of everyday life" (Kobayashi, Ikeda, and Miyata 2006, 605). As is seen below, this online mapping of offline life may account for much of the complex existence of tolerance/intolerance on the Net.

Whether or not the Internet is itself democratic and tolerant and thus breeds more tolerance has added the variable of technology to the portfolio of possible explanations. Patricia Wallace's *The Psychology of the Internet* (1999) was one of the first full-length studies considering the effects of the Internet environment upon human psychology, attitudes and behavior. Most recently, Joinson, McKena, Postmes and Reips (2007) have presented a compendium of research analyzing

4 For a review of many of these types of explanations see Moreno-Riaño (2002).

the psychological aspects of Internet behavior. While all of these approaches reject technological determinism, they do strongly suggest that the Net environment appears to engender significant differences in sociopolitical engagement, attitudes, and behaviors. Kobayashi and Ikeda (2004) have shown, for example, that various uses of ICT devices may affect how and with whom one bonds. In their study, it was discovered that PC e-mail use is reserved for more formal and distant relationships while communications via mobile devices is reserved for bonding between close friends and homogenous others. Both technological means promote social participation but one reaffirms one's view of self with other like selves. Sunstein (2001; 2008) has warned of this self-affirmation through technology and social networks since, in his opinion, these lead to echo-chambers, "cyberbalkanization," and, more recently, "information cocoons" that ultimately destroy democracy. It appears, then, that online political identity formation is rooted in "selective exposure, selective perception, and selective retention" of information (Jamieson and Cappella 2008, 75). As is shown below, however, tolerance/intolerance on the Internet is a complex phenomenon. As Dahlberg and Siapera suggest, "the Internet is not *essentially* democratic: rather…it is a contested terrain" (Dahlberg and Siapera 2007, 13).

Tolerance/Intolerance within the Net

Before the rise of the World Wide Web, the Internet resembled a tolerant political regime consisting of many groups and communities. Netizens conducted their interactions using postings and individual emails. For these participants, the Net seemed like a virtual state of nature. There was no licensing procedure. There was no formal censorship. Anyone could go online at any time and could say and do almost anything he or she pleased. Internal group politics was conducted largely by consensus, and the few rules that had to be obeyed were mostly technical rules written into the very code of the Internet. The overall ethos was laissez-faire, libertarian and tolerant. It inspired utopian speculation. Life in Cyberspace was personal, egalitarian and voluntary in contrast to what was perceived as the corrupt practices of elites and organized interests, and the prejudice and discrimination so abundant in the social life in the real world.

The period of time before the popularity of World Wide Web and the explosion of the online population appeared to be an age of pure tolerance. There was no discrimination based on race, religion, social class, ethnic origin, gender and the like. In fact, this lack of discrimination was considered one of the great strengths of the Internet. This tolerance was captured by the famous *New Yorker* cartoon of a canine sitting at a monitor proclaiming, "On the Internet, no one knows you're a dog" (Steiner 1993). Identity itself was flexible. Many people enjoyed participating in role playing games in which they pretended to be whatever they wanted to be.

Yet there were actions that could bring on sanctions. Even people who thought of themselves as extremely tolerant drew the line somewhere. There were three types of behavior that elicited intolerant responses. The first was irrelevant postings, a great "no-no." Because of limited disk storage and bandwidth, such behavior could not be tolerated. Inadvertently, we encountered this type of intolerance when anonymous Usenet judges accused (and convicted) us of spamming when we launched one of the first Internet surveys of the political attitudes and opinions of Usenet and Listserv subscribers. Without notifying us, the judges removed the survey from numerous Usenet groups, for which, in their determination, our questions were of insufficient relevance (Fisher, Margolis and Resnick 1996a, 1996b).

The second type of intolerance was scorn of "newbies," people who were not acquainted with "netiquette," the informal rules of the Net. Those who went online were expected to have at least minimal knowledge of how things were done, and if they made especially stupid mistakes they were kicked out of groups. This was sometimes justified in terms of shortage of bandwidth, but most often it was simply an expression of ordinary intolerance, a refusal to suffer novices gladly. Unlike those who engaged in irrelevant postings who knew the rules, but broke them, these poor folks just hadn't taken the time to obtain and study the fugitive documentation for proper netiquette.

The third type of intolerance seems quaint today. The early Internet was considered a noncommercial medium. You could "sell" ideas, but not things. Advertising was banned. There was a famous case of two lawyers in 1994 who posted an advertisement for their services to several thousand Usenet news groups. This caused an immense uproar, and they undoubtedly became the two most hated individuals in the history of the Internet up to that point (Loundy 1995). Now, of course, it's hardly possible to go online on the Web without encountering ads.

Though the Net prided itself on its tolerance, it also had to confront in practical terms a standard philosophical question. Must we tolerate the intolerant? The preferred libertarian way of dealing with people who wished to revel in their intolerance was to establish a special area for them so that the rest of us need not be disturbed by their rantings. However, there were people who did not harbor views most of society would label intolerant, but who were themselves intolerant of views differing from their own and were all too willing to express their hostility in unacceptable ways. These two types, of course, sometimes overlapped. Some degree of civility is necessary to carry on an extended fruitful discussion. Every once in a while so-called flame wars would erupt. A person would respond to an "offensive" communication with a scathing reply, often replete with obscenities and personal denunciations. This would prompt an equally intemperate reply, and a flame war would begin. Sometimes these flame wars would just burn themselves out, and the group would return to more civil discourse. At other times, the whole group would be destroyed as more and more people were turned off by the hostilities.

As mentioned earlier, Dahlberg and Siapera (2007) argue that the Net is a "contested terrain" and thus not essentially democratic. This same observation is applicable to tolerance/intolerance on the Net. While the very structure of the

Net was tolerant, this structural openness has allowed for a virtual public sphere in which tolerance and intolerance co-exist in a virtual state of hostility, where one's tolerance is another's intolerance and vice versa. Beyond issues of mere netiquette, the presence of intolerance online is real and substantial. While concrete figures are difficult to find given various standards of measurement,[5] the number of intolerant/hate websites on the Net has grown considerably since the birth of the Internet. According to The Simon Wiesenthal Center, in April 1995, the first extremist website went online. Today, the Center's Digital Terror and Hate 2.0 project identifies some 8,000 problematic hate and terrorist websites on the Net.[6] Out-Law.com reports that between 2000 and 2004 the number of hate and violence sites increased from 2,756 to 10,926.[7]

As of 2008, The Hate Directory (www.hatedirectory.com) has compiled a directory of fifteen Net site categories for the purveying of hate and intolerance primarily in the United States.[8] Within these categories exist 3,140 hate websites (e.g., hitlerisgod.com, hatred.isfun.net), file archives (e.g., ftp.nationalist.org), racist blogs and blog services (e.g., hitlerresearch.blogspot.com, wnblogger.net), listservs (e.g., subscribe@Aryan-Nations.org), usenets (e.g. alt.conspiracy, alt. flame.Chinese), IRCs (e.g., irc.whitepowerchat.com), online clubs and groups (e.g., groups.msn.com/SkinsOfTheRacialHolyWar), web rings (e.g., webring. racialloyalistcoalition.org), online racist games (e.g., resist.com.racistgames), podcasts and radio broadcasts (e.g., europeanbrotherhood.dyndns.dk:10040/ listen.pls), and racist friendly webhosting services (e.g., niggerfree.com). As noted in The Hate Directory as well as by The Simon Wiesenthal Center, intolerance on the Net, as manifested through numerous hate and terror websites, has begun to be communicated using Web 2.0 technologies including YouTube, Facebook, online games and radio clubs, and Second Life. A timely example of the use of such 2.0 technologies is AqsaTube. AqsaTube, launched in July 2008 (and re-launched in October 2008 from a Russian ISP), is a type of Arabic YouTube that

5 For example, the Southern Poverty Law Center states that the number of hate sites is somewhere between 400-600 (<http://www.media-awareness.ca/english/issues/online_hate/hate_and_free_speech.cfm> accessed 20 November 2008). HateWatch.org argues that currently there are between 450-500 "hard core" hate sites and numerous (between 1,500-1,750) sites that are problematic on the Net (<http://www.media-awareness.ca/english/resources/research_documents/statistics/internet/hate_sites_internet.cfm> accessed 20 November 2008). As seen below, there are still other figures that suggest a larger range of numbers.

6 <http://www.smartnewtown.org.nz/index.php?option=com_content&view=article&id=21:news8&catid=3:news&Itemid=5> accessed 20 November 2008.

7 <http://www.out-law.com/page-4640> accessed 25 November 2008.

8 Most European intolerant or hate sites appear to be U.S. based. According to the Council of Europe, in 2003, over half of racist websites were created and hosted in the United States given the latter's strong protection of First Amendment rights. See <http://www.cnn.com/2003/LAW/02/06/findlaw.analysis.ramasastry.cyberlaw/index.html> accessed 25 November 2008.

allows users to upload, view and share videos as well as featuring live streaming video. AqsaTube has been linked to Hamas and features videos of suicide bombers and terrorist leaders, terrorist training videos and children's videos educating the young in the importance of armed struggle. Ray and Marsh (2001) have shown that a number of these sites act as portals offering e-commerce, chat rooms, webhosting, and other networking tools as well as providing "how-to" information for carrying out acts of hate and violence.

It is evident that the forces of intolerance have become technologically savvy on the Net and more dangerous than ever. The Internet and its 2.0 technologies now allow all manner of intolerance to extend itself and reach millions of individuals. As Douglas (2007) has suggested, intolerance sites on the Net exist to provide opportunities for the building of community and solidarity among likeminded group members, the creation of links and relations between likeminded groups (networking), the deployment of recruitment activities, and education of new initiates, even young children.

Nevertheless, the Internet remains contested terrain. Douglas's observations also apply to groups and individuals who want to use the Net to expand tolerance both on and offline. One of the obvious ways in which this is being done is to build interactive websites to promote tolerance and erase its opposite. Amichai-Hamburger (2005) observes two ways in which the Net is being used for these purposes. First, the Net houses a number of tolerance-promoting resources. These include online educational sites such as the Southern Poverty Law Center's Teaching Tolerance website (www.tolerance.org) and the federally funded Understanding Prejudice (www.understandingprejudice.org). Both of these sites aim to distribute educational curricula as well as to assist in the development of teaching an ethic of tolerance and the creation of information networks among k-12 educators in the United States. Sites such as the International Tolerance Network (www.tolerance-net.org), the Foundation for Tolerance International (www.fti.org.kg), Youth Partnership (www.youth-partnership.net), and the International Network Against Cyber-Hate (www.inach.net) are extensive online networks and portals working to build cooperative relationship between various online and offline groups, NGOs, and state actors to further democracy, human rights, and tolerance in various parts of the world. Several of these sites provide email newsletters, marketing materials, calendars, databases, online reports, project updates, and links to other pro-tolerance websites and online initiatives. While there is some information on the number of intolerance promoting websites, very little exists regarding the number of tolerance advancing websites and their level of technological sophistication. The Hate Directory lists a total of sixteen hate-combating websites (e.g., www.unitedagainsthate.org, www.hatewatch.org, www.stopracism.com) but certainly many more exist.

Amichai-Hamburger's second observation is that the Net is used to advance tolerance through technological applications to filter and censor intolerance. One of the best examples of this pro-tolerance use of the Net is the 2002 Anti-Defamation League release of its ADL Hatefilter Filter 2.0, a free software program that would enable one to block any hate website from being displayed on one's computer. ADL's expertise in fighting intolerance and hate led to its partnership with Google's YouTube on December 11, 2008. In an effort to fight and curb online hate, intolerance, and extremism, YouTube created the YouTube Abuse and Safety Center. According to ADL, "The YouTube Abuse and Safety Center features information and links to resources developed by ADL to help Internet users respond to and report offensive material and extremist content that violates YouTube's Community Guidelines on hate speech."[9]

The Internet allows purveyors of tolerance/intolerance to build massive, coordinated digital networks of groups and activists. This process of "horizontal communication" (Dahlgren 2007) allows for the bonding of groups and individuals with common interests for online and offline action. One important example of such online activity is that of hacktivism. As Jordan (2007) suggests, hacktivism entails online direct action to spread tolerance and undermine oppression. Hacktivism can take the form of mass hacktivism such as the July 20-22, 2005 "virtual sit-in" by the Electronic Disturbance Theatre against the websites of the Border Patrol, NAFTA, and the California MinuteMen. Such a "virtual sit-in"—the simultaneous access of these sites by thousands of individuals—has the effect of shutting down the operations of these sites. A more sophisticated version of hacktivism is what is called digitally correct hacktivism. In such an example of radical online democracy, hackers develop a software application (e.g., CameraShy) for online use that allows for the free and secure sharing of sensitive hacking-related information across normally secure and censored digital walls and protective applications. Beyond simply a pursuit of the free flow of information or the blocking of a website, those who conduct online hacktivism have as their goal the destruction of what they consider to be oppressive, intolerant, and authoritarian organizations and viewpoints.

Besides the above uses of the Net for tolerance/intolerance, it is important to mention the rise of blogs as examples of how ICTs and CMCs are being used to advance or limit democratic values. Technorati, in its *State of the Blogosphere Report 2008* (http://technorati.com/blogging/state-of-the-blogosphere), suggests that the blogosphere is a universal and massive phenomenon. According to some of the report's figures, in 2007, the US blogosphere alone had 94.1 million blog readers and 22.6 million bloggers. As cited in *The Blog Herald* (www.blogherald.com), Technorati claims to be tracking, as of February 2008, over 112.8 million blogs, a number which, according to *The Blog Herald*, does not take into account the 72.82 million Chinese blogs as counted by The China Internet Network Information Center.[10] According to Barlow (2007) and Keren (2006), blogs are characterized by an ethos of emancipation from social intolerance, oppression, and arbitrary customs and authority. Keren (2006), in his in-depth study of nine blogs,

9 <http://www.adl.org/PresRele/Internet_75/5416_75.htm> accessed 15 December 2008.

10 <http://www.blogherald.com/2008/02/11/how-many-blogs-are-there-is-someone-still-counting> accessed 15 December 2008.

argues that blogs in general commonly assume a radical belief in the importance of boundless freedom and delivery from all rules and social conventions. This ethos of emancipation, according to Kahn and Keller (2007), permits blogs to be tools of tolerance and freedom for oppressed peoples and perspectives by freeing and delivering information to large publics and undermining the cloying grip of the traditional mass media outlets, outlets representative of dominant power centers. As examples, Kahn and Keller suggest that bloggers kept the story of Iraqi prisoner abuse alive on the Net through their circulation of images and that bloggers made the mass media accountable through their reporting of the dishonesty of *New York Times* investigative journalist, Jayson Blair. Furthermore, blogs represent some of the most open, transparent, and frank discussions on the Net, fostering an ethic of boundless freedom that may lead to a blurring of the private/public divide. While this seems disconcerting to some, for others blogs represent online tolerance in action.

We should note, however, that while blogs may facilitate boundless online freedom, they also bear certain characteristics that may validate Sunstein's concerns of the deleterious effects of echo chambers and information cocoons online. This leads to the conclusion that blogs, while chambers of boundless freedom, may ultimately become alcoves of narrow-minded prejudice and intolerance. Hargittai, Gallo, and Kaine (2008) have shown that bloggers tend to link to other bloggers who share their ideological convictions. Farrell, Lawrence, and Sides cite similar cocooning effects in the online reading habits of blog readers. Farrell et al. argue that blog readers seek blogs and materials that "have very similar criteria for what is important and a similar interpretative lens through which they understand events and issues" (Farrell et al. 2008, 5). This "selective exposure" facilitates polarization and bias. For Farrell et al., such blog readers are "carnivores" because they read blogs "that provide them with red meat that accords with their partisan or ideological predilections" (Farrell et al. 2008, 7). Keren's extensive qualitative study of blogs concludes that blogs are entirely antithetical to a democratic civil society or public sphere and, as such, to an ethic of tolerance online. For Keren, blogs are characterized not only by an ethic of boundless freedom, but also by a deep sense of melancholy, withdrawal and rejection. Blogs are illustrative of melancholic politics and are "filled with nicknames rather than people." They promote a "fetishism of ideas rather than a presentation of interests, solipsistic discourse rather than orderly exchange, and [they lack] clear frameworks of social obligation and political responsibility" (Keren 2006, 15-16). Echoing Sunstein, Keren argues that blogs and bloggers talk mainly to themselves and to others of their ilk. Their thin verbal discourse produces weaker group memberships online than do real world social bonds.

As Dahlberg and Siapera (2007) suggest, the Internet "operates…as constitutive of alternative political communities, new subject positions new possibilities for acting in concert, and ultimately radical new democratic cultures that challenge dominant political assumptions" (Dahlberg and Siapera 2007, 11). Whether it is pro-tolerance groups or groups intolerant of others, the Net's open system and its distributive and collaborative sites and applications can facilitate both tolerance and intolerance online. We now turn to a discussion of how the structure of the Internet itself impacts those who use it, and the ways that particular groups have devised to spread their message of tolerance or intolerance by means of the Internet.

The Impact of the Net on Tolerance/Intolerance

It seems reasonable to assume that the Net itself has some impact on the attitudes and dispositions of those who use it. Does using the Internet make people more tolerant or more intolerant? It can be argued that mere use of the Net could lead to more tolerance dispositions. Such an argument suggests that using the Internet increases tolerance because it exposes people to new and different viewpoints. They can easily encounter a range of attitudes and opinions, which they would not otherwise experience. This applies especially to those who live in isolated (or closed) homogeneous societies. The entire world of diversity is open to them online. The Internet is a public space, which resembles the dense urban environment of the public spaces of great cities, where people of dissimilar backgrounds and ethnicities gather. They learn that differences need not be equated with danger, and strangers need not present a threat.

Another argument counters that the cornucopia of views and perspectives on the Internet does not necessarily translate into encounters that breed tolerance. Putnam has observed that real world interactions often force us to confront diversity, whereas interactions online can lead to homogeneity in terms of views and outlooks. "Place-based communities may be supplanted by interest-based communities" (Putnam 2000, 178). Sunstein has also argued that rather than encouraging productive encounters among those who hold different views and attitudes, the Internet engenders fragmentation. While the Internet has dramatically increased the options available, most people do not avail themselves of them. People online have the ability to filter out whatever does not interest them. When people tailor their encounters according to their interests they need not confront views different from their own.

Sunstein claims that rather than leading to tolerance, this fragmentation creates its own problems. "If diverse groups are seeing and hearing quite different points of view, or focusing on quite different topics, mutual understanding might be difficult, and it might be increasingly hard for people to solve problems that society faces together" (Sunstein 2001, 61). Sunstein further challenges the optimistic evaluation of the Internet by pointing to the phenomenon of group polarization. There is evidence that when a group of like-minded people deliberate about an issue, the members tend to adopt a more extreme position. As people are exposed to the views of others in a group who have the same orientation, they become more convinced that they are right (Sunstein 2001, 65-72).

According to Sunstein the Net is a "breeding ground for extremism" because like-minded people are debating more and more among themselves without listening to contrary views (Sunstein 2001, 71). This would seem to be a bad thing, but he is careful to point out that such extremism might be good in certain circumstances. He cites civil rights, anti-slavery and gender equality as movements that were considered extreme in their own time. He also points out however, that even if there is homogeneity of opinions within each movement, society as a whole might benefit from a richer and more diverse set of ideas. These enclaves could serve as incubators for new attitudes, positions and programs which would add to the overall process of democratic deliberation. In order for this to occur, however, there is a need for the committed and convinced to reach out to those who hold different views.

This argument shows some of the political complexities of tolerance. Extremists are often the means for increasing tolerance in society. Their own intolerance may generate arguments and actions leading to the modification of intolerant practices by changing the ways in which particular issues are discussed, or they may serve as the vanguard of political movements for change and force new issues onto the political agenda. Whether or not the fragmentation and relative isolation of the Internet population is good or bad for society in the long run, if Sunstein is correct, the Internet as currently structured tends to make people less tolerant.

One of the few direct tests of Sunstein's theory can be found in the study of Robinson, Neustadtl, and Kestnbaum (2004). In perhaps the only study of its kind investigating the differences between Net users and non-users regarding their political tolerance attitudes, the authors test Sunstein's arguments through the General Social Survey Internet Use questions and attitudinal tolerance questions (that is, the Stouffer Items). Robinson et al. found that Net users "tend to be more tolerant on these GSS items independent of their demographic background" (Robinson et al. 2004, 245) and, thus, the effects of education and high income, though important, do not explain all of the levels of tolerance of Net users. While the differences between Net users and non-users, with Net users being more tolerant than non-users, are both monotonic and non-monotonic, it is important to note the tolerance characteristics of Net users. Consider the following: Net users support the view that controversial and minority writings should be available in libraries and spokespeople for such groups should be allowed to speak or teach;

a. Net users hold that children should be taught to think for themselves and not simply be expected to be obedient;
b. Net users oppose the view that African Americans are pushing too hard for equality and reject attributing a lower social status to African Americans on the basis of genetics or motivational factors;
c. Net users display a greater tolerance for premarital and homosexual sex but not for extramarital or teenage sex;
d. Net users demonstrate greater tolerance and support for sex education in public schools but not for giving birth control to teenagers;
e. Net users display a greater confidence in public institutions and possess a more positive outlook on life as well as a greater trust for their fellow citizens.

Obviously, these findings capture only a snapshot of a random segment of American Net users. However, these findings do provide evidence that the Internet may not solely foment intolerance, hatred, and cyberbalkanization and that, perhaps, we should not be as pessimistic about tolerance on the Net as Sunstein and others may suggest. More importantly, and this is a question that we do not answer here, is Robinson et al.'s finding that tolerance on the Net appears to be *independent* of demographic factors. Is there some dark energy to the Net that may lead to the expansion of online tolerance? It is difficult to answer this question. But the fact that the Net itself harbors so much intolerance along side tolerance may be a testament that its character, its very essence, can accommodate mutually exclusive worldviews and perhaps shape attitudinal predispositions.

So far we have considered structural arguments about the effect of the Internet. We now briefly look at some of the ways people are using the Internet to try to influence tolerance and intolerance directly. Obviously, there is some overlap with how tolerance/intolerance exist solely within the Internet and how the Internet is used to influence offline reality. Often times, offline groups and individuals use cyberspace not only to facilitate offline change (the subject of this section) but also to effect online change (the subject of the previous section). Most commentators refer to groups dedicated to increasing intolerance as hate groups. Hate groups were online for years before the advent of the World Wide Web. In 1985 the Anti-Defamation League published a report entitled *Computerized Networks of Hate* which described the operations of "Aryan Nation Liberty Net" which was on a computer bulletin board accessible to anyone with a modem and home computer. Even in those early years of CMC this bulletin board used tactics which have become commonplace on hate group sites today: spreading racist propaganda, recruiting new members, soliciting money and bypassing the prohibitions of other nations less tolerant than the US. Hate groups have also used Internet Relay chat channels, USENET discussion groups and listservs, both moderated and unmoderated. Though all these types of electronic communication have been used, the preferred forum now is the World Wide Web. The first American white supremacist website, Stormfront, was launched in March of 1995, and there have been literally thousands of racist and other hate sites created since then (Poisoning the Web 2001).

Not only do those hate groups, whose activities are legal in the United States, benefit from tolerance on the Internet, so do terrorist groups whose activities are clearly illegal. The active employment of the Internet by terrorists groups dedicated to destroying democracy illustrates the dilemma of trying to spread the democratic values of freedom and tolerance by means of the Internet. Rather than being part of the solution, it might be part of the problem. Terrorists have shown great facility in using the Internet to further their anti-democratic political agenda. They create websites to spread their propaganda, organize and recruit new members, and raise money. There are even websites which contain detailed instructions on how to make chemical and explosive weapons. They make extensive use of email, both encrypted and non-encrypted.

Law enforcement officials in the US have long been aware of the use of the Internet by both domestic and international terrorist groups, but they operated under severe restraints. Just after the terrorist attacks of 11 September, 2001 Steve Berry, a spokesperson for the FBI's National Infrastructure Protection Center, explained that they cannot monitor websites for logistical and legal reasons. He said, "However repugnant to our perception and to the general public and law enforcement their website or use of it might be, that does not give us the authority to block them. That's free speech. That's the country we live in" (Lyman 2001).

Law enforcement received new powers to combat terrorism when President Bush signed the USA Patriot Act on 26 October, 2001. The act includes giving the government broad surveillance authority to determine which websites a person has visited and to monitor the addresses of incoming and outgoing email (Davis 2002). Civil libertarians see the USA Patriot Act as a direct threat to constitutional freedoms. When it comes to the Internet, they fear a chilling effect of the new law because Americans will be afraid to communicate freely without fear of government surveillance (Free Expression Network 2002). Balancing free speech and public safety has become much more difficult in the post September 11 environment.

While the Internet has been used by anti-democratic terrorists organizations and hate groups to further all sorts of political and social causes including the most virulent racist, sexist and homophobic, it has also been used by those struggling for an increase in tolerance. The 2002 Webby award for the best activist website went to Tolerance.org, a project of the Southern Poverty Law Center. The site contains current news stories as well as numerous short articles designed to spread tolerance both online and offline. Among these are "10 ways to fight hate," "101 Tools for Tolerance," "Explore your Hidden Biases," and "Deconstructing Biased Language" (Tolerance.org 2008). Dahlgren (2007) cites the "permanent Net-based campaign phenomenon." These net-based campaigns are entirely virtually organized, managed, and deployed and often have offline counterparts. Alter-globalization groups such as ATTAC (www.attac.org) seek to generate enough online publicity or "offline noise" so as to pressure corporations and states to change policies and implement democratic reforms. Other such groups as the Association for Progressive Organization (www.apc.org), LabourStart (www.LabourStart.org) and Indymedia (www.Indymedia.org) have created massive digital networks of activists and independent and alternative media outlets to coordinate information, mailing lists, and online and offline action to challenge what they consider to be global injustice and oppression. All of these radical democratic organizations consider themselves to be extending democracy, tolerance, openness, and truth to all parts of the world.

The boundlessness of the Internet has also facilitated its use as a tool for tolerance and more democracy among non-state dissidents throughout the world. Hill and Sen (2005) suggest that the Indonesian revolution overthrowing Suharto should be considered one of the first revolutions that used the Internet. The authors argue that prior to Suharto's downfall, the Indonesian Internet was used to communicate publicly beyond the state's control and, as such, contributed to the development of an Indonesian public sphere. By the end of the 20th century, the Net had become thoroughly adopted and embraced within numerous sectors of Indonesian society. American moderated "Indonesia-L" (an email discussion list) was the first Net based activity to link and foster internal and external critics of Indonesias' New Order government. Known as *apakabar*, the email list had wide circulation within Indonesia and led to other influential email discussions lists and the use of the Net for establishing a presence by critics of Suharto and his authoritarian regime. The Net was a "weapon against state censorship" (Hill and Sen 2005, 131) and helped to create a place for a new politics, a new public sphere, and more open communication between government and citizens.

The Internet's low transaction costs as well as its universality have also had profound impacts on the work of non-state dissidents in the Middle East and China. According to McLaughlin (2003), dissidents in both of these parts of the world use the Net to communicate, plan, organize, and execute local dissident action within states with the goals of eroding authoritarianism and intolerance and building a strong international network of support. Two cases in point are those of Falun Gong (China) and the Zapatistas (Mexico). Falun Gong used email communication to stage numerous surprise demonstrations in China and uses its affiliated website (www.fofg.org) to inform and coordinate peaceful action throughout the world. And the Zapatistas (www.ezln.org.mx/index.html) have become the textbook example of using the Net to build an international network of support, information, collaboration, and solidarity. While some of this action cannot take place within the dissident's state, the goal is to use the Net to develop international support for greater tolerance and democracy in the dissident's political surroundings. The Internet's boundlessness has also been used to foster offline tolerance between traditionally hostile groups. As reported in Yablon (2007), the program "Feeling Close from a Distance" brought together in digital fashion Israeli and Arab high school students. The purpose of these digital "peace encounters" was to use the Internet to foster meaningful discussions regarding issues of equality, democracy and tolerance among groups that would most likely never meet and discuss.

What are we to conclude? Does the Internet increase tolerance or intolerance? It's hard to say. Structural arguments, such as Sunstein's, that polarization and fragmentation lead to extremism, are contentious.[11] It is possible that the tolerant become more tolerant, and the intolerant become more intolerant. It might depend upon the predispositions of those who participate in the discussions. Claims that the Net increases intolerance because it enables hate groups to recruit and to spread their messages can be countered by the fact that a great many groups also use the Internet to spread a message of tolerance both online and offline. Without additional empirical research it is difficult to reach any definite conclusion.

The Internet has certainly changed since the early days when it flourished under a policy of benign neglect. It has become a subject of government action

11 Interested readers should google "Sunstein" + "breeding ground for extremism" for a taste of the controversy.

and public policy debates around the world. We now turn to a discussion of some of the ways in which the old regime of pure tolerance has been modified by new regulations and concerns.

Tolerance/Intolerance that Affects the Net

There are actions and policies taken by governments and concerned groups which are intended to make the Internet a more tolerant or intolerant place, depending upon how you look at it. Different cultures and legal traditions have significant impact on the way the Net now operates. As Douglas (2007) suggests, the proliferation of tolerance/intolerance on the Net has raised a key policy issue for many governments, namely, to what extent should intolerance online be censored and to what degree should tolerance online be deliberately advanced? Many countries other than the United States ban racist and other extremist websites. Because of the First Amendment of the US Constitution, which protects even hateful political speech, the US government cannot remove such sites from the Internet. This has caused many neo-Nazi sites directed toward Europeans to switch to American Internet service providers (ISPs). As of 2003, according to the Council of Europe, over half of European hate websites were created and hosted on American servers.[12] Some ISPs have tried to avoid being used as conduits for hate groups by creating service contracts prohibiting subscribers from setting up hate sites. Organizations like the Anti-Defamation League have urged private individuals to use filtering software to keep such sites off their home computers and, as seen earlier, have even developed their own bias filter software (Poisoning the Web 2001).

While the First Amendment also protects ISPs, there have been attempts to convince them to remove objectionable websites from their servers. Sometimes this succeeds and sometimes not. Given the expansive and international nature of the Net, sites can easily migrate from one ISP to another, though even this strategy is not always successful. Pressuring ISPs has come under criticism by civil liberties groups. The Simon Wiesenthal Center has identified hate sites and pressured ISPs to get rid of them. While approving of the Center's campaign to expose such sites, the American Civil Liberties Union (ACLU) has criticized their attempts to pressure ISPs. The ACLU said: "It is particularly troublesome that an organization like the Wiesenthal Center that is dedicated to promoting tolerance would seek to erode the liberty most necessary for a free and tolerant society – free speech" (Anderson 2001). Civil liberties organizations equate tolerance with free speech, but even they recognize that free speech has its limits. They do not countenance fraud, criminal conspiracy, libel, child pornography and other types of speech, which have been recognized in most modern societies as beyond tolerance.

---

12 <http://www.cnn.com/2003/LAW/02/06/findlaw.analysis.ramasastry.cyberlaw/index.html> accessed 25 November 2008.

It is not always easy to navigate between the civil liberties model of tolerance, which sees any attempts to interfere with free expression as intolerance, and the anti-hatred and bigotry model, which insists upon limiting free expression in the name of tolerance itself. In 2000, several French anti-racism groups sued Yahoo! in France, accused it of trivializing the Holocaust by offering Nazi memorabilia for sale on its English language auction sites. While it is illegal in France to sell or display anything that incites racism, and the Yahoo! French language site, in fact, did not display such materials, French citizens could easily access Yahoo!'s English language sites. In November 2000, a French court gave the company three months to install a filtering system to prevent French users from accessing Nazi auction sites or other Yahoo! sites whose content was deemed to be racist. It threatened to fine Yahoo! 100,000 francs ($13,000) a day thereafter if it did not comply. In the beginning of January 2001, Yahoo! announced that from January 10 it would ban the sale of all Nazi and Ku Klux Klan memorabilia from all its sites, though it continued to take legal action in the US to resist the French court order.

Brian Fitzgerald, the senior auction producer at Yahoo!, announced the new policy but denied that the French court order had played a role in the company's decision other than to make Yahoo! aware of the seriousness of the problem and the need for a swift action. He said "we decided we don't necessarily want to profit from items that promote hatred or glorify hatred and violence." Given the timing, this statement of conscience on the part of Yahoo! was questioned by some commentators. While human rights activists hailed it as a great victory, some civil libertarians opposed the ban on free speech grounds. The ADL commended Yahoo! for coming up with a creative solution to combat the flood of Nazi memorabilia being offered for sale on online auctions. According to them, Yahoo! demonstrated corporate responsibility and sensitivity to the fact that, though it is not illegal to sell such memorabilia in the United States, it is offensive to many who frequent the auction site. The press release concludes "the Internet is a great tool for education and communication, but it continues to pose complex issues, requiring Internet companies to walk a fine line between free expression and inappropriate or hateful conduct." There was no mention of the French lawsuit in their press release, or the fact that Yahoo! was still challenging the decision (Tobias and Foxman 2001; Jesdanan 2001; CNN.com 2001; Guardian Unlimited 2000).

The decision not to sell Nazi memorabilia on online auctions was taken by Yahoo! either because the company became aware of its corporate responsibility or, what we believe is more likely, it decided to cave on purely business grounds because it was facing a complicated lawsuit and a lot of bad publicity. Finally, an American federal court in November of 2001 ruled that Yahoo! did not have to comply with the order of the French court because the First Amendment protects content generated in the United States by an American company from regulation by countries whose laws which do not have the same degree of freedom of expression as ours do. Yahoo!'s deputy counsel, Greg Warren said "It means that the ability of people in the United States to make information available on the Internet is ultimately going to be governed by the First Amendment, regardless of where it's accessed, not the lowest common denominator of accepted content in all countries." The tolerance inbuilt into our constitutional protections will be upheld by our courts, but this doesn't necessarily mean that it will always be maintained in practice. Despite the court victory Yahoo! did not revert to its earlier policy (Bergstein 2001).

Though this case began through a lawsuit involving private parties and eventually involved a foreign court issuing a legal order, governments have become much more involved in attempting to restrict and censor free speech online. As Jeffrey Rosen has recently suggested, the Yahoo! case was a landmark since "it made clear that search engines like Google and Yahoo! could be held liable outside the United States for indexing or directing users to content after having been notified that it was illegal in a foreign country" (Rosen 2008, 53). This means that Internet companies like Yahoo! and Google face more restrictions in places far from their own home country. Foreign governments are determining the limits of free speech by implementing policies that curtail tolerance and impose what many would consider to be intolerance. A common method of such activity is for governments to implement an online system of continual monitoring and control of all Net activity within its borders so that users always know that any online activity occurs within a nexus of surveillance. Yang (2006) has argued that China has some of the most sophisticated set of controls deploying social, political, technological, and psychological methods of censorship to control the massive number of Chinese online networks. Tunisia has implemented wide-ranging legislation disallowing the use of the Internet for political action and its state agency *Agence Tunisienne d'Internet* (ATI) maintains a master list of Internet subscribers enabling the government to deny or shutdown Internet access for specific individuals and groups (McLaughlin 2003).

Government has always assumed the role of cultural gatekeeper. The rise of the Internet has meant that governments must now extend this role to virtual reality. The case of Yahoo! is one in a long list of examples where tolerance/intolerance on the Net is affected by offline sociopolitical and cultural reality. More recently, Google has faced surmounting global pressure to censor content on its YouTube and Orkut websites when that content is deemed blasphemous, irreverent or otherwise politically, socially or culturally intolerable in a number of countries. Beginning in 2006, 24 countries have blocked access to Google and some of its applications. YouTube has been blocked, for example, in Turkey and Thailand, Blogger has been blocked in Pakistan, and Orkut has been blocked in Saudi Arabia (Rosen 2008). As these examples show, not all countries have adopted the same attitude towards free speech and religious toleration as the United States. Political tolerance is a matter of degree. Not only do we maintain a strict separation of church and state, but we have purged our criminal law of any overt religious content in the area of speech. Blasphemy, while still distasteful to the majority of Americans, is no longer a crime. We have learned to tolerate such acts of disrespect in the name of freedom of speech and expression, but not all democratic countries have followed us in decriminalizing sacrilegious actions. Such behavior, for instance, is still illegal in Italy.

In July of 2002, the Italian police shut down five websites which they deemed blasphemous and illegal, even though the websites were hosted in the United States. The sites were created in Rome, and the police were prodded into action by criticism in a Vatican controlled newspaper. According to the police, both God and the Virgin Mary were blasphemed, and next to their names appeared images of sex scenes. The police said they censored the sites so that the "precious freedom of expression" was not used to offend "the dignity of the people."

The Italian authorities could have tried to shut down the websites in America through legal action, but this would have involved them in a difficult First Amendment case. Or they could have attempted to put pressure on the American ISPs, which most likely would not have worked, given our tradition of religious toleration. The Italian police took the more direct route. They simply commandeered the alleged offender's computer in Rome, used his password, removed all the offending material from the site and replaced it with the symbol of the special police unit which was involved in the bust (*Associated Press* 2002; *BBC News* 2002).

What one society will tolerate, another will not. Differences in social and political attitudes have an impact on attempts by governments to regulate the Internet. While tolerating gambling under regulated conditions offline, the United States government has conducted a concerted campaign against online gambling. Other countries see nothing wrong with online gambling and are perfectly willing to regulate and tax it (Margolis and Resnick 2000, 157-81). While the United States finds online gambling intolerable, the French find using "English only" on a French website intolerable when that site is directed to French citizens. The French government even sued an English-language website in France affiliated with an American university because it offered services in English but not in French (Margolis and Resnick 2000, 12).

The old regime of pure tolerance on the Internet has changed because of the regulatory activities of governments around the world. In 1996 John Perry Barlow, an Internet activist (and Grateful Dead songwriter), wrote the widely distributed so called "Declaration of Independence of Cyberspace" in which he asserted that Cyberspace exists beyond government borders. Addressing governments, he proclaimed, "You have no moral right to rule us nor do you possess any methods of enforcement we have true reason to fear" (Barlow 1996). While such statements proclaiming Cyberspace as a government-free zone may seem hopelessly naïve, a number of international Internet companies along with Google, Yahoo!, and Microsoft and various civil society organization have been working to develop the Global Network Initiative (www.globalnetworkinitiative.org), a coalition to combat the censorship requests of governments throughout the world as well as to implement global standards for online freedom of speech and expression.

Governments have been more than willing to enter Cyberspace. As mentioned earlier, China exhibits some of the most sophisticated and stringent censorship in the world. The Chinese attempted to channel all external Internet traffic through filters to block sites the government thought inappropriate, but this turned out to be impossible given the enormous increase in Internet traffic. They began permitting commercial Internet accounts in 1995, and since then have issued at least 60 sets of regulations intended to control content. For example, Article 57 of the Telecommunications Regulations, which went into effect in September of 2000, prohibits, among other things, disseminating any material that "harms the prosperity and interests of the state,...arouses ethnic animosities, ethnic discrimination, or undermines ethnic solidarity,...undermines state religious policies, or promotes cults and feudal superstitions,...spreads rumors, disturbs social order, or undermines social stability,...[or] spreads obscenities, pornography, gambling, violence." Violations of such regulations can lead to serious consequences. ISPs can be fined or closed, and users face severe criminal penalties (Human Rights Watch 2002).

There are now Chinese Internet police whose job is to visit suspicious websites as well as to read the email of those suspected of criminal behavior. Chat rooms, which in the past have served as venues for spirited discussions of current affairs, must now provide a monitor who will filter out objectionable postings that cross the current political line (Eckholm 2002). On June 16, 2002 there was a fire in a Beijing Internet café which killed 25 people. Though the fire was allegedly set by children, it served as an excuse for a broad government crackdown. The government announced its intention to close 150,000 unlicensed Internet cafes throughout the country and passed new legislation requiring Internet cafes to install new software which can block designated foreign websites.

Intolerant governments know that having the Internet widely available is a risk. The simplest solution to the problem of the Internet spreading ideas of freedom, tolerance and democracy would be to shut it down entirely. Yet a total ban would be impossible for any society committed to economic development and modernization. The Chinese government has invested significant economic resources in fiber optic cable and a modern telecommunication infrastructure. As of July 2002, there were 45.8 million Internet users in China, a 72.8 percent increase since June of 2001 (Nua Internet Surveys 2002). In 2007, Deborah Fallows, a senior researcher at the Pew Internet and American Life Project, projected that in 2009 China's Internet users would outnumber those of the United States with recent estimates suggesting that this may have already occurred.[13] Thus, there is no way China can return to the days of almost total party control of information and communication. A degree of practical tolerance has been achieved even without a commitment to tolerance on the part of the authorities. It remains to be seen how long the liberating potential of the Internet can be suppressed.

People have used the Internet to escape from some of the political and social intolerance they face in their own daily lives. Young Iranians have gone online to express themselves in ways that would not be possible in Iran otherwise. Using the Internet has been especially liberating for Iranian women, whose freedom to speak

13 See <www.pewinternet.org/pdfs/China_Internet_July_2007.pdf> accessed 10 November 2008, as well as Barboza (2008).

and dress as they wish is ordinarily confined to the limits of their own houses. They can now discuss sexual matters and communicate their deepest feelings to others. Dissident Iranian political views have also been promoted on the Internet. The relaxation of official repression dictated by a dogmatic theology in Iran was attributed to political changes brought about by the election of President Mohammad Khatami, but the more likely causes were the same economic pressures operating in China. The Internet is such a powerful engine for economic development that even the government under his more religiously conservative successor, President Mahmoud Ahmadinejad, has been unwilling to stop it. Though there have been some half-hearted attempts to censor websites and restrict access, the government has apparently decided to live with the increased tolerance that the Internet has brought to Iran. According to Shaaban Sahidi, a former deputy minister at Iran's Ministry of Culture and Islamic Guidance, "Control has no meaning on the Internet. It would crash like the Berlin Wall" (Fathi 2002).

The Internet has been altered by the attempts of governments to regulate it. It is certainly no longer, if it ever truly was, a sovereign free space beyond the reach of any government. While not all of the attempts of states to impose their cultural views on the Internet have been successful, it is still evident that in many parts of the world, intolerant governments have molded the Internet in their own image. Still for many millions who live in repressive societies, the Internet holds out the hope for a freer life. While many states have delineated policies of censorship for Internet usage, a number of states, NGOs, and civil society organizations are using the Internet to bring about democratic change both on and offline. As Goldman, Booker and McDermott (2008) argue, there are a large and growing number of programs in the United States that use digital media as a "social and cultural technology" for "dialogue and positive social change" (Goldman, Booker and McDermott 2008, 192). This same observation is certainly applicable to other regions of the world.

In North America, Canada has used the Internet deliberately to advance and foster more tolerance and eradicate intolerance among its young. In 1997 The Canadian Human Rights Commission (CHRC) launched an online interactive video game "Erasing the Hydra of Hate" to teach 7th-12th graders "to understand how the seeds of hatred and racism are sown, and to learn what each person can do to stop them from growing."[14] The CHRC has also developed the "Hate on the Internet Project," an online initiative which according to O'Loughlin (2001) was meant to inform, educate, and empower private individuals and teachers concerning online intolerance. Currently, this initiative provides annual reports of hate on the internet as well as sponsors conferences and other initiatives to inform and educate the public as well as to influence public policy and corporate responsibility in this area. In the United States, organizations like the Southern Poverty Law Center, the Simon Wiesenthal Center, and the Anti-Defamation

14 <http://www.chrcccdp.ca/client/site/includes/print.asp?lang=en&print=1&url=%2Fpublications%2F1997_ ar%2Fpage4-en.asp> accessed 17 December 2008.

League have used the Internet to inform, educate, and protect against hate and intolerance on and offline. The "Global Action Project" (www.global-action.org), located in New York City, engages youth and digital media to encourage positive change and more tolerance in society against traditionally not accepted views and ways of life. In England, the Internet has been harnessed to improve the citizenship and democratic education of young people. The British Council deployed "Windows on the World" and "The Global Gateway" portal (www.globalgateway.org.uk) to integrate the National Curriculum as well as to strengthen the global and democratic competence of students through more "technology-based citizenship education" (Selwyn 2007). And UNESCO has funded several programs in India for the building of *Cybermohalla* (Cyber-neighborhood) and other Internet initiatives to "enable democratic access to information and communication technologies" among India's poor as well as to educate Indian youth in the democratic values of social and political critique and civic engagement (Asthana 2006).

While governments and corporations have become some of the leading forces affecting tolerance/intolerance on the Internet, a growing body of research demonstrates that offline patterns of behaviors and attitudes also have a substantial impact upon the online life of Internet users. While there is no necessary connection between offline tolerance/intolerance and online tolerance/intolerance, much work appears to suggest that online political behavior is heavily influenced by its offline counterpart. Numerous studies in the UK, Italy, and Australia, have shown that the Internet generally replicates offline behavior and, therefore, that outside forces influence the Net socially, culturally, and politically (Livingson, Couldry and Markham 2007; Calenda and Mosca 2007; Vromen 2007; Dahlgren and Olsson 2007). Nevertheless, despite the efforts of governments and NGOs to alter reality online and offline, the entrenched sociopolitical and cultural habits of individuals also exert a significant influence on the shape of the Internet.

Conclusion

Many of the actions that take place on the Internet, as well as many of the external actions that affect the Internet, undercut the overly optimistic outlook of those who proclaimed it a great engine for the spread of democratic values and tolerance. Not only have the interventions of governments made the Internet as a whole less tolerant than it was in the early days, but hate groups have attempted to use the tolerance that does exist online to undermine tolerance itself in the larger society. The authoritarian and intolerant attitudes assumed by democratic elitists have manifested themselves on the Internet, and these have worried many liberals. While it has not shaken the faith of those who believe in the free marketplace of ideas, it has undermined the plausibility of claims made by technocratic Utopians who believed that Cyberspace was and always would be a realm of freedom.

Not all democracies have the United States' extensive First Amendment concept of free expression, and for them it is perfectly natural to try to work out legal solutions to the problem of how much tolerance a free society can allow on the Internet, as well as in society at large. The Internet is a worldwide phenomenon, and it is proving impossible to impose America's understanding of tolerance on the rest of the world. While the very structure of the Internet with its tremendous diversity and possibilities may encourage tolerance, it may also lead to fragmentation by isolating people according to their own narrow interests. It would seem to have the potential to deepen democratic discussion and foster democratic values, but this potential may never be realized.

If we step back and ask ourselves whether, on balance, the Internet is more likely to have a positive or negative impact on tolerance, we must admit that it is difficult to know. If pressed, we would answer that, except for authoritarian non-democratic societies where we can see genuine glimmers of hope, most likely it will have little effect. Tolerance is another area in which what we call "the normalization thesis" will probably apply. Those who are very optimistic or pessimistic about the Net exaggerate its impact as an independent factor in social change. What people bring with them to the Net, rather than what they do on the Net, is more important in determining their fundamental attitudes and beliefs. The short history of the Net shows that, as it matures, it tends to reflect the real world. It seems likely, therefore, that even universal access to the Internet will be insufficient to bring about great changes in people's behaviors and attitudes, let alone great changes the dominant power structures—social, economic, political, religious and cultural—of most modern nations.

Chapter 5
Mass Media and Internet Democracy

The Noble Mission of Modern Mass Media

Western democratic theory posits the central importance of a "free press" or "Fourth Estate" for preserving citizens' rights and liberties in a modern society. Democracy's folklore, especially in the USA, extols the independent publisher, the courageous editor and the intrepid reporter as heroic icons whose critical mission is to protect the citizenry from the machinations of would be tyrants and corrupt public officials who would conspire with greedy allies to exploit the populace. Moreover, their facilitating the free flow of information is deemed necessary for citizens to fulfill their roles as the ultimate "deciders" in a democracy.

The Internet and related ICTs can provide citizens with access to unprecedented sources of information as well as to powerful new channels for exchanging that information with peers, elected representatives and with other public and private officials, but most people still seek out familiar commercial television and radio news programs and networks, newspapers, and news magazines on or offline to inform themselves about local, national and international affairs. Most also use these same sources for general information about their popular (and usually more pervasive) interests in sports, weather, crime, shopping, entertainment, business, religion or the like.

The rapid pace of modern living, however, has led to greater demand for information at the convenience of consumer. As regular Internet users form increasing proportions of the population, the familiar commercial media face growing competition from multiple sources to fulfill the "24/7" demand for "breaking news" about a broad variety of topics and interests. This competition ranges from upstart political bloggers, through compilers and distributors of general news to online publications and services that cater to more specialized topics or interests.

Pillars of Modern Democracy?

Their claims to comprise or to represent the Fourth Estate notwithstanding, privately owned news media are first and foremost profit-seeking businesses. Nowadays these heroic icons answer largely to international media corporations like Gannett or Newscorp or to conglomerates like Arvato-Bertelsmann or General Electric (GE). While profits have always been a motive, the corporate business model calls for news media to produce more profits than in the past. For such a

Fourth Estate to criticize its corporate masters raises problems. How deeply, for instance, can we expect NBC Universal's news operations to investigate GE's performance concerning completion of governmental contracts or compliance with environmental regulations? Similarly, can we realistically expect *The Wall Street Journal* to produce critical analyses of Newscorp's business operations in Mainland China, India, or the Middle East, let alone within the USA or the UK? Prudent editors and journalists are loath to slap the purse that pays them.

In addition to corporate ownership discouraging critical investigative reporting on sensitive topics, the business model itself hampers the news media's role as the citizens' watchdog. Sarah Oates' conceptual scheme for analyzing news media helps us to make this apparent. She divides "the media sphere into three main categories": news production, news content, and audience reaction (Oates 2008, 4). News production involves gathering, assembling and reporting information to the public. News content involves gate-keeping functions, such as selecting which stories to cover, determining the prominence to give them, and deciding the contexts or viewpoints in which to frame the stories' narratives. Audience reaction includes direct feedback, such as letters (including e-mail) to the editors or reporters, participation in media initiated opinion surveys or media controlled blogs. It also includes indirect feedback, such as increases or decreases in subscriptions, circulation, audience size, website visitors, page views, click-throughs and purchases of advertisers' products and services.

To produce news, media enterprises must invest capital. More importantly, however, to produce original news that fulfills their watchdog role, they must also employ labor. Producing original stories inevitably costs the most. The longer the time and the further afield they send reporters to investigate a story, the more costly their labor. It follows that most news media identify themselves with particular locales or areas, and they rely upon stringers employed by news services like the Associated Press or Reuters to provide the bulk of their stories about regional, national and international events.

Despite their nation's prominence in world affairs, major newspapers, broadcast and cable networks in the USA maintain fewer overseas bureaus and employ fewer foreign correspondents than in the 1970s. In June 2008 none had stationed a full time correspondent covering the war in Afghanistan even though the casualties in May exceeded those in the much more prominently reported war in Iraq. Six months later, when terrorists assaulted ten targets simultaneously in Mumbai hardly any American reporters were on location to cover the story. At the same time the American news media had almost no reporters on hand to explain—let alone cover—an ongoing sporadically violent crisis challenging the legitimacy of the elected government of Thailand.

Staff reporters are assigned mostly to cover uniquely local events. When syndicated reviewers or correspondents are already assigned to prominent new films, to touring companies and orchestras with nationally known artists, or even to important governmental officials or candidates for major office, coverage by local reporters can be minimized. Local political columnists and reviewers as well as editorial cartoonists can largely be eliminated in order to cut costs. Additional savings can be realized by partnering with local radio or television stations—sometimes owned by the same corporations in the USA—to reduce staff further and incidentally, to decrease the competition for market shares. The shared stories can appear in the newspaper, on radio, television, and on websites (sometimes jointly operated), where reporters and pundits can blog with the public.[1] The media also can invite their audience to e-mail news tips via the websites—or better yet—to submit publishable images, columns and videos which they can use gratis to augment their diminished reportorial capabilities.[2] Television news directors can replace highly paid news anchors—often referred to as "talents"—with less expensive personalities (Stetler 2008). And in extremis, local editors can downsize their news reporters further by assigning routine stories to educated freelance writers in India or other nations with lower pay scales. The freelancers can use information found online to prepare local events calendars, sports results, weather reports or to write summaries of particular regional, national or international events the editors select as having local connections or interest but don't require boots on the ground (Dowd 2008).

Prior to the expansion of the cable news and the popularization of the Internet, mainstream media had relatively few competitors through which advertisers could find a mass audience or from which the general public could get the information they desired about current events (Jamieson and Cappella 2008; Prior 2007). While it was always tactful not to offend significant numbers of advertisers or audience members, every now and then newspapers and broadcasters could present carefully researched investigative reports that enhanced their reputations and prestige (Godfrey 1999).

Nowadays, the Internet, cable and related ICTs present commercial broadcast and print news media with a dilemma. The business model for daily news reports requires advertising revenue to cover most of their operating cost. Where they once could count on regular viewers, listeners and readers to tune in at designated times for headlines and summaries or to subscribe to their publications for details and perspectives about public policy and current events, they now must compete for attention and for advertising dollars, not only with 24-hour cable and satellite

---

1 For example, between 1998 and 2008 the *Cincinnati Enquirer* reduced its reportorial staff by 60 percent (from about 125 to 50) even as it eliminated the rival *Cincinnati Post* by refusing to renew the 30-year joint operating agreement (Wessels 2008). The agreement had allowed the two dailies to share printing facilities, to offer discounts for joint advertising and to combine virtually all administrative functions, save those related to editorial policy and reporting assignments. See "News Paper Preservation Act…" and US Code: Title 15, Chapter 43.

2 Such submissions of course can enhance genuine news coverage. Often, however, they simply provide the media with information about the audience's current interests, which the news media can pursue, regardless of information's centrality to the media's avowed watchdog mission. See <http://www.cincinnati.com>, <http://www.stltoday.com>, <http://Foxnews.com> and related links for examples.

news services—foreign and domestic, on and offline—but also with thousands of great and small bloggers, media monitors, and online news compilers that serve up information about current events and public policy for fragmented portions of the general public.[3] In order to hold their readers, listeners and viewers, the once dominant mainstream media have adopted a number of strategies aimed at specific segments of their audience. These include emphasizing specialized coverage of local businesses, personalities, and neighborhoods within particular markets, offering podcasts for audiences to view or listen to at their convenience, consolidating operations by acquiring online and offline competitors, and by adopting more partisan viewpoints in place of broad coverage and professional neutrality. Friendly "soft news" mixed with a dash of sensationalism can please—and sometimes titillate—a goodly portion of the public. Accordingly, most local newspapers and local newscasts in the USA devote over half their coverage to soft news, sports, and weather. Broadcast networks now run partisan cable channels like Fox News Channel and MSNBC, niche channels like CNBC and Fox Business Channel, and integrated sports networks like Disney's ABC Sports and ESPN (Oates 2008, 26-34; Graber 2006, 19-35). This process of consolidation and specialization continues. In July 2008, for instance, a consortium led by NBC Universal (owned by GE) outbid Time-Warner to obtain the 24-hour cable *Weather Channel* from Landmark Communications (Walzer 2008).

Editors and publishers have the capacity to choose which public affairs to cover, which to emphasize, and how to frame the coverage, but the exigencies of the business model encourage them to research and pander to attitudes of beliefs of selected niches of the increasingly fragmented audience. Commercial media face the problem that access to the Internet and related ICTs like multi-channel cable and satellite (dish) TV provide affluent audience members—their advertisers' best prospects—with the means to select only those messages they desire to receive. Even though public affairs ordinarily do not play a central role in the daily lives of these prospective customers, almost all of them have been socialized to support the legitimacy of their nations' governmental institutions and public officeholders. This loyalty presents a disincentive for news media to emphasize critical information that might challenge the values or beliefs that most citizens (including advertisers) take for granted. Unless or until cataclysmic events impinge upon their daily routines, citizens generally seek affirmation of the legitimacy and righteousness of their government's motives and goals regarding domestic and foreign affairs, even when they disagree with particular policies or disapprove of particular public officials. Except in extraordinary circumstances, therefore, the large commercial

3 For examples of right, center, left, great and small political news sites based in the USA, point your search engine to Real Clear Politics, The Drudge Report, Townhall, EIN News, Cagle.Com (professional cartoonists index), Huffington Post, Daily Kos, Truthout, Juan Cole (informed comment), Gerry Lykins (northernkyfordean). Google turns up 208,000 entries for "media monitors" worldwide and a more manageable 680 entries for "news compilers." (Accessed 20 October 2008).

media provide news frames supportive of the current regime, or if critical, gentle the criticism in the manner of a loyal opposition.[4]

The horns of the dilemma become clear. The established commercial news media that remain broad chroniclers of public affairs are losing revenue and audience share to the emerging digital media. If they were to redouble their efforts to fulfill their vaunted role as people's watchdog evenhandedly, they inevitably would offend significant portions of their clientele. Among other things, they would probably continue to lose revenue from sponsors and advertisers, support from members of their audience, and access to governmental and private officials and their records. Alternatively, if they were to adopt news frames that favored particular parties or interest groups or that relied heavily upon connections to Internet based digital ICTs to attract an audience, their reportage would risk becoming indistinguishable from that which myriad partisan bloggers, videographers, and special interests produce daily.

While these developments hardly portend the imminent demise of established commercial news media—daily newspapers or radio and television broadcast news—they do show the declining audience appeal of regularly scheduled general news reports and publications and the pressure for news media to accelerate the convergence of new with old ICTs. Moreover, as younger "digital natives" replace their elders in positions of social, economic and political leadership, we expect this convergence will reflect decreased interest in written arguments and increased interest in multi-media presentations, (Hedges 2008). It is also likely to expand the demand not only for speedy news production but also for instantaneous news analysis.

Mass Media and Public Affairs in the Digital Age

In Chapter 1 we noted that despite the increased opportunities that successive ICTs have provided for more enlightened public participation in democratic politics, the actual increases never have fulfilled the expectations. Barring exceptional problems or events like droughts, plagues, great wars or economic depressions

4 Horton (2008) states that prior to 2007 CNN reporters were instructed not to use the word "torture" in the "domestic feed" when describing or criticizing interrogation techniques, such as "water boarding," that the USA has used on "enemy combatants" held at Guantanamo, Abu Grab, and secret CIA prisons, although the CNN International feed could use the term. When Horton appeared on PBS Newshour with Jim Lehrer, the producers told him that the word "torture" could be used "in the abstract" but not when he criticized the Bush administration's interrogation techniques (Horton 2008, 50). On a similar note, Phil Donahue has stated that MSNBC dropped his evening news show in 2003 because he opposed the United States going to war with Iraq, not because of low viewership. Although his viewership trailed Fox News Channel and CNN in his time slot, his audience was larger than any other MSNBC program on the cable news network (Remarks at "Inside Corporate Media—Can it Tell the Truth?" session at National Conference for Media Reform, Memphis, TN, 12 January 2007).

that impinge directly upon most citizens' daily lives, popular interests and tastes generally have given public affairs a low priority relative to everyday pursuits like making a living, attending to family affairs, shopping, sports, hobbies and other forms of entertainment. Why should we expect people to change their normal interests and behaviors just because Internet-based ICTs provide them with tools to gather and disseminate more information about public affairs?

When cataclysmic events do engender widespread public attention, however, many citizens who ordinarily do not follow public affairs closely turn to trusted sources for information about the actual situation, the plausible remedies, and the actions or policies needed in order to achieve them (Elkin and Soltan (eds.) 1999). For most of the last century the press, radio and television provided citizens of democratic countries this information. But as Internet usage has grown, public officials, party and interest group leaders, policy research centers, petitioners, bloggers and other political activists have begun to communicate their solutions to citizens directly and also to respond to citizens' questions, suggestions, opinions or reactions. These sources represent viable alternatives to the established news media for citizens whose interests or concerns about public affairs—regular or fleeting—relate to their particular areas of expertise.[5]

Reductions in reportorial staff combined with 24-hour news cycles mean that established news media have less time and fewer resources for checking the veracity of breaking news. Although hoaxes, spoofs, disinformation, propaganda and lies have long histories in public affairs, the Internet provides new opportunities to spread fabrications at lightning speed. While many, such as West African banking schemes and PayPal account re-registrations are transparently false or implausible, several groups, such as "The Yes Men" and the "Harding Institute for

5 In the 1940s and 1950s major newspapers had labor correspondents, and industrial unions ike the UAW sponsored or even produced their own radio shows and newspaper columns. As the USA's GDP changed from primarily manufacturing to service, however, labor's coverage by in influence over mass media waned. Service unions, whose potential members are more widely scattered than industrial workers, are generally harder to organize. Only in recent years have they begun to take better advantage of new ICTs. The leadership of the Service Employees International Union (SEIU) exemplifies this trend. The union of 1.9 million members endorsed Barack Obama for President in February 2008. It operates e-mail lists, websites and blogs, which it uses not only to foster its organizational activities, but also to champion public policies, such as a broad national healthcare plan for Americans. On November 19, 2008, barely two weeks after Obama became president-elect, the union sent the following message to its e-mail list:

Today, at 2:30pm EST, Andy Stern will be sitting down with his laptop for a live video Q&A with you on SEIU.org. He'll be debriefing us on today's Senate Finance Committee hearing on health care, and explaining our strategy moving forward.

Will you join us? Use this link at 2:30pm EST to watch: http://www.seiu.org/AndysDebrief

Missed it? Check-in on the SEIU.org blog to watch the archived video.

Thanks, Jessica Kutch SEIU Healthcare, New Media Campaign Manager.

Freedom and Democracy," have successfully developed elaborate impersonations of experts from World Trade Organization spokespersons to policy advisers to Senator John McCain's presidential campaign, that have garnered them featured presentations at International Business Conferences and coverage in prestigious news outlets, including *BBC World News*, MSNBC, Fox News Channel, *The New Republic,* and *The Los Angeles Times* (Yes Men 2008; Harding Institute 2008).[6] Short-staffed commercial news media frequently fail to produce public affairs coverage that exceeds the quality of stories produced by alternative media. Surveys from 1985 through 2007 by the *Pew Project for Excellence in Journalism* reveal steady declines in the mass media's credibility, trust and prestige among the general public (Ruby 2008).

Downsizing news staff also contributes to the long recognized problem of "yesterday's news." As the news media increasingly focus upon breaking stories, one story follows another without much context. The coverage of current events becomes nearly as disjointed as the audience's interests. Daily newspaper and broadcast news stories appear willy-nilly as though editors have lost their collective memories or (more likely) as though business managers have advised them to adopt the *Monty Python's Flying Circus* mantra: "And now for something completely different!" in hopes of attracting a larger audience. The lack of context seems unlikely to enhance the media's credibility among those who care about public affairs, however, and it may serve to confuse rather than to enlighten ordinary citizens. Indeed, survey evidence suggests that it has not stemmed the ongoing declines in newspaper readership and broadcast news, especially among adults under 45 years old. (See Bennett 2009, 1-76 and 193-220; "The State of the News Media" 2008; Newspapers, Network TV 2008; Ruby 2008).

That even the highly regarded *BBC World News* fell for the Yes Men's portrayal of a Dow Chemical Company spokesman who apologized and offered compensation for victims on the 20th anniversary of the Bhopal disaster, highlights another problem.[7] The UK and other European democracies have a tradition of underwriting substantial portions of the costs of public radio and television networks that produce and distribute news and entertainment programs whose content remains almost entirely independent of government control. In recent decades, however, EU countries have begun to follow the USA's practice of asking their public networks to

---

6 Readers can follow the links at these websites for examples of their work.

7 On December 3, 1984 near the center of Bhopal, Madhya Pradesh, India, a Union Carbide owned pesticide plant released 42 metric tons of methyl isocyanate (MIC) gas, exposing at least 520,000 people to deadly toxins that killed over 3,000 within hours. As many as 8,000 additional deaths occurred within two weeks of the disaster, and studies suggest that another 8,000 have died since from diseases related to their exposure. Union Carbide never settled with most of the victims, and litigation over the disaster and its long term environmental damage continues. After Dow Chemical acquired Union Carbide in 2001 it disavowed any liability, claiming that Union Carbide had settled the cases ("Bhopal Disaster", *Wikipedia*). On the prestige and credibility of the BBC, see Marshall (2008).

raise increasingly larger portions of their budgets from listeners, viewers and private sponsors. This semi-business model may engender the same types of self-censorship and reportorial downsizing that commercial news media face, (see Project Censored 2009; and "Television License," *Wikipedia*).

Mass Media, the Internet and 21st Century Democracy: Four Scenarios

As we write, the mass media are in flux. In order to maintain dominant position, traditional print and broadcast media (and their cable affiliates and rivals) are moving substantial portions of their operations online where they can compete directly for audience and advertising revenue not only with expanding journalistic enterprises like Town Hall or Huffington Post but also with more narrowly focused web publications as well as diverse bloggers and social networks. Simultaneously, the consumption habits of audiences are changing. Increasing proportions prefer using multimedia rather than print to gather information about virtually any subject from current events to entertainment. Moreover, they increasingly demand flexibility regarding when, where and how they can access media content. Manufacturers have encouraged (or perhaps created) this demand by developing and marketing devices and software—TiVo, Blackberry, iPhone, Bluetooth and the like—that combine numerous capabilities, such as Internet browsing, telephoning, texting, e-mailing, global positioning, digital audio and video recording and setting up mobile private networks. Indeed, the long expected convergence of communication media is technically feasible.

Future ICTs will undoubtedly provide Internet users with fantastic new ways to access greater numbers of information sources, but we remain skeptical about the extent to which these technologies will redistribute decision-making power regarding public affairs. We caution once again that easier access to information provides no guarantee that citizens actually will use such access to increase their knowledge of or participation in public and civic affairs. For example, even though nearly 75 percent of American adults claim to follow national or international news on television or the Internet, studies indicate that the growing number of cable television news channels and foreign and domestic news sources online has not produced a corresponding increase in the public's knowledge of national and international affairs. Moreover, notwithstanding their stated desire for unbiased news, Americans generally choose news sources that they feel share their viewpoints. Lastly, when asked to use available media to pick subject matters of interest, most Americans normally select movies, sports, music, drama or other personal pursuits over public affairs (Pew People and the Press 2008; Sunstein 2007, 46-96; Prior 2007, 27-141).[8]

8 The Pew Research Center reported that as of December 22, 2008, 40 percent of American adults chose the Internet as the source where they got "most of [their] National and International News." Television still led with 70 percent, but only 35 percent cited

We conclude this chapter by presenting four scenarios that illustrate the basis for our skepticism that new media will profoundly redistribute political power from decision-making elites to ordinary citizens. While we cannot dismiss the possibility that a new set of Internet and related ICTs will at long last fulfill the classical democrats' dream, we expect only minor accommodations. Historical patterns suggest that whatever forms communications media of the future may take, established democratic elites will mitigate their effects. They will acquire the new ICTs, or they will co-opt those users and interests that they perceive as probable challengers (Meisel 1962). The composition of elites and hence the power structure itself will change over time, but at a deliberate pace, not a revolutionary one.[9]

Scenario One: The Mass Media Reinforce the Status Quo

Lance W. Bennett has developed a model of "Managerial Democracy" that characterizes how mass media generally help incumbent political leaders and major social and economic institutions condition ordinary citizens to accept public policies and official actions that survey research indicates they actually disapprove. This acceptance stems from three factors. First, the mainstream media, which are largely owned by established interests, habitually define public issues by reporting what public officials or spokespersons for major social, economic, and political groups have to say. Because institutional representatives presumably possess (or can access) more information than most citizens, discussion in the mass media generally centers about the alternatives these representatives define. Second, unless there is considerable disagreement among the institutional elites, the mass media generally accept the superiority of institutional voices and distrust the quality of popular opinion. The media tend to minimize controversies over policy except when the elites make their disagreements public. We usually hear public opinion expressed regularly as a legitimate voice only on amorphous concerns, such as leadership approval or political party popularity. For most questions of policy, polls are seldom given as much weight as the voices of experts, political leaders or institutional representatives. Finally, even if mainstream media desired to look into discrepancies between institutional voices and mass opinion, staff reductions in news operations would leave them with few investigative reporters to assign to the task (Bennett 1989; 2009; Prior 2007).

The net result is that most news stories about public or civic affairs are presented from the perspective of established institutional leaders. As a result, citizens who do not ordinarily follow politics closely are likely to be exposed to proponents' points of view rather than to alternatives that might be shared by

---

Newspapers. (Multiple responses were allowed.) Among 18-29-year-olds, the Internet tied with Television (59 percent) as the main source, and only 28 percent cited Newspapers. <http://pewresearch.org/pubs/1066/internet-overtakes-newspapers-as-news-source> (Accessed 23 December 2008).

9 See Meisel (1962) for a discussion of Gaetano Mosca's theory of democratic elitism.

the bulk of the general public, including attentive individuals and groups who are not part of the current political establishment (Noelle-Neumann 1984). Even popular and scholarly historical accounts of political and civic affairs that feature viewpoints of ordinary people rather than those of political, social and economic elites remain relatively uncommon. (See Terkel 1997; Zinn 1999)

In short, Scenario One predicts that the principal effects of the mainstream media's moving their operations to the Internet will be to tame it in service of maintaining the distribution of social, political and economic power among ruling elites. The mainstream mass media will continue to transfer much of their coverage of public and civic affairs into cyberspace and to buy out, co-opt or otherwise absorb many of their smaller competitors in other areas of public interest, such as weather, sports, hobbies, religion, social networks and entertainment. Barring cataclysmic events like unanticipated economic depressions, invasions, or nationwide environmental disasters changes in the distribution of power will occur incrementally. The Internet will not actualize the classical model of participatory democracy.

Scenario Two: The Triumph of an Economic Model of Democratic Elitism

Where Scenario One projects incremental changes that follow patterns that resemble "circulation of elites" models within a democratic context, Scenario Two posits a somewhat less democratic future. Without denying the classical democrats' recognition that the Internet and related ICTs have great potential as accessible public utilities that open worldwide communication to all, Scenario Two recognizes that these same technologies also have the potential to provide ruling governmental and corporate elites with new tools with which to protect and enhance their privileged positions. Even though public funds financed most of the Internet's initial development, its operations largely have been privatized.

The business models of private companies that operate the Net, however, are generally designed to create profits rather than to provide services to all comers, most whom have little to spend. Among other things, profits are made through selling Internet access with differing tariffs for various speeds of transmission between the users' devices and ISPs, charges for transmitting data between ISPs, and fees involving advertising, user responses and sales. Additional profits arise from fees for use of intellectual property, such as copyrighted material or proprietary rather than open source software. As more and more users have begun to take advantage of the Internet's audio and video capabilities, there is a danger the current broadband capacity will be exhausted within the foreseeable future. In order to expand this capacity, therefore, the companies that own and operate most of the Internet's routers and connectors have proposed that they be allowed charge for prioritizing transmissions instead of treating all packets of information alike (Lessig 2001; Wakefield 2008).

This proposal is antithetical to the original Transmission Control Protocol/ Internet Protocol (TCP/IP) that was designed to make possible an open and unbiased system that could easily incorporate almost any kind of computer or network into a universal network-of-networks and would treat every information packet the same, regardless of its origin or destination (Goldsmith and Wu 2006). Indeed, the idea behind the original—and highly democratic—protocol has been dubbed "Net Neutrality," and classically inclined democrats have used it as a rallying cry against the corporate owner-operators' initiatives. The matter has become highly contentious in the USA and European Union. Critics argue that far from expanding broadband capacity or introducing innovative new forms of transmission, from which all users will benefit, the established media will ally with owner operators and use their privileged relationships with governments to expand their control over content and to favor messages of allies and supporters over those of competitors and dissenters. During his party's primaries and during his general election campaign President Obama promised to preserve the principles of Net Neutrality. As we write, the proposals are on hold in the USA, but attention to problems of worldwide economic downturns and ongoing wars will occupy most people's attention and may provide opportunities for the established mass media and their allies to attempt to impose their protocols once again. This would result in favored websites and users getting priority—at prices that they would be willing and able to pay—but their weaker and less well-funded competition could not afford. Moreover, ideas or services that severely challenge the owner-operators' dominance could be shut out altogether (Lindblom 1977; Head 1993; SavetheInternet.com 2009).

Scenario Three: Audience Fragmentation Produces Extreme Rhetoric, Intolerance and Inability to Compromise

We have cited scholars from diverse academic specializations who have argued that the multiplicity of choices the mass media offer through the Internet and other ICTs contributes to citizens eschewing more information about proposed solutions to contentious public affairs questions than when the media offered them fewer choices.[10] Evidence indicates that this paradoxical outcome reflects people's propensities to seek affirmation of their preconceived attitudes or opinions regarding any public issue or question of interest to them. The dual declines of daily newspaper readership and network news viewership decrease the likelihood that citizens will inadvertently encounter straightforward presentations of positions other than their own. Moreover, by fragmenting their public affairs coverage on cable, satellite and the Internet to match the interests of the attentive—and mostly partisan—public, the mainstream media encourage those who have little interest in public affairs to avoid them altogether. The news media will happily supply

10 E.g., Kathleen Jamieson, James Capella, Markus Prior, Cass Sunstein and Robert Putnam have diverse specializations that include Rhetoric, Communications, Public Opinion, Public Policy, Social Change, Economic Behavior, Political Theory and Law.

these citizens multitudes of radio stations, TV channels, websites, blogs, podcasts, downloads, mobile alerts, etc. that concern their particular subjects of interest.

Scenario Three projects these trends forward. It presumes that most citizens will continue to access media mainly to pursue interests other than news about public affairs and that increasing portions of the population will prefer multi-media to print presentations. The former presumption means that the majority of the habitual public affairs audience will have preconceived attitudes and opinions about the subjects or policies of interest, and that most will be seeking not merely information, but also confirmation of those preconceptions. The latter presumption means that well crafted rhetorical audio and video presentations will count as much as or more than well written storylines or logical explanations. As their business model instructs mass media to cater to their clientele, the media will use Web 2.0 interactive capabilities that allow users to specify the matters and (often by implication) the viewpoints or interpretations they seek.

While citizens can undoubtedly glean new information and interpretations from sources that cater to their ideological or partisan inclinations, the long-term effects are likely to narrow their perspectives. With practice, attentive citizens can develop personal search paradigms that exclude sources that frequently return subject matters or interpretations that they find discomforting. My *New York Times*, My *Wall Street Journal,* My social circle, My Favorite News Monitors or Compilers, My Favorite Blogs—the Internet and related ICTs provide the means for never having to encounter an argument or opinion with which you strongly disagree. As we discussed in Chapter 4, constant repetition of shared ideas within largely homogeneous groups tends to reinforce preconceived biases and to breed intolerance of opposing viewpoints, let alone serious consideration of moderation and compromise.

To be sure, there are hundreds of thousands of bloggers as well a millions of foreign and domestic websites that vie for visitors' attentions. Relatively few are devoted to politics and current events, however, and a majority of Americans admit they never (or hardly ever) read them.[11] Most political bloggers are essentially media monitors who add their own commentary and interpretations. They usually possess neither the time nor the resources to verify their stories, a situation that makes them vulnerable to planted stories or to payments for presenting particular points of view.[12] With few exceptions, they also lack the reputations or resources of the mainstream media to attract enough attention to drive traffic to their websites. Moreover, the exceptions often occur because mainstream media decide to carry

11 The answers were: "Never" 35 percent ; Hardly ever 29 percent; Sometimes 21 percent; Regularly 15 percent (*Pew Research Center for the People & the Press Biennial Media Consumption Survey*, April 2008).

12 Even regularly employed syndicated columnists, such as Armstrong Williams, Maggie Gallagher and Michael McManus accepted money from Bush Administration Departments in exchange for endorsing certain of their controversial policy initiatives. See Nationmaster.com (2009).

them, a co-optation strategy that we discussed above (see Oates 2008, 170-72 and 186-87 for examples.) President Obama's election and the worldwide recession may calm the online rhetoric and politics of confrontation in the USA and Europe, at least temporarily. It certainly will not change the rhetoric or focus of groups like Al Qaeda and others that foment racism, terrorism, jingoism, or similarly militant and uncompromising ideologies.

What about the majority, the "inattentive public," so to speak? Scenario Three projects that they will happily accept the media's invitation to "amuse themselves to death" (Postman 2006; Prior 2007). Even if the mainstream media and the owner-operators fail to eliminate Net Neutrality, they are finding new ways to market music, sports and other forms of entertainment online. Newly established channels, such as Hulu.com and Watch-livetv, offer network programs and cinema to online users worldwide "for free." The price paid is that users cannot fast forward, skip over or otherwise eliminate commercials that periodically interrupt the programming.[13] On a similar note, Apple forged a compromise with major record companies to free its iTunes downloads from Digital Rights Management (DRM) restrictions in exchange for allowing the companies to price their songs for \$0.69, \$0.99 or \$1.29 instead of the previously uniform price of \$0.99. At a time when the worldwide economic recession has made increasing numbers of users reluctant to spend money on outside entertainment, these types of marketing strategies may prove successful.

Unfortunately, none of these changes are likely to fulfill the classical democrats' desire to realize the Internet's potential to enhance the mass media's watchdog role and improve the quality of participatory democracy.

Scenario Four: The Audience Rebels: Citizens Become Attentive to Public Affairs and Demand Access to the Full Informational Potential of Internet

While this scenario seems unlikely at first blush, posting open and transparent information about (unclassified) governmental operations online could encourage citizens to become more attentive to public affairs as well as encourage the mass media to reinvigorate their role as the people's watchdogs. Implementing these types of governmental initiatives, which President Obama has publicly espoused, would improve citizens' knowledge and understanding of public policy, which, in turn, should improve the quality of participatory democracy over time. The democratic faith, after all, posits that citizens are capable of making enlightened decisions about their collective interests, directly through deliberative processes (when feasible) or indirectly through fair and honest elections of responsible representatives.

---

13 The former site is jointly held by NBC Universal and Newscorp through a private corporation. Thus, a Whois.net search turns up contact addresses only. The latter is so new that as of January 2009 no information about ownership is immediately available on Whois.net or Alexa.com.

Achieving such goals, of course, requires considerable effort. In most modern capitalistic countries such efforts would mean devoting greater resources to public purposes, such as increased access to education, expansion and maintenance of common infrastructure, environmental planning and regulation, as well as providing a host of complex and often controversial public projects, services and benefits that inevitably would take money away from private consumption and investment.

Democratic politics tends to be cyclical. The last two decades of the 20th century and the first decade of the 21st epitomized the triumph of modern capitalism and the global economy over the regulatory and socialistic regimes that arose after the Great Depression and World War II. The necessities of the current economic recession—the worst since the 1930s—may clear the way for a resurgence of governmental regulatory regimes that emphasize fiscal initiatives over the monetary economics that has been dominant for the past generation.

Will this crisis also invigorate the mass media's noble mission as the Fourth Estate? We remain skeptical, but we close this chapter with what some may read as an ambiguous judgment: fat chance!

Chapter 6
The Internet and Democratic Education

Education and Democracy

Hopes that the Internet's ICT capabilities will democratize access to all types of social and political information have their parallel in hopes that these same capabilities will democratize education. From the Enlightenment onwards, democrats have postulated that adult citizens possess the rationality necessary to determine their own and their society's best interests. Citizens govern society collectively, either through direct participation in policy-making or through their election of representatives. To exercise their capacity to govern a modern society effectively, however, citizens need both the information required for making decisions and the education necessary for understanding that information. Regardless of their particular differences, therefore, democratic theorists and practitioners have expressed common concerns for developing well-educated citizens (Dewey 1916; Jefferson 1964; Mann 1848; Mill 1963; Rousseau 1762; Van Setten 1998).

Despite lagging behind other democratic nations in adopting numerous welfare programs, such as unemployment compensation, social security, and universal medical care, the USA has generally devoted larger proportions of its resources to public education than have its democratic counterparts. Its official commitment to public education actually preceded the adoption of its Constitution. Article 3 of the Northwest Ordinance of 1787, passed under the Articles of Confederation, declared, "Religion, morality and knowledge, being necessary to good government and the happiness of mankind, schools and the means of education shall forever be encouraged." Public education for all children comports with liberal democratic ideas of fairness and individual self-development. Ideally, studying hard in school should increase a person's opportunities to succeed. The educational reforms of the "No Child Left Behind" Act (NCLB) implemented in 2002 paid homage to these values, notwithstanding the controversy it engendered over the federal government's standards intruding upon local control of school curricula (Cleary 2004).

Real societies are less than ideal. Because governmental resources are insufficient to provide support for every deserving cause, political struggles commonly concern choosing which causes to support and deciding how much to distribute among them. In the USA, for instance, the quality of public education varies by location. Public schools in localities with fewer resources and lower tax bases tend to have old physical plants and technology, out of date textbooks and library materials, and poorly paid teachers. Compared to richer localities, they offer lesser opportunities for students to get ahead. In attempting to improve the quality of education for poorer children, governments have instituted numerous programs, such as Headstart, Americorps/Vista, and subsidized meals in schools. These programs have achieved some success, but pollsters report that Americans worry about the quality of their children's education, and that they consistently place education among the top problems facing the country. In addition, Americans tend to rate the nation's public schools as mediocre, even though they usually rate their local public schools as somewhat better (Howell, West and Peterson 2008). These expressions of concern about public education, coupled with rumblings of discontent, have encouraged political leaders from both major parties to look favorably upon universal access to the Internet as a promising means to improve public school education, especially for otherwise disadvantaged students enrolled in the poorest school districts.

Politicians' enthusiasm for providing universal access to the Internet as a major program to improve public education is understandable. Internet access can connect students and teachers to digitized libraries that contain books, documents, sound recordings, videos, and other research and instructional materials that local school districts could never afford. While such access serves to enhance the resources available to everyone associated with local schools and libraries, those who are least well off stand to benefit the most. Public school financing consists of an amalgam of federal, state and local revenues, of which the federal government contributes only about 9 percent. Formulas vary from state to state, but local districts on average must raise about 43 percent of the revenues (Statistical Abstract 2008, Table 251). States legislatures raise and distribute the remainder.[1] In principle they seek to distribute those funds in a fair and equitable manner using formulas that account for the local districts' revenue-raising efforts, educational performance, children's needs and the like. In practice, however, funding formulas also involve political considerations, and in education, as in other areas of public policy, the better off are better organized and better able to secure the policies they favor (Schattschneider 1960; Verba and Nie 1972; Verba, Schlozman and Brady 1995). Critics allege—and courts sometimes agree—that numerous states' use distribution formulas that unfairly disadvantage children in the poorest districts (ACCESS 2009). Federal funding targeted to these districts for better Internet access (or other innovations) can bypass state legislative politics and make an immediate impact.

For political and educational leaders with limited dollars, the Internet's allure as a means for boosting the quality of public education is nearly irresistible. Seemingly small investments for Internet connectivity can virtually equalize educational opportunity among students, providing rich and poor alike with identical resources online for teaching, training and research. As the expanding market drives down

1 After passage of the No Child Left Behind Act, the federal portion increased about two percent between 2003 and 2006. During the same period, however, the state proportion declined slightly leaving local governments to fund about the same proportion as before.

the cost of computers and bandwidth, even the economically deprived students in the poorest districts will be able to enjoy the pleasures of learning online. The educational impact of previous technologies—public television and radio, instructional films, videos and sound recordings, special student editions of major newspapers and the like—would pale beside the power of the Internet. Of course such an optimistic expectation presumes that school districts will be assured a steady stream of funding to maintain and upgrade their technology.

Passage of the Telecommunications Act of 1996 revealed agreement across the political spectrum that with proper funding the Internet could become the next great educational equalizer. With the support of conservative and liberal technophiles like Newt Gingrich and Al Gore, the Act expanded the provision of subsidies for universal telephone service to include all levels of telecommunication services. It explicitly designated schools and libraries (as well as rural health facilities) as beneficiaries. Congress authorized the Federal Communications Commission to administer the program and to propose to Congress an allocation for the subsidy yearly. The subsidy, paid by long distance telecommunications vendors who could pass along the cost to their regular customers, became known as the "e-rate," where the "e" stood for "education," "equality" or "equal access" (Margolis and Resnick 2000, 141-45).

Capitalism and government educational policy, however, do not always mesh. Supporters had not reckoned that long distance telecommunications companies were struggling to fend off new competitors in the telephone business, while at the same time, they were attempting to grab a larger share of communications services on the Internet. Notwithstanding the initial lack of controversy over its authorization, the e-rate suddenly became a hot issue after AT&T and MCI (now part of Verizon) stopped rolling the subsidy into their base rates and started listing it as a separate charge on their customers' bills in May 1998. The National Taxpayers Union took up the cause, characterizing the rate as a new hidden tax, which they dubbed the "Gore Tax." Allies in Congress attempted to repeal this Gore Tax and replace it with money drawn from previously established federal excise taxes. The Clinton administration, its congressional allies, and local interest groups mounted a counter-offense that successfully staved off repeal.

As it happened, the e-rate proved to be enormously successful in fulfilling Bill Clinton's initial goal of establishing universal access to the Internet for all public schools. The National Center for Education Statistics (NCES) reported that 98 percent of all public schools were connected to the Internet by fall of 2000, including 94 percent of the poorest schools (the latter were defined as those with over 75 percent of their students eligible for a free or reduced price school lunch), 97 percent of all public elementary schools and over 99.5 percent of all public high schools had Internet access. Meanwhile the ratio of students to instructional computers with Internet connections fell from 12:1 in 1998 to 7:1 in 2000. These figures represented sharp increases from 1996 when 65 percent of all schools and 53 percent of the poorest ones had such access. Nevertheless, important differences remained. The poorest schools had lower proportions of their instructional classrooms wired for Internet connections, and their ratio of students to instructional computers stood at 9:1 (Cattagni and Westat 2001, 3 and Tables 1-4).

While the e-rate and funding from the NCLB have further improved these proportions, achieving near universal Internet access does not bridge the digital divide. The e-rate provides funding under four categories: "telecommunications services, Internet Access, internal connections and basic maintenance." (USAC 2008).[2] It does not pay for most computer hardware or for most instructional and communications software that must be purchased, maintained and upgraded. School districts must also pay their share for maintaining the online libraries, databases and instructional materials that their students access. In addition, teachers themselves need education and training in order to understand the strengths and weaknesses of computer-based instruction and in order to deploy the hardware and software effectively. Poorer districts lag behind richer ones on all of these factors (Cattagni and Westat 2001; NSF 2006). NCLB can provide some money to purchase and maintain computer hardware, software, and pedagogical equipment for instructional classrooms, but this must be part of a wider plan that explains how the money will produce measurable student improvement (Department of Education 2002).

The Internet is no longer a public utility. Huge commercial telecommunication companies, mostly based in the US, now own the fibers and cables that form its backbone. They make money through "peering arrangements" with other network owners that set fees for allowing data to traverse from one network to another across the Internet. They typically own the equipment at Network Access Points (NAPs), where Internet Service Providers (ISPs) house their servers and where information packets are exchanged between networks. Some network owners are also ISPs.[3] Except for providing information directly relevant to conducting governmental business online, the US government's role as a content provider is shrinking while the role of commercial content providers is growing (Weil 2000; Foster 2002).

The e-rate pays for securing access from private ISPs at a discount, but it does not pay for access to any particular content. The economic downturn that followed the terrorist attacks of 11 September, 2001, not to mention the current (2008-2009) worldwide economic recession, precipitated drastic reductions in advertising revenues that supported much of the "free content" on the Net. Commercial enterprises, which provide such content, must find new sources of revenues, cut back their services or go out of business. Well-known "dot.coms"

2 The Universal Service Administrative Company (USAC) administers the E-Rate under contract and supervision of the Federal Communications Commission (FCC).

3 In summer 2002, it became clear that Network owners had created a great overcapacity. Most telecommunications companies posted losses from their Internet operations, WorldCom and Global Crossing went bankrupt, and Quest Communications International barely avoided the same fate.

that supply public affairs content like those discussed in Chapter 5 as well as numerous providers of other types of content are struggling to condition users to pay fees for access to premium Web pages or to exclusive types services, many of which they once offered for free. If their efforts succeed, the Internet will become a service that provides tiered levels of access, much like cable television systems. Poor school districts, as well as lower income Internet users in general, could find themselves online but unable to afford access to the information they want to utilize (Mangalindan 2002).[4]

The question of whether or not poor districts have the wherewithal to take proper advantage of Internet access, however, begs a previous question. How much systematic evidence do we have that providing Internet access will improve public school education any better than would providing new textbooks, classroom materials, better physical plants and higher pay for teachers? Funneling federal funds into local school districts for high-tech solutions to educational problems may just avoid redistributing state funds from richer to poorer districts or reorganizing state school districts.

We do know that course by course comparisons—mostly in post-secondary educational institutions—show that students who use computer-based instruction for learning, including distance education, normally perform as well as those who use more traditional campus-based lectures and textbooks. But it also happens that in some cases they do significantly better, while in others they do significantly worse (Conger 2006; Varis 2006).

The Internet—to borrow Pippa Norris's apt description—is still in its adolescence (Norris 2001). It continues to grow and change at an astonishing pace. The total cost and final outcomes of adopting online education remain uncertain. While it seems unlikely that Internet technologies will hurt public education in grades K-12, critics caution that the more resources schools commit to these technologies, the less likely they will consider alternative strategies for improving education. In short, once educational institutions start down the high-tech road their psychological commitments and their maintenance costs increase. A blackboard can last as long as the building in which it is housed; computers need to be upgraded or replaced every three years. Many textbooks remain current longer than do computers and related communication software. In any case, they usually are cheaper to replace. Electronic classrooms also require more costly maintenance than do ordinary ones:

> No one seriously asks if technology-increased productivity compares with the previous ways of working, because the organization is no longer pursuing the old objectives and no longer works in the old way. No one seriously considers

4 This is also a problem at all levels of education across nations. Students, teachers, and researchers at public educational institutions cannot afford the cost of accessing full text online databases such as JSTOR, Medline, ProQuest, LexisNexis etc.

> abandoning the technology because it has become inconceivable to accomplish what is now being done without it (Lewis, Massey and Smith 2001, 129).

Regardless of its costs, the Internet's long-term impact on the quality of public elementary and secondary school education is unlikely to change the nature of the relationship between most students and teachers. Americans expect elementary and secondary public school teachers not merely to teach learning skills and to transmit knowledge but also to act as baby-sitters or surrogate parents and to help socialize their charges to liberal democratic norms with regard to personal, group, religious, civic and political activities and values. In most cases, fulfilling these expectations entails personal interaction between students and teachers in a public school facility. Access to the Internet facilitates the creation of alternative educational opportunities, such as home schooling, charter schools or special new private (often religious) schools where parents or instructors who don't meet state certification requirements for public school teaching can be in charge. Expanding these alternatives has drawn relatively few students from the public schools, however, nor has it caused disproportionate funding reductions for public schools, citizens' expressions of dissatisfaction with public education notwithstanding (Statistical Abstract 2008, Tables 217, 230 and 251).

The Internet's effect on higher education is likely to be more profound. At this level most students are expected to have sufficient knowledge, motivation, and learning skills to study and to carry out research without requiring as much direct personal supervision as they needed in high school. Indeed, as we shall see, instruction via the Internet is being marketed as a superior alternative to traditional classroom-based instruction.

Brave New Universities

Even though enrollment in public universities and colleges was more widespread in the United States than in most western nations, the American academy remained an elitist institution for most of the 20th century, drawing the lion's share of its students and faculty from affluent families. As late as 1960, 36 percent of students enrolled in programs of higher education attended private colleges or universities. For these relatively well off communities of scholars the American academy provided some refuge from the vicissitudes of the market economy. Scholars at universities and liberal arts colleges typically immersed themselves in study and in teaching. For most, the traditional mission of a university remained "the diffusion and extension of knowledge rather than the advancement" (Newman 1996, 3). They occasionally turned out a scholarly article, book or review, but a rather small minority produced the bulk of these publications (Ladd and Lipset 1975). Rhetorically, scholars in the liberal arts and sciences generally embraced the idea that their institutions valued education for its own sake, not necessarily for its immediate utility. Colleges of arts and sciences within the universities provided places where students and faculty could learn together, mature intellectually, and reflect upon how their knowledge ought to affect the conduct of private and civic affairs of the broader society. Those who chose scholarly careers might have found more lucrative employment outside academia, but it usually offered a less congenial environment for learning (Sperber 2000).

Of course higher education had a practical side. Great 19th century industrial merchants and barons like Andrew Carnegie, J.D. Rockefeller, James Duke, Ezra Cornell, Johns Hopkins, Cornelius Vanderbilt and Leland Stanford had endowed many well-known private universities. The specialized programs, schools, or colleges found within the universities provided training for various occupations and professions from farming and business through engineering, law and medicine. Patrons and clients of these institutions—governments, businesses, churches and philanthropies—expected that graduates would combine the virtues of educated citizens with the practical skills or knowledge necessary to secure desirable livelihoods.[5] And from the last decades of the nineteenth century American universities progressively leavened Anglo/American ideas that emphasized teaching, learning and citizenship with continental European ideas of academic research that emphasized the advancement of knowledge (Sullivan 1999).

Much of this has changed in recent decades. To accommodate the influx of postwar baby boomers and also to compete with the educational programs of the Soviet Union, higher education was expanded and its body of students was effectively democratized. Enrolments in public universities rose from 3.97 million enrollments in 1965 to 8.93 million in 1975. Private universities' enrollments grew more slowly: they rose only to 1.95 million to 2.35 million during the same period. The student population diversified as the new enrollments included larger proportions of women, minorities, and the less affluent (Statistical Abstract 2008, Tables 211 and 222).

In the aftermath of this great expansion, however, public universities and other higher educational institutions found themselves facing increased costs. They had new facilities and infrastructure to maintain, and they had bid up salaries in order to staff courses for their larger student population or to recruit scholars and researchers of great repute. When the American economy entered a long period of "stagflation" in the mid-1970s, therefore, higher education faced new financial problems. Increases in public appropriations lagged behind economic inflation, as did profits and asset values of corporate and philanthropic donors. Moreover, the baby boomer population bulge was moving beyond the traditional college age. In order to support their expanded programs and operations universities had to seek additional sources of revenue. Their efforts included recruiting and retaining new and non-traditional students, increasing alumni financial support, promoting revenue generating activities such as basketball and football teams or non-degree

5 Some critics argue that these programs also served to train the managers and professionals who would help socialize the expanding urban masses to accept the new industrial order (Zinn 1999, 262-64).

programs such as alumni travel or education in retirement. They also implemented businesslike evaluations of the revenue streams that stemmed from enrollments in particular academic programs, from research projects, from clinical income, or from other contracts for services. Lastly, encouraged by federal policy embodied in the Bayh-Dole Act of 1980, they entered into public/private partnerships to market inventions developed from federally funded research projects (Council on Governmental Relations 1999; Kirp 2004, 1-7 and 207-220.

These developments gradually transformed the collegial organization of most post-secondary educational institutions into a hierarchical organization resembling that of a corporate enterprise. Institutions of higher learning, particularly colleges and universities, had customarily been characterized as bodies of faculty and students primarily engaged in scholarly activities. Faculty committees and a few full-time officers generally had administered these activities. As satisfying the need for additional revenue made institutional life more complex, a separate class of career academic administrators arose to oversee the educational enterprise (Lazerson, Wagener and Moneta 2000; Marginson and Considine 2000). Even though higher education always played an important role in preparing a skilled and adaptable workforce, these administrators came to stress the economic benefits of that role, both personal and societal, as the main justification for their institutions to receive public and private subsidies (Bok 1993; Galbraith 1996; Sullivan 1999). Progressively, faculties were cast in the role of corporate employees and students in the role of full-fledged customers (Yudoff 2002; Kirp 2004, 1-7 and 101-148).

Still faculties remained an unusual class of employees, for most of their members, after a six-year trial period, had been granted career long tenure in their positions. Tenure was established to protect and encourage free inquiry in scholarly endeavors, especially teaching and research (AAUP 1940). As the need for new revenue became more pressing, however, the criteria for granting tenure tended to favor published scholarship and research supported by external funding more than factors like the quality of instruction students received or the impact of scholarly activities on communities outside the university. Ironically, therefore, the surest way to gain tenure at institutions of higher learning was to demonstrate that one's research not only merits publication but that it also satisfies the priorities of external funders. Exercise of independence in teaching and research, the original justification for tenure and a bulwark for democratic self-criticism, is rarely a central consideration.[6]

In leading universities the rewards for producing good research came to include a diminution of responsibilities for teaching regularly scheduled courses. Meanwhile, the proportion of part-time faculty increased from less than 22 percent

6 An expansion of the size and number of academic journals followed the expansion of faculties as more researchers began to turn out more research, driven in part by new requirements for tenure. Whether or not this expansion has increased the total value or overall quality of scholarship is a matter of debate, not unlike the debate over whether or not the expansion of major league franchises has contributed to the overall quality of baseball.

in 1970 to more than 47 percent in 2005. Having teaching assistants, adjunct, visiting and other non-tenure stream faculty teach courses in lieu of higher paid professors may cost less, but that calculation does not consider whether or not these substitutes have the expertise to provide students with the same quality of content and instruction (Bok 1993, 155-177; Statistical Abstract 2008, Table 286; Fogg 2001).[7]

During the 1980s the academy itself was affected by the conservative turn in American politics. Many of the new private foundations were conservative, as were the policies of the Reagan and both Bush administrations. American universities had sometimes been characterized as bastions of political liberalism during the 1960s and 1970s, but this was accurate only for faculty in the social sciences, law, humanities, and to a lesser extent fine arts. Faculties of the physical and biological sciences, medicine, business, engineering, agriculture and other applied fields were substantially conservative; and overall, the political orientation of the faculty of the "divided academy" was, if anything, slightly conservative (Ladd and Lipset 1975, 60).[8]

By the mid-1990s signs of a corporate culture pervaded most American universities (Bromell 2002; Kirp 2004). The ratio of full-time administrators to full-time faculty had risen. Faculty who retired were replaced by part-timers and graduate students, especially in those disciplines which brought in fewer research dollars from external sources. Universities not only encouraged faculty to seek research dollars and contracts from external sources, but they also actively lobbied state legislatures and Congress to receive funds earmarked for their specific institutions. In fiscal 2008 earmarked appropriations from Congress alone exceeded $2.35 billion, up from $538 million in 1998 (Brainard and Hermes 2008).[9] Administrators commonly likened students to "customers" whose patronage—notwithstanding rising tuitions—their institutions needed to attract and retain. Pressures increased to raise the teaching loads of scholars who failed to bring in research dollars, and politically conservative academics attacked the professorate in general and the institution of tenure in particular (Huber 1992; Sykes 1988). Perhaps in response, efforts to unionize faculties also increased.

When popularly accessible computer mediated communication through the World Wide Web and multi-media browsers like Netscape Communicator and Microsoft Internet Explorer arose in the mid-90s, this new corporate culture

---

7 The rate of growth of part-time faculty accelerated during the 1990s.

8 These generalizations are based on aggregate distributions of a sample of 60,028 faculty members at 303 universities, four-year colleges, and junior colleges. They do not account for differences within and among particular educational institutions. See Ladd and Lipset (1975), 4.

9 Accounting for inflation congressional earmarks peaked in real dollar value in fiscal 2003. *The Chronicle* has two searchable databases of earmarked academic grants from 1990-2003 and for 2008 at: <http://chronicle.com/premium/stats/pork/legacyindex.php> and < http://chronicle.com/stats/pork/> respectively. (Accessed 28 January 2009).

became a catalyst for a radical restructuring of higher education. Higher education had always been a labor-intensive task, but heretofore there had been no fully acceptable way to cut labor costs by eliminating lectures and classroom discussions. The new technology had the potential to overcome this limitation and perhaps, at long last, to break the professorial guild. Indeed, the very manner in which the educational product had been marketed provided the justification for such changes. The anticipated savings, combined with high-tech delivery of the product, would certainly please their financially strapped customers; and if the product still resulted in a sufficiently trained workforce, those savings alone would also please their patrons and clients (Bromell 2002; Taylor 1998). Since the early 1980s similar changes have occurred at universities in Europe, Canada, Australia and the advanced industrial sectors of other regions (Braun 1999; Lewis, Massey and Smith 2001; Manicas and Odin 2004).

In sum, the stage had been set for the adoption of Internet technologies to bring about profound changes in the conduct of teaching and research in higher education. The next two sections discuss the likely changes and their likely consequences for higher education, and more generally, for public education and liberal democracy.

The Internet and Higher Education

The Internet and related media provide the means to alter, enhance and otherwise improve traditional forms of instruction and research. Instructors commonly place syllabi and assignments online; they utilize course management systems to facilitate and to monitor students' study habits and research; they computerize classroom presentations to enhance or replace lectures and face-to-face discussions; and they use e-mail, live chat and asynchronous forums and networks to improve communication with and among students whether on campus or at a distance. Beyond this, remote access to digitized libraries and databases can enhance or replace on-campus resources, both for coursework and for original research (Atieh 1998; Harknett and Cobane 1997; Katz and Associates 1999).

We can imagine idyllic campuses in an ideal democracy where faculty members guide students through the fundamentals of their academic disciplines, where rigorous study builds good character, and where students and mentors use the knowledge gained to contemplate questions of philosophic import. Combining this setting with access to the Internet's vast stores of information could lead to an enlightened civic-minded public whose good works, according to liberal democratic theory, would result in a better life for all (Dewey 1916, 94-116).

The most obvious problem with this scenario is its cost. No modern society has offered so rich an education to any but its elite, and arguably, no democratic society would find it feasible without diverting substantial resources from other public and private commitments. In the United States an intimate association of students and teachers "without the distractions of…outside work or other competitive involvements" can be found only at leading private liberal arts colleges or at select undergraduate colleges of major public and private research universities (Trow 1997, 294). For most of these leading institutions the cost of acquiring new information technology is not a primary concern. Notwithstanding the premium tuition they usually charge, most have large waiting lists of qualified students who desire to matriculate. They can use the technology largely to enhance the value of the education that results from the close student-teacher relationships already in place, and if necessary, they can charge an additional premium for this technological enhancement.[10]

Higher education for the masses takes place mostly at public institutions and generally focuses upon the transmission of knowledge. It has less concern for building character or shaping society's leaders through personal interaction between students and mentors. Studies are less intense than at elite institutions, student to faculty ratios are larger, and in the United States most students combine their studies with substantial outside employment during the school year in order to meet educational and other expenses. Outside employment may enrich their studies, but that usually is not a requirement (King and Bannon 2002). The key concern is for students to gain skills and knowledge necessary to certify them as trainable employees in their chosen fields, and not incidentally, to earn a sufficient income to pay off their college loans. While adopting information technology can enrich the curricula at these institutions, it costs money to do so. At most colleges and universities, therefore, adoption tends to be justified as providing wider access to courses, and inevitably, as cutting the per capita cost of delivering the educational product.

The second problem is that the great majority of undergraduates, the customers so to speak, are interested mostly in securing employment and a good income directly upon graduation or in gaining entry to graduate or professional programs to increase their skills, prestige and potential income. They are far less concerned about honing their critical thinking, developing philosophies of life, improving social and political values, entering public service, becoming community leaders, participating in civic or cultural affairs, or realizing other benefits of a rigorous education. To gain a general education and appreciation of cultural ideas will suffice.[11] That the majority of undergraduates view their education as a personal

10 Elite universities in the USA have recently attempted to attract a greater proportion of less well off students. See Gutmann (2008).

11 These assertions are based upon the annual surveys of freshmen entering four-year colleges and universities conducted by the UCLA Higher Education Research Institute and the American Council on Education taken each fall. Patterns illustrated in the table below have remained substantially the same since 1995. The 2001 survey, based on responses of 281,064 students at 421 four-year institutions, was largely completed before September 11. The 2006 survey included responses from over 270,000 freshmen at nearly 400 four-year institutions (See Appendix to this chapter).

economic investment is understandable. Not only does it comport with the corporate marketing of higher education as a commercial product, but it also reflects the diminution of public funding for higher education: In 1990 the ratio of state and local appropriations to tuition was 3:1; by 1998 this ratio had shrunk to 2.2:1, and by 2007 it was down to 1.8:1. Nearly 60 percent of students surveyed in 1997 had assumed an average debt of $16,700 to complete their educational programs; these figures rose to over 66 percent and $21,900 in 2007 (Statistical Abstract 2001, Tables 275 and 277; Statistical Abstract 2008, Table 281; Reed et al. 2008).[12]

This brings us to the third problem involved with simply adopting information technologies to enrich established curricula: the technologies themselves provide a means for new enterprises to upset the near monopoly that traditional institutions have enjoyed as providers of higher education. Where most degree programs still require students to attend class at a physical campus, instructional programs that use the Internet can eliminate this requirement. By delivering degree programs online, virtual institutions can maintain scanty physical plants devoid of expensive laboratories, classrooms, libraries, dormitories, or offices. By employing minimal numbers of full-time (let alone tenured) faculty, staff and librarians they can drastically reduce the customary labor costs of instruction. At the same time they can hold out the promise of equal access to higher education for everyone who can login to the Internet (Blaustain, Goldstein and Lozier 1999; Duderstadt 1999; Leonard 2000).

The United States is a market-dominated society where citizens commonly express an ideological bias against economic planning and regulation by government.[13] Adopting information technologies for instruction via the Internet allows university administrators to respond to pressures from politicians, taxpayers, and students-cum-customers to decrease the cost of delivering higher education. Additionally, these technologies provide opportunities for new types of higher learning enterprises—private and public; for profit and not-for-profit—to emerge. Most of these enterprises strive to deliver higher educational products comparable to those of traditional university programs of mass education, but with greater efficiency and at less cost (Atieh 1998; Baker 1999; Blumenstyk 1998; Bromell 2002; Grimes 2000; Kirp 2004, 207-220; Kolowich 2009; Lewis, Massey and Smith 2001; Lips 2000; NASCULGC 1999; Olsen 1999; Shea 1998).

In the United States today, online institutions that offer certificate or degree programs usually see "nontraditional students"—men and women aged 25 and

12 The *Statistical Abstract*: 2008 did not include comparable figures on the proportion of students who borrowed money to finance their higher education costs nor their average debt. See Reed (2008).

13 See Burns et al. (1998, 172 ff.) for a discussion and references on American ideology.

over who are regularly employed—as their primary customers.[14] The arguments for enrollment commonly focus upon economic advantages:

1. The U.S. Department of Labor (or some other authority) predicts that the great majority—perhaps as many as 80 percent—of new positions in a rapidly changing job market will involve Information Technology.
2. In order to stay competitive today's workers will have to keep acquiring new skills and knowledge.
3. Distance learning via the Internet can match traditional rates of tuition and can save students time and money by decreasing indirect costs—transportation, home help, wardrobe, room, board, and the like.
4. Online courses offer flexible hours and self-paced learning that cater to the needs of people who must work for a living.
5. Students who successfully complete courses online acquire marketable skills and learn as much as or more than students who complete similar courses in traditional college settings (Atieh 1998; Russell 2002).

This rationale fits the needs of non-traditional students who already embarked upon careers or who on average have more specific vocational goals than their younger less experienced colleagues. Missing, however, is the idea of a college or university as a place where learning extends much beyond formal coursework. There is little concern for developing civic leadership and character, for examining the nature of society or for pondering philosophical implications of implementing particular public policies (Resnick 2000). Nor is there much concern for the modern university's role in the research to expand our knowledge. The appeal, after all, is to "people whose geographic location, work demands, physical or social conditions, personal circumstances, or family and community responsibilities impede their access to traditional university-level education" (Atieh 1998, 9). Distance learning via the Internet is presented as the quintessential means of achieving success by adapting oneself to particular job requirements set by corporate America (Blasi and Heinecke 2000; Hales 2000).

An online education may be found lacking in comparison to the traditional programs at elite colleges or universities, but it looks more competitive when compared to standard programs for mass education. Even though some studies contradict claims of "edupreneurs" that students learn as much or more online as in standard programs, the evidence remains inconclusive. Moreover, Web 2.0 interactive tools are making it easier to develop and customize online pedagogy that will speak to younger students who have grown up using the Internet (Carnevale 2000; Noble 1998; Prensky 2001a and 2001b).

---

14 Actually, only 25 percent of undergraduates in the United States are "traditional" full-time students who enrolled directly after high school and who depend upon their parents for a substantial portion of their financial support (Evelyn 2002; Yankelovich 2005).

Similarly, even though claims that instruction online really costs less than does standard instruction remain unproven—a number of startups have failed, including non-profits such as the California Virtual University and the American branch of Britain's Open University—we have not yet completed the stage of venture capital investment and its attendant market shakeout. Once this stage is over, edupreneurs assure us that the efficiencies of free markets and the economies of scale will drive down the costs of hardware and software (Arnone 2002; Gladieux and Swail 1999; Institute for Higher Education Policy 1999; Kirp 2004, 205-263; White 1999).

If competition from online learning enterprises erodes the traditional base of non-elite colleges and universities, the latter must share part of the blame. Having marketed a college degree as an investment designed to produce a profitable return, they have helped to destroy the idea of a university as a gathering place where scholars and students engage in a mutual enterprise of learning and research, regardless of the immediate economic benefits. Forget the lofty educational ideals of Newman or the democratic ideals of Dewey. Forget about developing knowledgeable and engaged citizens. The university has begun to resemble an education factory designed to transmit technical skills and produce a trained workforce with maximum efficiency.

Assessing the Consequences

Mindful that their patrons and clientele desire more bang for their educational dollar, yet faced with increased costs, institutions of higher learning have adopted more businesslike practices. Differential markets for higher education are openly acknowledged. The best students clamor to gain admission to the most prestigious—and often most expensive—undergraduate programs. Although some scholarships are available, those with both the skills to qualify and the money to pay have the best chances of gaining admission.

Established institutions of higher learning that offer bachelor, master and doctoral degree programs for most students are harder pressed to make ends meet. Increasingly, they evaluate the quality of courses or programs by the number of students enrolled and retained. Productivity involves achieving higher ratios of students to full-time faculty, often using low paid teaching assistants to break large classes into smaller discussion sections.[15] Threatened by the potential loss of students to less expensive two-year community colleges or to virtual educational

15 The University of Cincinnati's course plan for the 2003 summer session provides a model: "All summer-session courses will be taught on a contingency basis. This will allow much more readily for expansions and reallocations so as to accommodate any course that is able to enroll at a level that is sufficiently profitable for the University to support. There is no longer any 'regular budget' for summer-session courses." The formula for determining the breakeven point includes all costs associated with the course (faculty, staff, and TA salaries and benefits, plus miscellaneous costs).

institutions, they have sometimes ignored or lowered their standards for admission in order to maintain enrollments.[16] Additionally, they have begun to offer distance-learning courses on their own or in partnership with other educational providers (Allen and Seaman 2008; NASULGC 1999; Kirp 2004, 164-206; Olsen 1999; Young 1999).

Private-sector companies see the USA's post-secondary instructional market as more easily penetrable than the larger K-12 market, where government funded competition and regulation make it more difficult for them to turn a profit.[17] In their view, campus-based "bricks-and-mortar" educational institutions with traditional two-year associate and four-year bachelor degree programs are stuck with maintaining expensive physical plants and semi-permanent employees. They cannot match the prices that efficient well-managed online for-profit educational providers can offer the mass education market for accredited courses, certificates, and degrees. The good will and prestige that accrue to graduates of traditional programs at established non-elite institutions justify some premium for their tuition, but accrediting boards and systematic studies have concluded that their for-profit competitors offer course content and instruction that is sufficient to merit accreditation of numerous degree programs. In short, those that provide Internet-based distance education cannot be summarily dismissed as "digital diploma mills" (Noble 1998; Olson 1999; White 1999).

The presumption that for-profit distance education providers can expand their reach from niche markets into mass education that encompasses the core disciplines of the liberal arts and sciences, however, has yet to be proven. For most students, effective K-12 education involves some interpersonal relationships with teachers and fellow students, not merely digitized interaction via networked communication devices. Critics contend that most post secondary students also need to spend some quality time with their instructors and with one another. Can interactive applications, such as "Second Life," foster similar relationships? The dropout rate among distance learning students has been a perennial problem, regardless of the medium of instruction.

Distance educators insist that Internet based courses can offer individualized instruction that matches or exceeds the personal attention that students typically experience on the crowded campuses of non-elite institutions (Katz 1999). This argument is not new: the edupreneurs who ran the for-profit correspondence schools during the "roaring 20s" made the same points. Just as correspondence

16 The controversy over whether or not such admissions have led to increased costs for remedial courses or to a general "dumbing down" of standards are beyond the scope of this chapter. So too are the controversies over the impact of affirmative action on admission standards.

17 Lips (2000) estimated the K-12 public expenditures on operational costs at $350 billion and the post secondary expenditures at $250 billion. We estimated these to have grown to approximately $550 billion and $375 billion by 2008 (Statistical Abstract 2008, Tables 251, 280 and 281).

school instructors found that responding to students via the post required large amounts of time, anyone who has employed the Internet to enhance a campus-based courses or used it to teach distance learning courses has found that preparing such courses and responding to student communications usually demand more time than do traditional classroom-based courses. For profit institutions that offer post-secondary course usually have been:

> ...compelled to reduce their instructional costs to a minimum, thereby undermining their pedagogical promise. The invariable result has been not only a degraded labor force but a degraded product as well. The history of correspondence education provides a cautionary tale in this regard, a lesson of a debacle hardly heeded by those today so frantically engaged in repeating it (Noble 1999).

Over and above labor costs, the distance learning via the Internet requires the same institutional investment in communications hardware and software, and the same access fees to proprietary courseware and databases. Unless Internet education providers are willing to foot the bill, their students must purchase and maintain their own communications access as well as computer hardware and software. In short, the economic viability of post-secondary education in the liberal arts and sciences via the Internet, as opposed to more specific professional or vocational training, remains unproven.

As Noble points out, however, this has not stopped academic administrators from touting the economic advantages substituting Internet-based pedagogy for traditional face-to-face meetings. Traditional institutions have tended to follow two general strategies in order to survive what administrators see as the new competitive environment. The first is to highlight the cultural values that higher education tries to foster among its graduates and to tout them over and above the personal economic benefits of a college degree. Democratic values like equality, diversity, social mobility, scientific progress, moral enlightenment, and enriched quality of life can be realized in affluent post-industrial societies like the United States. The second strategy is to model institutional practices more closely on the operations of profitable private corporations. This involves de-emphasizing non-economic values and adopting hard-nosed businesslike criteria to measure performance.

Non-elite institutions might have chosen the former strategy when faculty played a decisive role in university administration. The strategy will still succeed for specific schools or subject areas, where non-elite institutions can establish programs of excellence designed to attract good students. As an overall strategy, however, it goes against how most colleges and universities have sought public support. With faculty acquiescence universities have been marketed as an economic investment, and as we have noted, surveys indicate that most students have now accepted this view.

Even though lip service is still paid to the idea of a university as a special place for study and thought, and from which will emerge the next generation of political and civic leaders, most educational institutions already have adopted aspects of the second strategy. They have revamped criteria for evaluating research, teaching and community service to reflect their impact on university budgets. They have downsized full-time faculty through attrition and relied increasingly upon low paid part-time instructors and graduate students to teach undergraduate courses. They have begun replacing classroom lectures with interactive sessions on the Internet. They have cut research costs through use of digital libraries and networked computers, reduced support for non-lucrative scholarship, and they have begun to charge a fair price for services they once provided freely, such as computer setup and maintenance or access to special databases. Finally, they have become as much concerned with retaining their undergraduate students as satisfied customers as with challenging them to develop their intellects (AAUP 2003).[18]

To differentiate themselves from online competitors some urban institutions, such as the University of Cincinnati, have invested heavily in value-added features of campus life. Even though UC students are mostly commuters, and about half work 20 or more hours per week to pay for their education, the University has constructed a "MainStreet" where students are supposed to gather to spend significant portions of their day.[19] Such value-added projects, which are designed to maintain or increase undergraduate enrollments, also serve to increase a university's bonded debt.

In order to generate more revenue to pay back debt over the long term, therefore, UC has invested in conference centers on campus and community redevelopment corporations in neighborhoods surrounding campus. These are in addition to established alumni programs, university paraphernalia, varsity athletic enterprises and exclusive contracts for on-campus sales with food, beverage and clothing vendors as well as management of the UC Bookstores. As UC's president is expected to be an effective fundraiser, she or he serves ex officio as a trustee of the University's fund-raising arm, the UC Foundation, and the Foundation in turn has a representative on the University's 14-member Presidential Search Committee. The Committee has used Heidrick & Struggles, a worldwide corporate executive search firm, to find and approach candidates in its 2002-03 and 2009 searches for a new President (UC 2009). Faced with declining appropriations from state legislatures, public colleges and universities throughout the United States have taken similar actions (Breneman 2002).

The aim of reducing instructional costs comports with the economic values held by most students, public officials and conservatively inclined corporate and philanthropic donors. The second strategy, therefore, is easier to adopt than the first.

---

18 "Contingent Appointments," AAUP (2003) has links to reports on this and related items discussed above.

19 Ironically, students were charged special fees for the construction costs of the MainStreet project. See King and Bannon (2000) for national figures on students who work.

It stands a better chance of winning the university plaudits for good management and gaining it capital investment for technological development. Whether it actually reduces costs and maintains the high quality of education students deserve remains to be seen, but nay saying to the advancement of technology is hardly a viable position.

Unless students and faculties can agree upon and promote new alternatives, the next stage in the evolution of higher education for the general public will most likely entail full adoption of the corporate model of education as an investment product. We already have for-profit enterprises like the University of Phoenix, Jones International and DeVry Universities, Kaplan Inc. and Knowledge Universe using information technologies online for degree programs. Course management systems, such as Blackboard or eCollege can facilitate presenting online courses by standardizing procedures for attendance keeping for virtual classroom meetings, information posting and exchange, online testing, grading and so forth.

As characteristics of introductory courses offered by traditional campus-based universities begin to resemble those offered by online institutions, we can expect even greater standardization. Course management systems can provide additional features, such as subgroups with their own work areas, podcasting of lectures and presentations, external links and course use statistics. They can also include ancillary educational services like integrating registration, enrollment and final grade submission online, or business services like providing smart cards for faculty, students and staff to obtain products and services on campus or from nearby private vendors. Further enhancements include partnering with major publishers to provide prepackaged electronic textbooks and supplemental materials that can be uploaded and integrated directly into the management system. Needless to say the course management companies are expanding into broader academic markets, such as kindergarten through high school, as well as to more specialized training centers of governmental agencies, corporations, and professional organizations.[20]

Why spend money for faculties at separate institutions to develop and teach introductory courses that have the same essential content? Wouldn't it be cheaper to develop online courses that not only could be accessed at the students' convenience but also could be taught by the world's best teachers? Non-elite institutions no longer

20 Blackboard's home page <http://www.blackboard.com> provides links ("Solutions") to each of these markets. Its partners' page boasts: "Innovative e-Learning… with superior content. That's why Blackboard partners with academic publishers to provide easy ways to supplement online courses with content-rich materials. Designed for use with the Blackboard Academic Suite technology, Blackboard Course Cartridges® are text- and discipline-specific content solutions developed by leading educational publishers. With over 25 publishers, 40 imprints, 60 disciplines, thousands of titles and countless possibilities, we're making it easy for you to add compelling, interactive instructional material to your online courses." <http://www.blackboard.com/Communities/Partners/Course-Cartridges.aspx>. The University of Cincinnati is among the foremost campus-based institutions that use Blackboard's ancillary services. See <http://www.blackboard.com/sites/innovationstories/uc/> (all pages accessed 31 January 2009).

would need to limit their course instruction to their own (mostly undistinguished) faculty. Eventually, many of their undergraduate programs—perhaps even entire schools or colleges—could be marketed as franchises of greater, more distinguished institutions (Blumenstyk 1999b; Duderstadt 1999). Indeed, these prospects have led an increasing number of American universities to assert ownership and control over the intellectual output of their faculty (Twigg 2000; Booth and Turk 2009).

Some analysts argue that universities can use corporate-like management to balance short-term objectives demanded by the new educational market with established long-term objectives of cultural enrichment (Baldwin and Chronister 2001; Breneman 2002; Braun and Merrien 1999; Katz and Associates 1999; Marginson and Considine 2000). Inexorably, however, the logic of corporate management of the higher education market leads to ending professorial tenure as we know it. Traditional institutions must spend more money just to recruit and retain their most profitable undergraduate customers. Must they also be obliged to carry their workers through lean times as well as fat? Academic freedom needs to be protected, but in the new competitive market of higher education tenure also must be balanced against economic exigency (Baldwin and Chronister 2001; Lively 1998; Margolis 2004; Wilson 1999).[21]

Barring faculty and student agitation in support of strategies and alternatives to preserve the intellectual culture of the traditional campus-based university, the lines between most traditional higher educational institutions and the upstart educational enterprises that rely upon information technology seem likely to disappear. While the particular mix of partnerships, mergers, buyouts, consolidations, spin-offs and the like cannot be specified as yet, established institutions will restructure their delivery of higher education in businesslike manners that maximize efficient use of information technologies for instruction and minimize the need for personal instruction by highly paid professors. Basic courses available in most disciplines, like the basic fare available from fast food franchises, will be offered in a limited number of standardized forms, and factors like ease of access and convenience of information delivery will be stressed. Institutions will strive to become the students' portal to higher education, the only connection they will ever need, at least for their undergraduate training. A good local or branch campus will stress advantages like the availability of personal consultation, meeting rooms, laboratory facilities, entertainment centers, low priced health clubs, and similar services and facilities,

21 The AAUP 1940 Statement of Principles cites demonstration of economic exigency as an acceptable reason for eliminating tenured positions at particular educational institutions. It does not contemplate eliminating tenure altogether (AAUP 1940). Colleges and universities in the USA have found new ways to create non-tenure stream ranks for appointments that nonetheless teach full time. The University of Cincinnati, for instance has created "qualified" academic titles of "clinical," "research" and "field service" for instructors, assistant, associate and (full) professors who can work full time, but "shall not be eligible for tenure." *Rule* 15-15-02- <http://www.uc.edu/trustees/rules/RuleDetail.asp?ID=212>.

not unlike stressing the advantages offered by a good local or branch bank. Non-traditional students will find that the restructured institutions also offer plenty of programs that employ information technologies suited to part-time study. All of this will be advertised at suitably competitive prices.

Outstanding professors and researchers will still be found in the best undergraduate colleges and universities and in the best graduate programs. Gifted students will still be able to attend select undergraduate institutions on scholarship or for a higher price, but most students will be spared the challenges of a rigorous education. The public will also be spared the burden of supporting a tenured professorate. That intellectual class will no longer be allowed to draw pay to support its inclination to study and to think. Costly travel to attend professional meetings will be reduced by holding such meetings online. Graduate and professional studies, which offer increased economic benefits to those who earn advanced degrees, will be supported by tuition and by grants or contracts for research. The campus of the future will be hailed as a triumph of the free market. Students, politicians, donors, and taxpayers will approve. What could be more democratic?

Actually, the loss will be considerable, but only from a classical democratic perspective. Characterizing students as customers or as investors in educational programs that yield degrees leaves out traditional concerns about democratic citizenship. In particular, it ignores the idea of the best and brightest acquiring civic virtue through political participation (Putnam 2000). If higher education's central mission is to provide citizens with the skills to thrive in the market economy, then why should the emerging generation of leaders bother to examine social policy?

The Internet was developed primarily with taxpayers' money, not through private investment. Once it grew popular and appeared potentially profitable, it was auctioned off to commercial telecommunications companies. These companies promptly commercialized the Internet, and unhampered by governmental regulation, they extended its capacity to transfer data far beyond what their customers required. Their Internet operations showed enormous profit for a while, but as we have lately discovered, this profit may have been illusionary, perhaps even fraudulent. As we have noted, the current market incentives are to develop new ways to increase what users pay for accessing and transmitting information over the Internet.

To realize the Internet's potential to democratize education will require treating full access to the Internet as a public good available to all. This means assuring that educational institutions not only can connect to the Internet but that they also have the wherewithal to pay for the proprietary data and services necessary for their students to take full advantage of that access. How resources will be allocated for education is a political question, one that will involve a struggle among parties, interest groups, and governmental agencies. The outcome will influence whether or not students will receive a high quality education in their public schools and universities in the 21st century.

Even though "education" has an exalted place in the election campaign rhetoric and the list of policy priorities of modern democratic nations, we must remember that however critical an educated population is supposed to be for a nation's social, economic and political success, it remains only one of many policy concerns that people consider important. In the next chapter we examine how established political actors make use of the Internet to help them achieve their particular goals. We also examine the extent to which new political actors, parties and interests have been able to use the Internet and related ICTs to insert new values and policy preferences into the political process.

Appendix

Table A.1 Results from 2001 and 2006 UCLA Higher Education Institute Freshman Surveys

Reason noted as very important in deciding to go to college	**All (%) 2001 2006**	**Men (%) 2001 2006**	**Women (%) 2001 2006**
To get training for a specific career	71.8 69.2	68.5 64.8	74.4 72.7
Get a better job	71.6 70.4	72.0 70.4	71.2 70.4
Make more money	70.0 69.0	74.4 71.9	66.5 66.6
Gain a general education and appreciation of ideas	64.5 64.3	58.0 51.5	68.9 69.9
Prepare for graduate or professional school	56.9 57.7	50.2 51.0	62.4 63.1
Make me a more cultured person	40.5 (NA)	34.6 (NA)	45.3 (NA)
Improve reading and study skills	41.1 (NA)	37.7 (NA)	43.9 (NA)
Objectives considered essential or very important	**All (%)**	**Men (%)**	**Women (%)**
Being very well-off financially	73.4 73.4	76.1 (NA)	71.1 (NA)
Raising a family	73.1 75.5	72.7 (NA)	73.4 (NA)
Becoming an authority in my field	59.7 58.2	61.6 (NA)	58.1 (NA)
Helping others who are in difficulty	61.7 66.7	52.8 (NA)	68.8 (NA)
Obtaining recognition from my colleagues	51.2 53/8	51.7 (NA)	50.8 (NA)
Developing a meaningful philosophy of life	42.4 (NA)	43.1 (NA)	41.8 (NA)

Source: <http://chronicle.com/stats/freshmen.htm>.

Chapter 7
Parties, Interest Groups and the Internet's Impact on Democratic Participation

Plus ça Change?

Classical democrats believed the Internet would empower political parties, activists and interest groups of every stripe—especially those the established mass media and political institutions generally ignored, played down, or denigrated—to inject their ideas into the public square. The Internet gave every citizen the means to communicate directly with virtually anyone who had access to the Internet. Citizens who wished to spread their opinions or concerns about civic affairs no longer would need to persuade (or to pay) the established mass media to make their ideas available to a wide audience. For a modest investment in a website, they could publish their ideas online, and they could use the Net's communication capabilities to form new interest groups and political parties. The expected proliferation of political uses of the Net would enhance the quality of democratic participation. In Chapter 2 we argued that the preliminary evidence indicates that the Internet has produced changes in the ways that citizens inform themselves about political and civic affairs, but it has not produced the surge of participatory politics nor the redistribution of political power that classical democrats anticipated.

In this chapter we assess the impact of changes that have taken place and speculate on the likelihood that present trends will continue. It is of course far too early to make definitive judgments. After all, popular usage of the Internet stems only from the introduction of graphic browsers for the World Wide Web, in the mid-1990s, and most citizens who made regular use of digitized media from early childhood—digital natives, so to speak—are still under 30 years of age. Most of them will take another decade or so to ascend to positions of social, political and economic leadership. Nevertheless, we can review current trends, and we can use previous experience with modern communications technologies to suggest why certain developments seem more likely than others to continue.

In the next section we discuss the weakening of traditional political party organizations in the USA and elsewhere during the 1970s and 1980s followed by their subsequent transformation and rejuvenation. We will suggest that the changes were less severe than commonly perceived, and that by and large the major interest groups that supported the parties hardly changed. In the USA, for instance, no serious third party challenges have arisen to the near monopoly of governmental power the Democratic and Republican parties enjoy. At best, a plural elite form of democratic politics has produced incremental adjustments necessary to maintain the established power structure. Indeed, the evidence indicates that since the 1970s dominant business interests, allied with public officials of both major parties and bolstered by the (mostly) friendly mass media they own, have tilted public policies disproportionately toward the preferences and to the benefit of higher income groups. Moreover, the globalized economy has helped spread to other nations not only American models of capitalism but also expensive styles of media-driven candidate-centered electoral campaigns.

In the final section we argue that the established political interests have largely tamed the Internet. Innovative political uses of the Net that challenge the established political order have made an impact, but their impact pales in comparison to the marketing goods and services (including social networks) online. In short, politics that affect the Net generally reinforce the influence of dominant social, political and economic interests. These interests have become quite adept at marketing their political preferences and their preferred candidates in much the same way they market services and commodities online. Far from empowering political parties and interest groups the established mass media and political institutions have generally ignored, increased access to and usage of the Internet has generally been accompanied by a shift of economic resources and power from the poorest classes to the richest both within and between nations.

Political Parties and Mass Democracies

One of the more egalitarian theories of elite democracy postulates competition among viable political parties as a necessary condition. Mindful that most citizens have neither the time nor the interest to acquire sufficient knowledge to make informed decisions regarding complex questions of public policy, numerous elite democratic theorists and practitioners have argued that instead of seeking citizens' opinions on specific issues, responsible party leaders should offer voters broadly defined platforms and principles. Through periodic elections voters can choose rationally among these competing slates of candidates knowing that, once elected, the parties' nominees will support specific programs and policies that refine and implement their parties' stated principles.

This model has two great attractions. First, it provides a degree of democratic control without making unreasonable demands upon most voters' knowledge of public policy. Second, it recognizes that in contrast to membership in most organizations or interest groups—excepting religious or ethnic/tribal affiliation in some stable democratic nations—party "membership" commonly involves little more than a self-declared identification with a political party. Whereas about half of the adult populations of the UK and USA have no formal association memberships, the great majority nonetheless identify with a political party (Brooks 2006; Zukin 2006). The idea of political parties providing the means for implementing elite models of democracy of course has a long pedigree that goes back at least to Edmund Burke and the 18th century Rockingham Whigs.[1] As we discussed in Chapter 1, 20th century theorists like Anthony Downs (1957), E.E. Schattschneider (1942), and Joseph Schumpeter (1962) went so far as to assert that the essence of modern "democracy" is a competitive electoral system in which leaders and organizations offer voters choices among candidates who support generally described principles and policies. If elected, they gain the power to develop, refine and implement public policy alternatives in accordance with party principles until the voters choose to retain or dismiss them at the next scheduled election (see also R.T. McKenzie 1966). Moreover, unlike interest groups the parties govern in their own name.

Ideally, political party platforms and programs aggregate and address the concerns of the individuals and groups that support them. Such aggregation involves negotiation among these supporters in order to resolve policy differences, a process influenced by the institutional arrangements used for determining the electoral outcomes. Countries like the USA and UK, for instance, use single member districts in which the candidate with the plurality of votes ("first past the post") wins. As a result, the parties usually seek to attract broad-based groups of voters, and this in turn encourages supporters to work together to develop coherent platforms before the election. In countries like France, Germany and Israel, which use institutional forms that assure more proportional representation, party bases tend to be narrower, single party electoral majorities are more difficult to obtain, and negotiations to resolve policy differences often must take place after the ballots have been cast.[2] In any case, successful aggregation of interests contributes to citizens' confidence in the fairness and legitimacy of the political system.

Because party and interest group leaders and activists generally are better informed about public affairs and more knowledgeable and supportive of the political system than ordinary citizens, they and their organizations can act as stabilizing forces that preserve and protect democratic processes. Based upon their separate reviews of studies of mass behavior in Western industrial nations, William Kornhauser and Seymour Martin Lipset both concluded that too much direct political participation by ordinary citizens frequently led to breakdowns of liberal-democratic processes and to the institution of totalitarian regimes. In the *Politics of Mass Society* (1959) Kornhauser laid great emphasis on the role of parties and interest groups acting as buffers between the ruling elites and the masses. In stable democratic systems elites are likely to receive public demands

1 See AbsoluteAstronomy.com and Margolis (1979, 44-46 and 95) for elaboration and citations.

2 The French National Assembly uses single member districts two rounds of voting: the first requires a majority for outright election; the second a plurality. Parties may withdraw candidates between rounds and throw their support to a compatible party (or parties) with whom they hope to form a majority coalition after the second round. See "Elections in France," *Wikipedia*; "Electoral Systems in Germany" German Culture 2009; "Elections in Israel," Israel Ministry 2009.

relayed through parties and interest groups in an organized manner rather than from individual citizens or—worse yet—from mobs of citizens directly. At the same time by providing independent sources of information parties and interest groups protect individual citizens against manipulation by unscrupulous elites. In *Political Man* (1959) Lipset too emphasized the stabilizing influences of voluntary associations in democratic states. He concluded that higher national levels of economic development and higher socio-economic status of citizens encouraged greater numbers of voluntary associations; and contact with such associations encouraged tolerance by exposing citizens to diverse sources of information and to competing points of view.

By the early 1960s party and interest group based models of democratic elitism became quite popular among social and political theorists in the USA and UK because they comported with the findings of the new wave of scientifically generated studies of political behavior.[3] These studies demonstrated that most citizens had neither the knowledge nor the interest to fulfill the civic responsibilities expected of them in many classical models of democracy. Instead of placing unreasonable burdens upon the citizenry, a realistic theory would strive for a balance: a few highly motivated leading citizens and a few with little or no interest. The great majority should form an Aristotelian middle class, a moderate center that supported the processes and institutions of the polity, but whose members became directly involved only when particular political issues piqued their interest.[4]

As we have discussed, classical democrats contend that elitist models depict impoverished democratic processes that downplay the knowledge and skills for governance ordinary citizens can acquire through political participation. Classical democratic models have viewed successive ICTs from the penny press through radio, television and the Internet as potential means for mass publics to participate directly in politics rationally and responsibly. Regardless of their differences, however, both classical and elite theories have generally postulated robust political parties and diverse voluntary associations as necessary for modern democracies to sustain what Gabriel Almond and Sidney Verba dubbed an "allegiant-participant" civic culture (1965, 30).

Classical and elite theorists may agree that political parties, voluntary associations, and proper socialization of civic leaders play necessary roles in sustaining modern democracies, but that does not mean that they share the same criteria for evaluating the adequacy of actual party and group dynamics or of the socialization mechanisms in place at any given time. The rising popularity of party and group based elite theories of democracy among political scientists during the early to mid-1960s was superseded by chaotic developments that called into question the empirical adequacies of the theories. If every interest really had a fair

3 Variations of these models emphasized educational systems that socialized political, civic and interest group leaders to resolve conflict through bargaining and compromise.

4 For elaborations, citations and critiques of these scientifically-based elitist theories, see Margolis 1979, 95; Margolis 1983; Miller 1983; and Chapter 1 of this volume.

chance to make its case, then why did certain racial and ethnic minorities, women, and the poor have so much difficulty achieving a semblance of equality in such diverse areas as housing, health care, education and employment? If the political system was sensitive to each group's needs, then what led ghettoized blacks to riot? If organized political activity was the *sine qua non* of elite models of democracy, then why did the Johnson and Nixon administrations treat organized opposition to the Vietnam War as though it were illegitimate? If political socialization bred faith and trust in political institutions and processes, then what accounted for the rise of Countercultural and New Left Movements? And what accounted for the precipitous decline in citizens' trust in these institutions following the 1964 presidential election? Lastly, why did New Left type protests in the United States seem to inspire (or perhaps reflect) similar protest movements in several European democracies, particularly France and Italy?

Even though his empirical measures were inexact, C. Wright Mills had been one of the earliest critics to attack the empirically based elite models on their own terms. By the mid-1960s his loosely measured indicators of a "power elite" gained considerable credibility. There was no denying that the United States Congress, arguably the most powerful elected legislature in the western world, was becoming overshadowed by the executive and its vast bureaucracy, not only in the area of foreign policy, but also in de facto control of the budgetary process. As the military's size and budget grew with American involvement in Vietnam, it became increasingly difficult to deny that the military-industrial complex controlled sufficient resources to have its way in the most important areas of public policy. The executive, the military, and their corporate allies justified elite models of democracy as realistic approximations of classical models of democracy, but the latter:

> are not adequate even as an approximate model of how the American system of power works. The issues that now shape man's fate are neither raised nor decided by the public at large. The idea of a community of publics is not a description of fact, but an assertion of an ideal, an assertion masquerading…as fact (Mills 1957, 300).

Where Mills' critique of the elite democratic theories most directly influenced ideas and actions of the New Left, the upheavals of the late 1960s also raised doubts among mainstream political scientists concerning the adequacy of the party and interest group structure that undergirded democratic elitism. Sidney Verba and Norman Nie (1972) used the scientific methods elitist theorists favored to demonstrate that parties and interest groups in the American political system were disproportionately composed of and responsive to the needs and desires of citizens who were already socially and economically advantaged. Moreover, this skewed representation among interest groups was exacerbated by what appeared to be a precipitous decline in the roles of political party organizations. Prior to World War II local party officials maintained steady contact with their parties' supporters, particularly in urban areas. The postwar expansion of the welfare state, coupled with the increasing application of civil service rules to state and local government, the loss of talented volunteers as great numbers of women entered the workforce, and the rise of television as a campaign medium, were eroding many of the functions that precinct and ward officials performed for citizens in exchange for their loyalty at the polls. Instead of contacting party officials, citizens increasingly turned to elected representatives, executives and bureaucrats to find jobs for the unemployed, support for those in trouble with the law, aid in securing government services, or help in obtaining licenses, contracts, and the like.

A new style of expensive electoral campaigns was emerging, one that used new communication technologies, particularly television and computerized mailing and telephone lists, to allow candidates and elected officials to communicate directly with their constituents (Agranoff 1972; Keefe and Hetherington 2003, 22-24). The net result was a diminution of the influence of local party organizations over nominations and elections, and a corresponding growth of independent campaign organizations devoted largely to electing individual candidates.[5]

Many believed that personal campaign organizations, often run by professional managers and consultants, were rapidly displacing party organizations:

> Candidates—for minor offices and major ones, incumbents and challengers—all have their own organizations....Within these units the key decisions are made on campaign strategies, issues, worker recruitment, voter mobilization, and the raising and spending of campaign funds....[P]rofessionals conduct public opinion surveys, prepare [videos] and advertising; raise money; buy radio and television time; write speeches; provide computer analyses of voting behavior; and develop strategies, issues, and images. Less and less of campaign management is left to chance, hunch, or the party organization (Keefe and Hetherington 2003, 23).

In reaction to the perceived decline of parties a group of American political scientists whose scholarship focused on political parties formed a national Committee for Party Renewal.[6] Besides advocating responsible party organizations that aggregated policies and interests into coherent platforms, the Committee's major aims included restoring the importance of local party organizations for connecting citizens to their governmental officials, mobilizing voters during election campaigns, and conveying information that voters could use to distinguish among the advertised and reported claims candidates and policies that pervaded the mass media. An important means for achieving this was to reform campaign finance laws so that a

5 The growth of these organizations is facilitated by not only by primary elections, which—in contrast to most western democratic nations—remove formal control over nominations from party officials, but also by campaign finance regulations that limit the amounts that political party organizations can contribute directly to any candidate's electoral organization (See Keefe and Hetherington 2003, 105-142).

6 Later called the "Committee on Party Renewal."

greater portion of the funding was funneled through national, state and local party organizations (Epstein 1986, 338-40; White 2001, 44-45).

The Committee's goal of restoring close relationships between local precinct officials and voters was never achieved, but its efforts to strengthen party organizations' finances seconded state and national party officials' pressure on Congress to allow their committees more flexibility to fund individual candidates' congressional and senatorial campaigns. Congress did amend the Federal Election Campaign Act (FECA) to allow state and national party committees to contribute more money to federal candidates' campaigns than could any single individual, interest group or political action committee. It also exempted certain party expenditures from funding limits and permitted national and state committees to exchange funds (within specified limits) in order to coordinate their campaigns.[7] Moreover, the national and state parties eventually succeeded in getting the courts to affirm their First Amendment rights to make unlimited "independent" expenditures in support of any federal candidate. This allowed them to spend as much as they wished to legally elect a candidate, provided that they did not plan, consult or otherwise attempt to coordinate their expenditures with those of the candidate's campaign organization (Keefe and Hetherington 2003, 108-113).[8]

It turned out that fears of the demise of party organizations' electoral influence underestimated their resilience. True, the power of local party organizations that used precinct workers and rallies to contact voters—retail politics, if you will—diminished as candidate-centered campaigns deployed capital-intensive ICTs to reach voters "wholesale." By the late 1970s, however, the national Republican and Democratic parties had learned to use the FECA rules to raise money for centralized campaign operations that took advantage of the new technologies, and by the mid-1980s they were supplying state party organizations with funding, training, and technology that could be deployed in primary and general elections. While the Republican Party generally led the way in adopting the new technologies during the 1980s, both parties strengthened their state party organizations, and even some local party organizations showed signs of transformation and renewal (Kayden 1989; Gibson et al. 1985 and 1989).

When the World Wide Web burst upon the scene in the 1990s, the major parties' national and state organizations had the technological capacity to take advantage of it, but most lagged behind minor parties until 1996. Even as late as 1998, their webmasters said they found the Internet most useful for communicating with party activists and mobilizing or channeling the energies of known party supporters.

7 The cumulative amount of money individuals and political action committees contribute directly to candidate organizations still exceeds total that the state and national committees contribute. See Keefe and Hetherington (2003, 106-25) and Currinder (2009).

8 This of course creates the paradox that a political party can "support" its candidate with actions, appeals, or policy statements that have nothing to with—or may even contradict—those its candidate actually supports. The case is *Colorado Republican Federal Campaign Committee v. Federal Election Commission,* 518 U.S. 604 (1996).

Most did not find it particularly useful for recruiting new supporters, and it took Bill Bradley's successful fund-raising efforts during the early presidential primaries of 2000 for them to realize that the Web had made it economically feasible to solicit and accrue small donations from people who visited their parties' or their candidates' websites (Margolis and Resnick 2000; Gibson et al. 2003; Margolis, Resnick and Levy 2003). Indeed, by 2002 campaign webmasters whose sites emphasized mobilization ranked fund-raising among the top three of 11 proffered goals (Foot and Schneider 2006, Table 7.5).[9]

By fall of 2004 Howard Dean's erstwhile campaign manager pronounced the Internet revolution complete (Trippi 2004). Virtually every major party candidate for state and national office had an interactive website as did most Democratic and Republican party committees from the national and state down to the counties and cities of metropolitan areas. The webmasters had become strategic members of the candidates' and parties' campaign organizations (Foot and Schneider 2006, 187-210; Howard 2006, 143-169). Online fundraising and mobilization was becoming commonplace, and audio and video clips were not unusual. By 2008 these clips—often independently produced—had proliferated among candidate's "friends" (and enemies) on social networks like Facebook, MySpace and YouTube. Meanwhile, parties and candidates in western European nations and other technologically advanced countries were adapting the American online campaign techniques to suit their own institutional circumstances.

Throughout this revolutionary period, however, a remarkable stability remained in the viable choices available to voters. Democratic and Republican Party candidates won nearly every partisan election, and when they chose to make their preferences known in formally non-partisan contests, such as those for Mayor and members of Council in cities like Chicago, Cincinnati and Dallas, their favored candidates usually carried the day. The major interest groups associated with the parties hardly changed, and voters began to profess stronger identification with and loyalty to the major parties than they had during the 1970s. The Internet had facilitated a revolution in campaign strategies and techniques, but to what extent had it brought about the sorts of changes classical democratic theorists had hoped for? The final section of this chapter addresses this question.

Assessing the Changes

Where classical democratic theorists argue that the Internet and related ICTs provide sufficient amounts of easily accessible information for ordinary citizens to make sound judgments about choosing political leaders or parties and determining

---

9 Most websites, however, aimed only to involve visitors by inviting them to use interactive features to learn about candidates, issues and events, to subscribe to email lists, or to provide information about themselves and their willingness to volunteer for a variety of campaign activities. See Foot and Schneider 2006, 69-100.

public policy, elite theorists counsel caution. Although they accept that democratic governance requires that public officials take account of people's preferences, elite theorists recommend that they should almost always be implemented at a deliberate pace that avoids radical courses of action. They point out that notwithstanding those new ICTs, most people still have neither the interest nor the knowledge necessary to make sound prospective judgments about complex questions of modern governance. Better to leave most policy planning and implementation to legitimately elected (and appointed) officials, and to treat election outcomes as though they were retrospective referenda on whether or not to retain incumbent leaders and their policies. As we pointed out in Chapter 1, these elitist views are compatible with Dahl's classical criterion of effective participation as long as citizens have effective means to communicate their policy views and preferences to the general public as well as to political leaders between elections.

It follows that the relative stability of the party structures of technologically advanced nations that we normally label "democratic" since the mid-1990s is not necessarily a reliable indicator of the Net's impact on policy change. In addition to forcing parties and candidates to change electoral strategies and tactics, expanded Internet usage may empower newly formed (or previously ignored, underfunded or unpopular) groups of citizens to force governmental elites to respond to their policy demands. Several types of indicators bear on this question of empowerment.

First, we can look at studies that measure the extent to which the most influential lobbying groups have changed over time. Second, we can examine political websites of prominent candidates, parties and interest groups to determine whether or not they are using the collaborative participatory aspects of "Web 2.0" to replace centrally directed interactions.[10] Third, we can examine the extent to which policy outputs indicate that increased Internet usage is reducing the social, political and economic inequalities of citizens both within and among nations. While none of these areas can give us definitive answers, the preponderant evidence indicates that expanded use of the Internet since the mid-1990s has not as yet produced the changes that classical democratic theorists hoped for.

These days hardly anyone argues that the governance of modern democratic nations resembles that of "banana republics" or "company towns" where public policies primarily served the interests of one or two powerful groups. Nevertheless, governments consistently promulgate policies that tend to favor the concerns of particular interests, such as major business enterprises in capitalistic societies, over those of others (Lindblom 1977). Consider, for instance, democratic governance in the USA, the capitalistic country that operates the world's largest national economy. While economic plans for the recession-cum-depression of 2008-2010 of the Bush (Republican) and Obama (Democratic) administrations differed in emphases, both shared the common thread that taxpayers had to subsidize major business and financial enterprises because they played too critical a role in the

10 The definition of Web 2.0 remains somewhat nebulous. See "Web 2.0," *Wikipedia*.

American economy to be allowed to fail. The close relationship between the US government and business of course runs well back in history. Among the many 20th century examples, the values espoused by Andrew W. Mellon, Secretary of the Treasury under Presidents Harding, Coolidge and Hoover (1921-32), and Charles E. Wilson, Secretary of Defense during President Eisenhower's first term (1953-57) epitomize this relationship.

Mellon was a great businessman, banker, financier and philanthropist who believed in low taxes and small government, but most of all, he believed in a balanced budget. He had run a successful lumber business, taken charge of and expanded his father's banking enterprises, and underwritten the development of numerous companies, including the Aluminum Company of America (ALCOA today), the Carborundum Company (industrial abrasives: Carbo PLC today), and the Koppers Company (Koppers Holdings Inc., today), whose core businesses still operate coke ovens that produce carbon-based chemicals from coal tar. He also financed the Mellon Industrial Research Institute, now part of Carnegie-Mellon University. By the mid-1920s he had become the third richest man in America, behind J.D. Rockefeller and Henry Ford. As the nation's longest serving Treasurer, he pushed what we now call "trickle down" economics:

> His theory was that big business would prosper in proportion to the lightening of its tax load and its profit would be transferred to the rest of the nation. During much of his tenure, general prosperity and times of peace enabled Mellon to implement his measures. The Great Depression, however, …brought him under increasing criticism. Despite the downturn in the economy, Mellon continued his policy of balancing the budget by cutting spending and increasing taxes, which worsened the effect of the Depression on the ordinary citizen (U.S. Treasury 2009).

Wilson was a gifted electrical engineer who earned his reputation at Westinghouse Electric through supervising development of electrical parts for automobiles, and during World War I, through the development of dynamotors for the Army and Navy. In 1919 he became chief engineer and sales manager for Remy Electric, a General Motors subsidiary. From there he rose through GM's ranks to become the company's President in January 1941. The country recognized his subsequent direction of GM's huge World War II effort by awarding him a Presidential Medal of Merit in 1946. He was still GM's President in 1952 when President-elect Eisenhower announced his intention to nominate him for Secretary of Defense.

Despite the Republican Party having obtained majorities in both houses of Congress for the first time since the election of 1928, Wilson's nomination did not proceed smoothly. True, Wilson had successfully steered GM into the boom of the late 1940s and early 1950s, pushing sales to more than 3 million units annually. At the same time, however, GM continued to be one of the nation's largest Defense Department contractors, and its workforce had grown larger than the combined populations of Nevada and Delaware. Wilson owned $2.5 million in GM Stock (about $19.5 million in today's dollars), which he saw no reason to sell.

Senators of both parties (as well as many others) felt such ownership inevitably would create a conflict of interest. In a closed confirmation hearing before the Senate Armed Services Committee, Wilson defended both his investments and his integrity. When Senator Robert Hendrickson (R-NJ) asked him if, as Secretary of Defense, he could make a decision adverse to GM's interests, he replied:

> I cannot conceive of one, because for years I thought what was good for our country was good for General Motors and vice versa. The difference did not exist. Our company is too big. It goes with the welfare of the country (Hyde 2008).

The answer—honestly intended to put the matter to rest—was a political blunder. Because the hearings were closed, reporters ended up boiling down second-hand misquotes from Senators and their staff members into what became Wilson's most memorable dictum: "What's good for General Motors is good for the country!" In the end Wilson agreed to sell his stock, and the Senate confirmed his appointment 77-6, but the statement plagued him throughout his tenure.[11]

The values that Mellon and Wilson took for granted—a certainty that their big business interests meshed with those of the country and that ordinary citizens always benefited from policies that favored those interests—became gospel in the first decade of the 21st century. When Dick Cheney, George W. Bush's two-term Vice President, had served as Secretary of Defense under his father's (George H. W. Bush) administration, he had developed relationships with defense contractor, Brown and Root, a subsidiary of Halliburton.[12] After leaving office, Cheney joined the American Enterprise Institute, a conservative think tank based in DC, and he simultaneously served a second term as Director of the Council on Foreign Relations.[13] In 1995 he became—lo and behold—Chief Executive Officer of Halliburton where he remained until July 2000, when Bush asked him to join his ticket as the Vice Presidential candidate. During Cheney's tenure as CEO, Brown and Root's defense contracts, government subsidized loans, and credit guarantees soared, as did its parent company's direct business with the Defense Department (Bryce 2000).

Cheney left Halliburton with a retirement package that included deferred salary, stock and stock options worth over $33 million. He saw no reason to consider his separation from the company incomplete. Unlike Wilson he chose

11 The misquotation's notoriety inspired Al Capp to create the ruthless business tycoon, General Bullmoose, as a recurring character in his highly popular "Li'l Abner" comic strip. Bullmoose's mantra: "What's good for General Bullmoose is good for the USA!" did much to preserve Wilson's gaffe for posterity.

12 Brown and Root was one of a consortium of four companies that had provided most of the infrastructure for the U.S. bases and logistics for the Vietnam War during President Lyndon B. Johnson's administration.

13 His first was during his last term in Congress from 1987-89.

not to divest himself of the stock; he placed it in a so-called blind trust instead. When investigations by Senator Frank Lautenberg (D-NJ) and others showed that the Iraq War had greatly enriched his stock's worth, he promised he would donate the profits to charity and forsake the tax deduction. Tax laws that apply to the very rich are quite complicated, however, and it is questionable whether or not Mr. and Mrs. Cheney's use of special 2005 tax provisions to give more than 50 percent of their annual gross income to charity actually fulfilled that promise (See Hoffman 2006 and Nichols 2003).

It is easy to find objections to this type of behavior online from journalists, bloggers, public officials and concerned citizens, but it's hard to connect these objections to actions in the real world. The general public's lack of action suggests that they have low expectations regarding most politicians' ethics and that they believe their chances of organizing groups that can successfully change such objectionable behaviors are too low to justify the effort. Better to work hard to promote the immediate interests of one's family and friends.

Far from being atypical, the cases we have discussed above simply illustrate a general pattern that social scientists and investigative journalists have found. Most interest groups disproportionately represent those citizens whose preferences public policies already tend to favor. These groups' leaders and political liaisons not only succeed in establishing and maintaining friendly relations with relevant public officeholders, party officials, and candidates, but also in developing procedures with their political allies to handle anticipated political problems, events or demands (see Strolovich 2007). As we have observed, most members of these favored groups have more wealth, income, and education than the majority of their compatriots. Moreover, they are not inclined to give up their advantages:

> By and large, organized group representation in Washington is about maintaining the status quo. Regardless of the political ideology of an interest group, its method of operation and its avenues of influence in the political system are fairly stable; its goals are to maintain established relationships and sustain the existing balance of power in its policy domain. When those conditions are met, the organization may then seek to broaden its scope of influence. Only in rare instances do events [create] political vacuums in Washington (Shaiko 2005, 1).[14]

Interest groups maintain these relationships by providing policymakers with resources in exchange for desired public policy decisions. Resources may include information, expertise, mobilization of members and allied groups, fundraising, donations and independent expenditures at election times, and present or future employment opportunities for friends, relatives or the policymakers themselves. As election costs and federal budgets have risen over the past quarter century,

14 Shaiko cites "The terrorists acts of September 11, 2001" as creating a political vacuum, i.e., "the absence of a coherent policy domain—one devoted to homeland security (ibid.)."

increasing numbers of well-funded interest groups and multi-client lobbying firms have established offices around K-Street in Washington. The groups and their clients include not only traditional social and economic policy advocates, but also state and local governments; and by most standards they have been highly successful in securing decisions and policies that benefit for their members and clients (Birnbaum 2006; Loomis 2007). The lobbying efforts of state and local governments usually reflect the policies and decisions favored by established interest groups among their electorates. Indeed, reputational and case studies at the state level from 1980 through 2007 indicate a remarkable stability in the hierarchy of power among interest groups within the states (Nownes, Thomas and Hrebenar 2008). This does not mean that researchers find no significant differences when they compare the power structures of the various states, nor that they always find agreement within various types of groups, such as business, professional, or labor, regarding which policies best satisfy their particular concerns. But it does mean that expanded Internet usage—including expanded usage by established groups—has not produced anything like the redistribution of political power that classical democrats have advocated. If anything, the privileged interest groups—particularly large private corporations—have increased their level of success relative to others in obtaining public policies they favor.

Although most business interests usually favor the Republican Party's policies over those of the Democrats, they find it prudent to maintain good relations with public officials from both parties. Other established groups also pursue similar strategies. In any country with a competitive electoral system it is usually cheaper and easier for these groups to earn the gratitude—or at least gain the ear—of political decision-makers by using a portion of their resources to support their electoral campaigns or to provide services or information that can help them to carry out their responsibilities.[15] In the USA and UK, some business groups have ingratiated themselves (or perhaps pervaded the policy process) so successfully that their governments now consider them too important for the nation's economy to be allowed to fail. In a related vein, the third ascent of Silvio Berlusconi to the office of Prime Minister of Italy demonstrates his ability to parlay his huge mass media and financial interests into legitimate political power. Once again, all of these developments have taken place, notwithstanding citizens' easy access to the Internet's technical capabilities to rally those who oppose their government's policies.

---

15 The K Street Project, launched in 1995 by Republican strategist Grover Norquist and House Majority leader Tom DeLay, attempted to pressure lobbying organizations to hire and promote Republicans if they expected to succeed in getting legislation through the Republican dominated Congress. While the project had some success, the complexities of the policy process, coupled with scandals involving Republican lobbyists like Jack Abramoff, and followed by DeLay's retirement from Congress took much of the steam out of the project, even before the 2006 election restored the Democrats to the majority position in both the House and Senate. See Loomis (2007).

While organized groups' under-representation of the interests of the poorer, less educated and otherwise disadvantaged portions of the population is widely recognized, the control that public officials, political parties, candidates and interest groups impose on user interactions on their websites attracts less attention. As we noted in Chapter 3, for the past ten years Lawrence Lessig has worked to explain how the program codes that underlie the Internet limit the abilities of users to structure their online activities. He has also been one of the champions of "open code" rather than the propriety or "closed" code that lies behind most of the Net applications that ordinary citizens use. In championing open code, however, he does not ignore the need for governmental regulation to protect sensitive publicly and privately held data as well as the need for new types of copyright protection. But Lessig wants transparency. He knows that sophisticated users will find ways around regulatory limitations written in open code, but he argues that as citizens, users should know what the closed code does and why government regulators deem shielding it from public scrutiny to be necessary.

> Closed code would make it easier for the government to hide its regulation and thus achieve an illicit regulatory end....[Open code] is no simple defeat of government's ends but instead a trade-off—between publicity and power, between the rules' transparency and people's obedience. It is an important check on government power to say that the only rules it should impose are those that would be obeyed if imposed transparently (Lessig 1999, 224).

Where Lessig makes a general point about closed code, Philip Howard describes how parties and candidates use it to make seemingly open websites integral parts of closely controlled campaigns:

> The code staffers write, the material schemata that take shape as they make hardware and software decisions, give their political organization an important performative power. Especially when it come to Web site design, code reveals and conceals features of the organization to the outside world, enabling candidates or parties to show different aspect of their ideologies to different people (Howard 2006, 168-69).

Political consultants can help their clients use closed code embedded in their websites to constrain political choice by denying access to some content and using hypermedia links to direct the routes by which visitors discover new information. The code's design forms an "exoskeleton that structures the distribution of political content," the purpose of which is to direct how people form their opinions and express their preferences (ibid., 177).

The Internet has affected the style by which most well funded parties and candidates run their campaigns, but it has not changed their desire to control the messages the public receives. Foot and Schneider found that campaign website managers frequently reported tensions between their desire to maintain strategic ambiguity in releasing campaign information to the public and their desire to take advantage of the Web's capacity to provide information in depth. Managers want to direct certain types of information to particular groups of voters just as businesses want to aim advertisements for certain products to particular groups of customers. Because any user can access information on a public website, deciding which information to expose to a particular user is more difficult on the Web than deciding which messages to send to particular groups via email. The solution adopted by the major party presidential campaigns in 2000 and 2004 (and by some congressional campaigns in 2002 and 2004) was to invite the visitors to "personalize the campaign site." They presented user-friendly Web questionnaires to elicit information about visitors' backgrounds and interests, planted cookies on their computers, and used the information to direct the visitors exclusively to preselected website pages whenever they returned (Foot and Schneider 2006, 61-65).

By 2008 many more campaign websites followed similar principles, but they deployed considerably more audio and video messages on their sites. Many of the videos were also linked to channels on YouTube. In addition, the Obama campaign made an early effort to tap into the enthusiasm of many of their candidate's youthful supporters through social networks like Facebook and MySpace.[16] The Obama campaign website also encouraged supporters to set up their own independent sites. A series of short videos featuring enthusiastic campaign workers—disproportionately young women—provided instructions not only about how to set up and register the sites, but also examples of information and messages to post—just in case the supporters had not already come up with material on their own.

In our view the Obama campaign found a way to decentralize and localize the campaign without really relinquishing control over the official campaign themes. The campaign separated itself from the independent efforts of its supporters, yet it remained linked to their websites, positioned to distribute its official messages and to reap the benefits of the successes its local supporters might achieve. At the same time, because it had no direct control over its supporters' independent actions, the official campaign could distance itself from responsibility for any blunders that locally based supporters might commit.

That the Obama campaign received a flood of small donations (under $200) from supporters drew the news media's attention, but the campaign received a flood of large donations as well. Indeed, the Campaign Finance Institute's systematic study of Federal Election Commission data revealed that small donations comprised only 26 percent of Obama's funding, approximately the same proportion of funding that George W. Bush received from small donations (25 percent) in 2004. The key differences were: 1) 49 percent of Obama's donations came in amounts of $200 or less, compared to only 31 percent of Bush's donations; 2) More than half of Obama's 403,000 medium sized donors ($201-$999) were repeaters who started

16 The McCain campaign soon registered their candidate on the social networks, as did rivals of both nominees during the primary election period, but they never gathered as many online "friends" as Obama.

out by giving less than $200; and 3) Obama's use of innovative social networking tools to interweave appeals for contributions with those for campaign volunteers attracted huge numbers of new donors who were not part the traditional reception-attending large donor crowd. The bulk of Obama's campaign money still came from large donors, however, and ironically, much of it was raised by bundling techniques developed by George W. Bush's 2000 and 2004 presidential campaigns (Malbin 2008).

The principles of central direction and control by campaign managers also apply to the websites of major interest groups that involve themselves in public policy issues. Information rendered by visitors who register is used to place them on appropriate mailing lists or to direct them to appropriate pages and external links. Donations or memberships are often solicited. From time to time leaders may poll registrants or members regarding the selection of projects, policies or issues to which the organized group should give high priority, but the leadership of course determines the choices offered for consideration. In effect, Boss (William Marcy) Tweed's dictum still applies: "I don't care who does the electing, so long as I get to do the nominating."[17] Top down communication within parties and interest groups remains the norm.

The extent to which widespread Internet usage is associated with reducing social, political and economic inequalities of citizens within and among nations is the final criterion we use in this chapter to assess the Net's impact on the policymaking process. We already have described the general stability of the interest group and party structures since the 1970s, and we have noted that this status quo tends to preserve policies that confer advantages on a polity's more affluent citizens. The studies we reviewed also indicated that while political uses of the Net have moved political elites to alter the strategies by which funds are raised and electoral campaigns are run, neither the preponderant sources of the funds nor the electoral outcomes reflect the momentous changes that classical democrats desired. Nevertheless, the cumulative effects of incremental changes in the power structure could produce what amounts to a revolution over time.

While indicators are never entirely reliable, several commonly accepted measures of the wealth of nations suggest that despite all the talk of a global economy raising standards of living for all nations, the richest nations of the world remain largely unchanged. At the end of World War II the victorious allies designated five permanent members of the Security Council of the United Nations and gave each veto power over those resolutions that required mandatory compliance from all member nations. The economic power of these five nations—China, France, the Russian Federation, the UK and the USA—remains surprisingly strong. The

17 Tweed was the leader of the Democratic Party Machine of New York City from 1858 until 1871. The organization was known for wastefulness and corrupt leadership, but also for policies that helped immigrants and the poor. It operated through the Tammany Society, also known by the name of its headquarters, "Tammany Hall." (See "William M. Tweed", *Wikipedia*).

CIA World Factbook estimates the purchasing power of their combined GDPs to comprise 41 percent of the World's purchasing power. In fact, each of these nations ranks among the top 10 on this standard. By the same measure, the combined purchasing power of the European Union, Brazil, China, India, Japan, Russia and the USA, represents 70 percent of the World's purchasing power ("Country Comparisons" 2009).

Per capita measures of GDP give a somewhat different picture. City-states, tax havens and oil rich nations of the Middle East join the higher ranks, while the rankings of China and India drop below the median of $8,800. The per capita GDP of virtually every sub-Saharan country except South Africa falls well below that median. The per capita income of course is even less. The variations between total GDP purchasing power and per capita GDP also suggest considerable disparities in the distribution of wealth among the citizens of most nations. The second aspect of our criterion, however, was whether or not the situation within nations is becoming more equitable.

If the USA is at all representative of relatively affluent nations, the simple answer appears to be "no." Since 1947 the US Census Bureau has reported the annual family incomes for of each of four quintiles up to the 80th plus the income of the families at the 95th percentile. For the postwar period (1947-1974) the distributions showed relatively equal shares of income growth for each group with a marginal shift of incomes toward the lowest four. The family incomes of the richest group grew by 89.3 percent. Income growth of the other four varied between 97.5 and 102.9 percent, with those in the middle (40-60th percentiles) gaining the most. After 1974 the picture changed drastically. From 1974 to 2005 the real incomes of the poorest 20 percent increased by 10.3 percent while those at the 95th percentile grew 62.9 percent. The percentage growth for the rest of the groups was distributed monotonically: 18.6, 30.8, and 42.9 percent respectively for the 40th, 60th and 80th percentiles. In short, the rich got richer and the richest group enjoyed six times the income growth of the poorest. Translating the growth into inflation adjusted dollars over this period, annual family incomes at the 95th percentile increased by approximately $67,000 while those at 20th percentile barely increased by $3,000. The net result was that income shares of the top five percent in the years prior to the 2008 economic downturn resembled those of the top five percent during last years prior to the Great Depression (Bartels 2008, 6-13; U.S. Census Bureau 2009, Table 672).

So how did the expansion of Internet usage affect these trends? If anything, the disparities between the family income shares of the top 20 percent and the rest of the populations accelerated between 1995 and 2006. And to the extent that many other capitalistic democracies emulate or are directly affected by the USA's economic policies, increased Internet usage also is unlikely to have played a significant role in restructuring the social and economic order.

While these data and the findings from other studies we have discussed are compatible with numerous explanatory hypotheses, they clearly do not support the hypothesis that increasing citizens' access to the Internet will lead to their using the Net for political and civic purposes that enhance democratic values like fairness and equity. Indeed, the increasing dependence of political parties upon large donations to support media driven election campaigns, the consolidation of economic power into large globally based corporations, the continuing desire of most citizens to use the Internet for commercial rather than civic purposes, and their willingness to consume rather than create information all portend reinforcement of current socio-economic and political power structures.

Chapter 8
Internet Democracy in the 21st Century

The Internet has been heralded as one of the leading change agents, if not the main one, of the 21st century. Given its structure, breadth, depth, and ease of access, the Internet, so we are told, will leave nothing untouched. Internet enthusiasts have argued that the dynamic nature of the net will facilitate not just rapid change but also positive and revolutionary change throughout society.[1] As we have argued in this book, one key area where revolutionary change has been predicted and expected is in politics, more particularly democratic politics. Political scientist Russell J. Dalton captures this "change is in the air" ethos in his recent book *The Good Citizen* (2008) when he writes:

> Politics in the United States and other advanced industrial societies is changing in ways that hold the potential for strengthening and broadening the democratic process.…If we do not become preoccupied with the patterns of democracy in the past, but look toward the potential for our democracy in the future, we can better understand the American public and take advantage of the potential for future progress (Dalton 2008, 19).

While Dalton chides political theorists and scientists who deny the future promise of democracy given its past patterns of failure, e-democrats have exhibited a utopian impulse in their discussions of democracy and the Internet. As Richard J. Bernstein argues, a utopian impulse is characterized by the notion of an emancipatory critique:

> [It is] a refusal to accept the status quo, a condemnation of social injustice, and a defiant creative imagination that dares to project an ideal of a more socially just world…[it] is not about the future: it is directed to the present and to concrete reality. It is the source of energy and motivation for the practical striving to transform existing reality in order to approximate a more ideal, socially just world (Bernstein 2008, 38).

E-democrats cite past and current dysfunctions within democracy to demonstrate that traditional institutional arrangements, while useful, have taken modern

1 Borgmann (2002) notes that the reactions to the "prospects" of various forms of recent technologies (i.e., information technology, biotechnology) are "as divided as they are to carnival rides—they produce exhilaration in some people and vertigo in others" (p. 9). This same observation is apt in discussion of ICTs and democratic politics.

civilization as far as they possibly could. The present political landscape needs a brave new democratic arrangement, and the Internet fits the bill.

As we noted in Chapter 1 and throughout this book, enthusiasts have argued that the Internet will revitalize if not radically transform democracy. The Internet will facilitate the fulfillment of Dahl's requirements for democracy—effective participation, voting equality, enlightened understanding, and control over the political agenda. The Internet will help to realize C. Edwin Baker's democratic prerequisite of the widest possible dispersion of communicative power (Baker 2006). And this realization will satisfy what many democratic theorists consider to be the essential characteristics of "democracy *qua* democracy"—citizen participation and informed, responsible citizens (Colby, Beaumont, Ehrlich and Corngold 2007, 26-29).

While we have acknowledged that the Internet has facilitated changes in national and international politics, we have also argued that an overwhelming amount of evidence indicates that revolutionary changes in democratic political participation have not occurred. Politics on the Net is largely a replication—a mirror image—of politics in the real world. Rather than the Internet transforming politics, the impact of politics has largely shaped and harnessed the Internet to do its bidding. This same conclusion is applicable to the myriad ways in which individuals use the Internet for political activities. In these cases, it is individuals and their ideologies—their *Weltanschauungs*—that harness the power and potential of the Internet and other ICTs to perform their bidding. Thus, rather than the Internet possessing some inherent transformative power that turns all that it touches into gold, the Internet often becomes a conduit for channeling the passions and practices of the actors of politics.

These considerations hark back to questions about the extent to which the design of the Internet can continue to incorporate the philosophical assumptions of the Enlightenment when billions of new users from nations with non-western (and often less democratic) traditions eventually demand that the Internet's rules also reflect their values. For example, just as the Chinese government demands formal recognition of its nation's influence over the global marketplace, so too we can expect its leaders to demand more formal participation in setting the codes by which the Net operates. We raised these questions in the Introduction and they have lurked behind our discussions of privacy, deliberative democracy, democratic education, openness of mass media, and the like, but at this stage answers remain largely speculative. Nevertheless, if we are correct that Politics on the Net reflects politics of the real world far more than vice-versa, we ignore them at our peril.

Understanding the influence of the Internet upon democratic politics requires that we assign to the Internet neither the role of history maker nor the role of a passive technological entity. Robert L. Heilbroner reminds us:

> That machines make history in some sense—that the level of technology has a direct bearing on the human drama—is of course obvious. That they do not make all of history, however that word be defined, is equally clear. The challenge,

> then, is to see if one can say something systematic about the matter, to see whether one can order the problem so that it becomes intellectually manageable (Heilbroner 1994, 54).

It is not very difficult to reject the argument that the Internet is a passive technological entity. The Internet and other ICTs have facilitated numerous developments that simply would not have occurred—or would have taken much longer to occur—without its existence. The rise of blogs, the CNN/YouTube presidential debates, and a host of other technologically dependent developments exist today because of the digital context that the Internet provides. In this sense, we can demonstrate a causal relationship. But is it possible, as Michael Cornfield has recently argued, that the increased level of popular political participation during the 2008 American presidential campaigns as well as the 100 percent increase in the communications citizens initiated with their U.S. Senators or Representatives were caused primarily by "the rise of digital, computerized, portable communication systems, the technology and prevailing social uses of it bound up in the word 'internet'"? (Cornfield 2008, 68). Is it really the case that American politics is experiencing a "civic surge" due to the Internet and that, consequently, this same effect can be expected in other countries where citizens' access to the Internet is widespread?

Robert Dahl's list of criteria for democracy represents an important step toward systematizing and ordering the question of whether or not the Internet and other ICTs can transform democracy and perhaps even herald a utopian e-democracy. Given our assessment of the evidence, however, we cannot conclude that political uses of the Internet have satisfied Dahl's criteria. Political uses of the Internet have affected aspects of democratic politics, such as electioneering and lobbying techniques, but they have hardly enhanced or furthered democracy. Even though the potential for more effective participation, greater voting equality, more enlightened understanding, and more substantive control over the political agenda certainly exists, patterns of political activity associated with the Net generally reflect the predominant patterns of offline political activity. Does the Internet provide all members of a democratic voting polity a chance—a substantially equal chance—to make their views known about a proposed policy before it is adopted? Absolutely not. At this point in time, no democratic polity has offered a list of policy proposals on the Net and invited all of its voting age citizens to make their views known before the policies are adopted. In the USA, the most recent example is President Barack Obama's $787 billion economic stimulus plan, a plan that affects every American citizen and yet a plan for which no input was invited from the voting public. This observation is related as well to Dahl's argument that true democratic processes include citizens having control over the political agenda.

Just as the Net has not been used to foster effective participation in contemporary democracies, neither has it been utilized to nurture a political culture in which citizens create and develop the political agenda. As Sniderman and Bullock (2004) remind us, democracies are too often "menu dependent," with bills of fare that originate with bureaucrats, parties, or established interest groups not with ordinary citizens. While attempts in the USA to use the Net to increase public input in the process of rulemaking have resulted, at times, in more than 250,000 online responses, those who respond tend to be activists mobilized by parties or interest groups from their proprietary email lists. Most proposed rules pass through the *Federal Register* quickly and quietly with little public comment. It is clear that even these relatively large numbers are minute in comparison to the numbers of citizens whom the proposed regulations might directly affect. The general reluctance of public officials to call attention to their proposed rules and regulations does not intimate a desire for a robust e-democracy (Coglianese 2007).

In the arena of voting, the Net has not fared much better. E-voting, the means of casting and counting ballots using secure public and private computer networks is fraught with security and privacy hazards in the USA and European Union countries like the Netherlands (*International Herald Tribune* October 30, 2006). And even if e-voting could be deployed effectively and securely, does the simple act of voting on a slate of candidates selected by established political parties and their interest group allies, or a political menu crafted by these same elites provide voters with effective participation and control over the political agenda?

Just as pertinent to this discussion is the question of enlightened understanding. Given the propensity of Internet political usage to mirror offline reality, it is difficult to envision robust public squares online where citizens have the opportunities to learn about alternative policies and their outcomes and to discuss and deliberate these policies. Nor are there many places online where candidates or elected officials regularly engage in substantive discussions or debates about important public policies or controversies. The primary use of the Internet and related ICTs in the most recent American presidential nomination campaigns is a case in point. Political parties and campaigns used the new media as one-way vehicles to raise money, to place new items on the political menus, and to mobilize and communicate with supporters (Haynes and Pitts 2009). While these parties and campaigns undoubtedly considered their actions as encouraging "political participation," it is a neutered sort of participation, one that is centrally managed to control and dictate the who, how, when, and where of participation.

Another unfortunate reality is the general tendency of the Net to foster echo chambers. While the Internet possesses a large number of diverse political voices and communicative outlets, most citizens use their freedom of choice to personalize their information menus to seek sources that confirm rather than challenge their political views or biases. This reminds us of the relevance of Cass Sunstein and Markus Prior's arguments that modern democracies need media that present contrasting viewpoints in a rational and engaging manner.[2]

If the political uses of the Internet have not approximated the fulfillment of Dahl's criteria for democracy, what then remains? A more modest appraisal of

2 E.J. Dionne has recently suggested that even though the Net does indeed foster echo chambers, the predominant "free-wheeling open debate" may eventually cancel out the echo chamber and produce a more positive deliberative ethos. See Mathewes (2008).

the Internet's impact upon democratic politics raises three important observations. First, the increased use of the Internet in and for democratic politics may also lead to an increase in the grassroots and political influence of those who use it. The educational uses of the Net provide ordinary citizens with easier access to higher education as well as online educational activities that advance core democratic values. While some online universities exist as diploma mills, many are reputable. Moreover, a large number of traditional and elite bricks and mortar universities have now taken their brands and curricula online.[3] As research has consistently demonstrated, higher levels of education are strongly correlated to higher levels of tolerance and democratic values. Furthermore, increased political participation on the Net, however one measures or understands its immediate impact, can have a positive effect over time upon the health and vitality of a democratic polity. We concede that it is difficult to quantify this effect and that political elites try to direct this participation. But the synergy of thousands of citizens involved in campaigns through researching and acquiring information, making monetary donations, sending and receiving campaign text messages (even "tweets") and emails, reading and contributing to blogs, sharing wikis and viewing and sharing YouTube videos can add to the health index of a democracy, the social capital of a community, and the efficacy of citizens. There are countless examples in Europe, Asia, and North America where the ICTs were used to build coalitions and communities of action and information with tangible results upon the political process. While the number of citizens engaged in these efforts is small in comparison to the number of citizens in each polity, their existence and their success give us reason for optimism.

The second observation gives us cause for concern. While there is a grassroots desire to use the Internet to enhance and transform democracies throughout the world, democratic governments have responded through an interpretation of e-democracy as e-government. As Bekkers (2005) has suggested, it is difficult to define e-government given its lack of theoretical foundations. Various empirical accounts characterize it broadly as information based government focuses heavily on the provision of online services to citizen-consumers (West 2005). This transactional characteristic also includes governmental considerations for a more efficient and automated public sector where "the Internet [is used] as an instrument to improve government structures and processes and to foster the culture and values of public administrations" (OECD Observer 2003). While relatively few accounts of electronic government add the implementation of some forms of democratic processes to encourage more robust political participation (e.g., Thomas and Streib 2003), the overwhelming majority focus on the implementation of a business e-commerce model to government so that e-government is simply public business done online.

3 Among these elite institutions is the University of Southern California which recently unveiled the nation's first solely online master's degree in teaching. See Riley (2009).

Admittedly, e-government is a sophisticated, efficient, and customer sensitive manner in which to provide public services to all citizens. Citizens can now connect online and schedule trash pick up, file and pay taxes and bills, acquire important public information, and suggest to governments improvements and commendations regarding the performance and delivery of public services. In this fashion, e-government has indeed brought government closer to its citizens and thus there is an aura of accountability and transparency in such efforts. But the aura could be merely an illusion. E-government efforts have indeed brought public services closer to citizens, but these same efforts have not brought the public policy and legislative process closer to citizens. There still exists a wide chasm between citizens and the formulation of public policy, a divide that e-government does not—and most likely will not—bridge any time soon. E-government efforts in North America as well as in Europe have reinterpreted democratic government as the efficient provision of public services (customer service) and democratic political participation, namely citizenship, as consumerism. This is a deeply flawed anti-democratic vision. E-government characterizes citizens as consumers of public services with rights to receive courteous and timely treatment and adequate information. Citizens are to become informed and contented e-consumers.[4]

Advocates of e-government consider the Internet as a way to modernize the public sector and democratize the relationship between individual citizens and their government (Bekkers 2005; Esterling, Neblo and Lazer 2005), in much the same manner as the Internet has brought dramatic improvements to e-commerce. Information can be accessed and services can be delivered at the convenience of the citizen. No more having to visit a government office, no more trying to reach a bureaucrat by telephone, no more waiting for forms to arrive in the mail. E-governments will realize modern representative democracy by employing ICT features to implement policies expeditiously and to provide services efficiently. With transparent organization and user-friendly programming, elected officials and bureaucrats can employ ICTs to exchange relevant information with their peers as well as with their citizen clientele individually or in groups. As a bonus these exchanges should increase efficiency by reducing duplication of records and services among governmental agencies and by giving administrators better feedback from citizens regarding the effectiveness of the policies and services they provide.

But this bureaucratic e-democracy model dodges a critical question, namely, to what extent ought democracies to encourage their citizens to employ new ICTs to deliberate and determine which policies and services government *should* provide? Using ICTs to encourage greater deliberation that leads to citizens deciding policies would be the very embodiment of a more robust democratic political engagement.

4 E-consumers also tend to be passive. Their heavy use of technology often makes their communication impersonal. With headsets on and their hands busily texting they pay less attention to one another's behavior in public spaces. They may feel angry, but they're unlikely to riot in the street. See Venkatish (2009).

If citizens of a democracy are supposed to exercise the ultimate authority to choose and to dismiss those who decide the great political issues, shouldn't their role in governance be more than that of customer? Customers, after all, are largely concerned with transactions that satisfy their personal private demands and those of persons or groups they hold dear. They generally do not raise questions about how their private transactions might help or hinder resolving broader problems that affect the quality of life—perhaps even the survival—of the society as a whole. Viewed from this perspective, the advancement of a bureaucratic, e-commerce based model of e-democracy is not an advancement. Rather, it is a frightening step backward.

The growing commercialization of the Internet exemplifies the commodification of everything. It inevitably involves the denigration of public goods because they don't fit into business models. Moreover, critics like Benjamin Barber see the Internet's commercialization as contributing to the manufacture of artificial wants and needs and to the infantilization of the citizenry:

> Digitalization encourages and facilitates both speed and nonlinearity, the latter a kind of artificial rupture in temporality in with our "normal" linear experience of time is deconstructed into nonsequential fragments. Ruptures in temporality may catalyze art and creative innovation…but are corrupting to normal consciousness and to responsible and predictable behavior of the kind traditionally associated with mature adulthood (Barber 2007, 98-99).

Slow is replaced by fast; books and newspapers are replaced by videos; complex is replaced by simple. If a problem can't be solved quickly, it's hardly worth pondering. There are close to 100 million websites online. One might expect not only a fragmentation of audiences but also a great variety of paths those audiences would take to diverse websites of interest. If one runs through Alexa.com's most trafficked websites of OECD nations, however, there is a surprising commonality among the top 25. Familiar names like Google, Yahoo!, YouTube, eBay, MySpace, Facebook, Flickr, Friendster, Wikipedia, Msn.com, blogger.com and YouPorn.com repeatedly appear. There are relatively few news media sites and few if any governmental ones.[5]

Our final observation is related to what Giovanni Sartori called "confused democracy"—the fact that in the contemporary world most claim to approve of democracy though they "no longer know (understand, agree) what it is" (Sartori 1987, 6). Sartori's comments, at the time, were directed at normative and empirical democratic theories for bricks and mortar democratic arrangements. Today, they are applicable to all of the major democratic theories in existence—direct, minimal, representative, aggregative, participatory, deliberative, and all their offshoots. They apply even more to the meanings of e-democracy, online political participation, e-citizens (netizens), e-citizenship, and electronic voting. The offline conceptual ambiguity that exists regarding these terms is mirrored in their online

5 www.Alexa.com (accessed 10 April 2008).

counterparts. Consider, for example, the understanding of e-democracy advanced by the U.K. Hansard Society, an important e-democracy research center. In 2003, The Hansard Society provided a clear definition of e-democracy as the "efforts to broaden political participation by enabling citizens to connect with one another and with their representatives via new information and communication technologies" (Chadwick 2006, 84).[6] More recently, The Hansard Society has suggested that e-democracy is:

> more likely to be many small, independent projects, each engaging a handful of people on focused, topical issues. Technology is matched to the nature of the issue and local forums emerge so that people can think things out and get to know each other offline as well as online…This is long tail democracy in action; hundreds, even thousands, of micro-projects, issued based, choosing the right technology. They're temporal; projects come and go. Growth is viral, dynamic, evolutionary and sites have a natural, short lifecycle—mayfly not tortoise. People have multiple and varied roles in many campaigns or consultations and so it doesn't just become noise, all of this is aggregated and listened to where it counts (Hansard Society 2008).

The Hansard Society has thus conceptualized and defined e-democracy in two very different manners.

Another leading e-democracy organization on the Internet is e-democracy.org. Registered as Minnesota E-Democracy, e-democracy.org advances as its mission the goal of expanding "participation and stronger democracies and communities through the power of information and communication technologies and strategies" ("About," e-democracy.org). As its website states, the year round goal of e-democracy.org is "the use of the Internet to improve citizen participation and real world governance through online discussions and information and knowledge exchange" (ibid). As these definitions demonstrate, democracy on the Internet is a highly fluid and dynamic concept and practice, one that appears to resist efforts to define and manage it. This mirrors offline political reality in numerous ways.

Beyond Giovanni Sartori's dictum of "confused democracy," one simply has to consider the numerous attempts by political scientists to operationalize, measure, and quantify the concepts of democracy, political tolerance, democratic creed, citizenship, civic participation, and political participation. Even in the real world scholars and politicians alike have found it extremely difficult to grasp the essential nature of and relationships among these concepts. How much more difficult, then, to grasp what these concepts mean and how they work in the highly transitory and constantly changing context of the digital world? As the Internet and other ICTs evolve, we expect these concepts and their digital representations also to change

6 As cited in Chadwick (2006) from http://www.hansard-society.org.uk/edemocracy.htm (accessed 3 April 2003).

in ways that make it even more difficult to grasp their meaning and forecast their consequences.

As political scientists who teach and do research we face the danger of falling back on the traditional recommendation of providing our students with more and better education for citizenship. We would love to see a global commons, where citizens deliberate questions of world social and economic policy using relevant information gleaned from the Internet. Our modest hope, however, is that we as educators and researchers will utilize Internet-based ICTs to learn to change ourselves even as we work to educate our students and perhaps the general public at large. Most faculty are what Marc Prensky (and others) have called "digital immigrants" while most of our students are "digital natives." In contrast to Barber, Prensky argues that educators should accept the fast-paced, nonlinear, world of short attention spans that digital natives share. A gaming specialist, he hammers away at building video games from which students (and others) can gain information—perhaps even wisdom—through play. He argues that psychological research provides some support for the proposition that using logical linear lesson plans tends to retard rather than help digital natives to learn (Prensky 2001a; 2001b).

Our suggestions for change are not as radical as Prensky's. We believe that new ICTs must be incorporated into our teaching methods if we are to communicate effectively not only with our students but with increasing portions of the public at large. We place our hopes with new programs that use ICTs to illustrate and enhance the knowledge we intend to impart and the values we intend to encourage. Questions of citizens' roles in achieving just, orderly and democratic societies have been around for a long time because they are difficult to answer, and because events beyond a society's control may require those roles to change.

If Internet democracy is to be defined, let alone to exist, citizens need to appreciate Max Weber's maxim that "politics is a slow boring of hard boards." Solving political problems by rational democratic means takes time, patience, and effort. Instantaneous solutions grabbed from the Internet via ICTs are unlikely to succeed.

Bibliography

"1940 Statement of Principles on Academic Freedom and Tenure with 1970 Interpretive Comments," Washington DC: American Association of University Professors <http://www.aaup.org/statements/Redbook/1940stat.htm>, accessed 6 April 2009.

"1960s," *Wikipedia, The Free Encyclopedia* <http://en.wikipedia.org/w/index.php?title=1960s&oldid=268626251>, accessed 5 May 2008.

"About," *E-Democracy.org* <http://e-democracy.org/about.html>, accessed 15 March 2009.

"About Aryan Nations," *Aryan Nations* <http://www.aryan-nations.org/about.htm>, accessed 6 May 2008.

Abramson, J.B., Arterton, C.F. and Orren G.R. (1988), *The Electronic Commonwealth: The Impact of New Media Technologies on Democratic Politics* (New York: Basic Books).

"Advanced Search: 'Internet Voting'," *ePractice.eu.2009* <http://www.epractice.eu>, accessed 8 February 2009.

Agranoff, R. (comp.) (1972), *The New Style in Election Campaigns* (Boston: Hobrook Press).

Allen, I.E. and Seaman, J. (2008), *Staying the Course: Online Education in the United States, 2008* (Needham: Sloan Consortium).

Almond, G. and Verba, S. (1963), *The Civic Culture; Political Attitudes and Democracy in Five Nations* (Princeton: Princeton University Press).

Almond, G. and Verba, S. (1965), *The Civic Culture. Political Attitudes and Democracy in Five Nations* (Boston: Little, Brown).

Alvarez, M.R. and Hall, T.E. (2004), *Point, Click and Vote: The Future of Internet Voting* (Washington, DC: Brookings Institution Press).

Amichai-Hamburger, Y. (2005), *The Social Net: Understanding Human Behavior in Cyberspace* (Oxford: Oxford University Press).

Anderson, D. and Cornfield, M. (eds) (2003), *The Civic Web: Online Politics and Democratic Values* (Lanham: Rowman & Littlefield).

Anderson, K., "Battling online hate," *BBC News Online* <http://news.bbc.co.uk/2/low/americas/1516271.stm>, accessed 30 August 2001.

"AqsaTube," *Aqsa Tube Online Videos* <http://www.aqsatube.com>, accessed 5 November 2008.

Arneberg, P. et al., "The Provision of E-learning in the European Union," *NKI Distance Education* <nettskolen.nki.no/in_english/megatrends/Book1.pdf>, accessed 7 February 2009.

Arone, M., "International Consortium Readies Ambitious Distance Learning Program," *Chronicle of Higher Education* <http://chronicle.com/free/v48/i42/42a02801.htm>, accessed 28 June 2008.

Arterton, F.C. (1987), *Teledemocracy: Can Technology Protect Democracy?* (Newbury Park: Sage).

"Association pour la taxation des transactions financières pour l'aide aux citoyennes et citoyens," *ATTAC* <http://www.attac.org/spip.php?rubrique4>, accessed 13 November 2008.

Asthana, S. (2006), *Innovative Practices of Youth Participation in Media* (Paris: UNESCO).

Atieh, S. (1998), *How to Get a College Degree Via the Internet: The Complete Guide to Getting Your Undergraduate or Graduate Degree from the Comfort of Your Home* (Rocklin: Prima Publishing).

Austin, R. (2007), "Reconnecting Young People in Northern Ireland," in Loader (ed.), pp. 143-57.

Bachrach, P. (1967), *The Theory of Democratic Elitism: A Critique* (Boston: Little, Brown).

Baldwin, R. and Chronister, J. (2001), *Teaching Without Tenure: Policies and Practices for a New Era* (Baltimore: Johns Hopkins).

Baker, C.E. (2006), *Media Concentration and Democracy: Why Ownership Matters* (New York: Cambridge University Press).

Baker, R. (1999), "The Education of Mike Milken: From Junk-Bond King to Master of the Knowledge Universe," *The Nation*, 3 May, 11-18.

Barber, B. (1984), *Strong Democracy: Participatory Politics for a New Age* (Berkeley: University of California Press).

Barber, B. (2007), *Consumed: How Markets Corrupt Children, Infantilize Adults, and Swallow Citizens Whole* (New York: Norton).

Barber, B.R. (1994), *An Aristocracy of Everyone: The Politics Education and the Future of America* (New York: Oxford University Press).

Barboza, D., "China Surpasses U.S. in Number of Internet Users," *New York Times* <http://www.nytimes.com/2008/07/26/business/worldbusiness/26internet.html?_r=1>, accessed 16 December 2008.

Barker, E. (ed.) (1960), *Social Contract: Essays by Locke, Hume, and Rousseau* (New York: Oxford University Press).

Barlow, A. (2007), *The Rise of the Blogosphere* (Westport: Praeger).

Barlow, J.P., "A Declaration of Independence of Cyberspace," *Electronic Frontier Foundation* <http://homes.eff.org/~barlow/Declaration-Final.html>, accessed 8 February 1996.

Bartels, L. (2008), *Unequal Democracy: The Political Economy of the New Gilded Age* (New York: Russell Sage Foundation and Princeton: Princeton University Press).

Bauman, Z. (2001), *Liquid Life* (Cambridge: Polity Press).

Beckett, S. (1954), *Waiting for Godot: A Tragicomedy in Two Acts* (New York: Grove Press).

Beer, S. (1962), "New Structures of Democracy," in Chambers and Salisbury (eds).

Bekkers, V. (2005), "E-Government and the Emergence of Virtual Organizations in the Public Sector: An Exploration of the Interplay Between ICT and Socio-Organizational Networks," in Bekkers and Homburg (eds), *The Information Ecology of E-Government* (Amsterdam: IOS Press).

Bekkers, V. and Homburg, V. (eds) (2005) *The Information Ecology of E-Government* (Amsterdam: IOS Press).

Benkler, Y. (2006), *The Wealth of Networks* (New Haven: Yale University Press).

Bennett, L.W. (1989), "Marginalizing the Majority: Conditioning Public Opinion to Accept Managerial Democracy," in Margolis and Mauser (eds).

Bennett, L.W. (2001), *News: The Politics of Illusion*, 4th Edition (New York: Longman).

Bennett, L.W. (2009), *News: The Politics of Illusion*, 8th Edition (New York: Longman).

Bentley, A. (1908), *The Process of Government* (Chicago: University of Chicago Press).

Berelson, B., Lazarsfeld, P. and McPhee, W. (1954), *Voting: A Study of Opinion Formation in a Presidential Campaign* (Chicago: University of Chicago Press).

Berger, A., Kirshstein, R. and Rowe, E. (2001), *Institutional Policies and Practices: Findings from the 1999 National Study of Postsecondary Faculty, Institution Survey* (Washington, DC: U.S. Department of Education).

Bergstein, R.J., "Technology: Yahoo! not subject to French ruling on Nazi-related auctions, U.S. judge rules," *The Nando Times, AP Online* <http://www.nandotimes.com/technology/story/166434p-1593321c.html>, accessed 22 February 2003.

Bernstein, R.J. (2008), "Democratic Hope," *The Hedgehog Review* 10:1, 36-59.

Berthon, P. and Williams, C.B. (2007), "Stages of e-democracy: Towards an Open-Source Political Model," *International Journal of Information Technology and Management* 6:2/3/4, 329-342.

"Bhopal Disaster," *Wikipedia, The Free Encyclopedia* <http://en.wikipedia.org/wiki/Bhopal_disaster>, accessed 30 November 2008.

Bimber, B. (1998), "The Internet and Political Transformation: Populism, Community, and Accelerated Pluralism," *Polity* 31:1, 133-60.

Bimber, B. (2003), *Information and American Democracy: Technology in the Evolution of Political Power* (Cambridge: Cambridge University Press).

Birnbaum, J.H., "'Clients' Rewards Keep K Street Lobbyists Thriving," *Washington Post* <www.washingtonpost.com/wp-dyn/content/article/2006/02/13/AR2006021302239.html>, accessed 28 March 2009.

Blair, J. (2001), "The Dreams of Webzines Fizzle Out: Online Magazines Scramble for Readers and Ads," *New York Times*, 9 March.

Blasi, L. and Heinecke, W.F. (2000), "From Rhetoric to Technology: A Transformation From Citizens to Consumers," in Cole (ed.).

Blaustain, H., Goldstein, P. and Lozier, G. (1999), "Assessing the New Competitive Landscape," in Katz and Associates (eds).

Blumenstyk, G., "An Entrepreneur Sees Profits in the Future of his 'Power Campus,'" *Chronicle of Higher Education* <http://chronicle.com/weekly/v45/i06/06a04101.htm>, accessed 2 October 1998.

Blumenstyk, G., "A Company Pays Top Universities to Use Their Names and Their Professors," *Chronicle of Higher Education* <http://chronicle.com/weekly/v45/i41/41a03901.htm>, accessed 18 June 1999.

"Blogs," *Internet Public Library 2008* <http://www.ipl.org/div/blogs>, accessed 22 February 2009.

Bohman, J. (2004), "Expanding Dialogue: The Internet, the Public Sphere and Prospects for Transnational Democracy," *The Editorial Board of the Sociological Review* 52:1, 131-155.

Bohman, J. and Rehg W. (1997), *Deliberative Democracy: Essays on Reason and Politics* (Cambridge: MIT Press).

Bok, D. (1993), *The Cost of Talent: How Executives and Professionals Are Paid and How It Affects America* (New York: Free Press).

Booth, T. and Turk, J.L., "Ownership Rights—The Sale of Online Course Content," *CAUT Bulletin* (Canadian Association of University Teachers) <http://www.cautbulletin.ca/en_article.asp?articleid=1860>, accessed 31 January 2009.

Borgmann, A. (2002), "On the Blessings of Calamity and the Burdens of Good Fortune," *The Hedgehog Review* 4:3, 7-24.

Boyd, A. (2003), "The Web Rewires the Movement," *The Nation*, 4 August, 13-18.

Brainard, J. and Hermes, J.J., "'Colleges' Earmarks Grow, Amid Criticism," *Chronicle of Higher Education* <http://chronicle.com/free/v54/i29/29a00101.htm>, accessed 28 March 2008.

Braun, D. (1999), "New Managerialism and the Governance of Universities in a Comparative Perspective," in Braun and Merrien (eds).

Braun, D. and Merrien, F.X. (eds) (1999), *Towards a New Model of Governance for Universities: A Comparative View* (London: Jessica Kingsley Publishers).

Breneman, D., "For Colleges, This Is Not Just Another Recession," *Chronicle of Higher Education* <http://chronicle.com/weekly/v48/i40/40b00701.htm>, accessed 14 June 2002.

Bromell, N. (2002), "Summa Cum Avaritia: Plucking a profit from the groves of academe," *Harper's Magazine*, February, 71-76.

Brook, J. and Boal I.A. (1995), *Resisting the Virtual Life: The Culture and Politics of Information* (San Francisco: City Lights).

Brooks, A.C. (2006), *Generations and the Future of Association Participation* (Chicago: William E. Smith Institute for Association Research).

Bryce, R., "The Candidate From Brown and Root," *Austin Chronicle: Weekly Wire* <http://weeklywire.com/ww/current/austin_pols_feature2.html> , accessed 28 March 2009.

Buchstein, H. (1997), "Bytes that Bite: The Internet and Deliberative Democracy," *Constellation* 4:2, 248-263.

Budge, I. (1996), *The New Challenge of Direct Democracy* (Cambridge: Polity Press).

"Bush administration payment of columnists," *NationMaster.com* <http://www.nationmaster.com/encyclopedia/Bush-administration-payment-ofcolumnists>, accessed 10 January 2009.

Burns, J.M., Peltason, J.W., Cronin, T.E. and Magleby, D. (1998), *Government by the People*, 17th edition (Upper Saddle River: Prentice-Hall).

Calenda, D. and Mosca, L. (2007), "Youth Online: Researching the Political use of the Internet in the Italian Context," in Loader (ed.), pp. 82-96.

Caplan, B. (2007), *The Myth of the Rational Voter* (Princeton: Princeton University Press).

Carey, K., "Graduation Rate Watch: Making Minority Student Success a Priority," *Washington, DC: Education Sector* <http://www.educationsector.org/usr_doc/Graduation_Rate_Watch.pdf>, accessed 2 May 2008.

Campbell, A. and Converse, P. (1972), *The Human Meaning of Social Change* (New York: Russell Sage).

Carnevale, D., "Turning Traditional Courses into Distance Education," *Chronicle of Higher Education* <http://chronicle.com/free/v46/i48/48a03701.htm>, accessed 4 August 2000.

Castronova, E. (2005), *Synthetic Worlds. The Business and Culture of Online Games* (Chicago: University of Chicago Press).

Cattagni, A. and Westat, E.F. (2001), *Internet Access in U.S. Public School and Classrooms: 1994-2000* (Washington, DC: National Center for Educational Statistics (NCES 2001-071): U.S. Department of Education).

"Center's Digital Terror and Hate 2.0 project," *Simon Wiesenthal Center* <www.wiesenthal.com/ireport>, accessed 13 November 2008.

Chadwick, A. (2003), "Bringing E-Democracy Back In," *Social Science Computer Review* 21:4, 443-455.

Chadwick, A. (2006), *Internet Politics: States, Citizens and New Communication Technologies* (New York: Oxford University Press).

Chambers, W. and Salisbury, R. (1962), *Democracy Today* (New York: Collier Books).

"Charles Watson-Wentworth, 2nd Marquess of Rockingham," *AbsoluteAstronomy.com* <http://www.absoluteastronomy.com/topics/Charles_WatsonWentworth,_2nd_Marquess_of_Rockingham#encyclopedia>, accessed 13 March 2009.

Charlton, E., "May 1968, France's fast-forward revolution," *The Age* <http://www.theage. com.au/news/world/bhistoryb-france-is-still-torn-over-its-revolution-forty-yearson/2008/ 04/28/1209234751594.html>, accessed 5 May 2008.

"China's Net population on the Increase," *Nua Internet Surveys* <http://www.nua.ie/surveys/?f=VS&art_id=905358195&rel+true>, accessed 23 July 2002.

Cigler, A. and Loomis, B. (2007), *Interest Group Politics*, 7th Edition (Washington: CQ Press).

Cleary, R.E., "The No Child Left Behind Act of 2002," *Cosmos 2004* <http://www.cosmos-club.org/web/journals/2004/cleary.html>, accessed 26 January 2009.

Clift, S., "The Future of E-Democracy—The 50 Year Plan," *Publicus.net* <http://www.publicus.net/articles/future.html#E-Citizens>, accessed 14 April 2008. 9

Coglianese, C. (2007), "Weak Democracy, Strong Information: The Role of Information Technology in the Rulemaking Process," in Mayer-Schönberger, and Lazer.

Cohen, J. (1997), "Deliberation and Democratic Legitimacy," in Bohman and Rehg (eds).

Colby, A., Beaumont, E., Ehrlich, T. and Corngold, J. (2007), *Educating for Democracy: Preparing Undergraduates for Responsible Political Engagement* (San Francisco: Jossey-Bass).

Cole, R.A. (ed.) (2000), *Issues in Web Based Pedagogy: A Critical Primer* (Westport: Greenwood Press).

Coleman, S. and Gøtze, J. (2002), *Bowling Together: Online Public Engagement in Policy Deliberation* (London: The Hansard Society).

Committee on Political Parties (1950), "Toward a More Responsible Two-Party System," *American Political Science Review* 44:3, (part 2).

"Community Economic Development Center," *Centre for Sustainable Community Development* <http://www.sfu.ca/cedc/>, accessed 15 August 2003.

"Conference disagrees on solution to hate sites," *Outlaw News* <http://www.out-law.com/page-4640>, accessed 25 November 2008.

Conger, S.B., "If There Is No Significant Difference, Why Should We Care?," *Journal of Educators Online* <http://www.thejeo.com/Basu%20Conger%20Final.pdf>, accessed 27 January 2009.

Connolly, W. (ed.) (1969), *The Bias of Pluralism* (Chicago: Aldine-Atherton).

Converse, P.E. (1972), "Change in the American Electorate," in Campbell and Converse (eds).

"Contingent Appointments and the Academic Profession," AAUP Policy Statement *Washington DC: American Association of University Professors* <http://www.aaup.org/AAUP/pubsres/policydocs/contents/conting-stmt.htm>, accessed 6 April 2009.

Cornfield, M. (2004), *Politics Moves Online: Campaigning and the Internet* (New York: A Century Foundation Report).

Cornfield, M. (2008), "Come and Play: Citizenship and the Internet," *The Hedgehog Review* 10:3, 66-79.

"Country Comparisons: GDP (purchasing power parity); and GDP – per capita," *The World Factbook* <https://www.cia.gov/library/publications/the-world-factbook/docs/rankorderguide.html>, accessed 30 March 2009.

Currinder, M. (2009), "Campaign Finance: Fundraising and Spending in the 2008 Elections," in Nelson (ed.).

Dahl, R.A. (1956), *A Preface to Democratic Theory* (Chicago: University of Chicago Press).

Dahl, R.A. (1970), *After the Revolution? Authority in a Good Society* (New Haven: Yale University Press).

Dahl, R.A. (1989), *Democracy and Its Critics* (New Haven: Yale University Press).

Dahl, R.A. (1998), *On Democracy* (New Haven: Yale University Press).

Dahlberg, L. (2001a), "The Internet and Democratic Discourse: Exploring the Prospects of Online Deliberative Forums Extending the Public Sphere," *Information, Communication and Society* 4:4, 615-633.

Dahlberg, L. (2001b), "Democracy via Cyberspace: Mapping the Rhetorics and Practices of Three Prominent Camps," *New Media and Society* 3:2, 157-177.

Dahlberg, L. and Siapera, E. (eds) (2007), *Radical Democracy and the Internet: Interrogating Theory and Practice* (Basingstoke: Palgrave Macmillan).

Dahlgren, P. (2005), "The Internet, Public Sphere, and Political Communication: Dispersion and Deliberation," *Political Communication* 22:2, 147-162.

Dahlgren, P. (2007), "Civic Identity and Net Activism: The Frame of Radical Democracy," in Dahlberg and Siapera (eds), pp. 55-72.

Dahlgren. P. and Olsson, T. (2007), "Young Activists, Political Horizons and the Internet: Adapting the Net to One's Purposes," in Loader (ed.), pp. 68-81.

Dalton, R.J. (2008), *The Good Citizen: How a Younger Generation is Reshaping American Politics* (Washington, DC: CQ Press).

Davis, C., "Kiss Your Privacy Goodbye: Online Anonymity Post 9/11," *The Internet Law Journal* <http://law.case.edu/student_life/organizations/tilj/content.asp?id=127>, accessed 6 February 2009.

Davis, S. (1996), *American Political Thought: Four Hundred Years of Ideas and Ideologies* (Englewood Cliffs: Prentice Hall).

Deibert, R.J. (2000), "International Plug 'n' Play? Citizen Activism, the Internet, and Global Public Policy," *International Studies Perspective* 1:3, 255-272.

Department of Education (2002), "Rules and Regulations," Part IV, *Federal Register* 67:231, 71709-71771.

Dewey, J. (1916), *Democracy and Education* (New York: Macmillan).

Dewey, J. (1927), *The Public and Its Problems* (New York: Holt and Company).

"Digital 4sight 2001," *Digital 4Sight* <http://www.digital4sight.com/>, accessed 9 September 2000.

"Dilbert," *Dilbert Comic* <http://www.dilbert.com/comics/dilbert/archive/dilbert20030731.html>, accessed 1 August 2003.

Douglas, K.M. (2007), "Psychology, Discrimination and Hate Groups Online," in Joinson, McKenna, Postmes and Reips (eds).

Dowd, M. (2008), "A Penny For My Thoughts?," *New York Times*, 30 November.

Downs, A. (1957), *An Economic Theory of Democracy* (New York: Harper).

Dryzek, J.S. (1990), *Discursive Democracy* (New York: Cambridge University Press).

Duderstadt, J. (1999), "Can Colleges and Universities Survive in the Information Age?," in Katz and Associates (eds).

Dudley, R.L. and Gitelson, A.R. (2002), *American Elections: The Rules Matter* (New York: Longman).

Duncan, G. (ed.) (1983), *Democratic Theory and Practice* (New York: Cambridge University Press).

Dunn, J. (1999), "Democracy and Development," in Shapiro and Hacker-Cordon (eds).

'Dutch government scraps plans to use voting computers in 35 cities including Amsterdam', *International Herald Tribune* <http://www.iht.com/articles/ap/2006/10/30/europe/EU_GEN_Netherlands_Voting_Machines.php>, accessed 15 March 2009.

Duverger, M. (1974), *Modern Democracies: Economic Power Versus Political Power* (Hinsdale: Dryden Press).

Eckholm, E. (2002), "Taboo Surfing: Click Here for China," *New York Times*, 4 August.

Editorial Introduction (2003), "The Commodification of Everything," *The Hedgehog Review* 5:2, 5-6.

Eisenhower, D.D., "Eisenhower's Farewell Address to the Nation," *Kennedy Assassination Homepage* <http://mcadams.posc.mu.edu/ike.htm>, accessed 14 August 2003.

"Electoral System of Germany," *German Culture* <http://www.germanculture.com.ua/library/facts/bl_electoral_system.htm>, accessed 13 March 2009.

"Elections in France," *Wikipedia, The Free Encyclopedia* <http://en.wikipedia.org/wiki/Elections_in_France>, accessed 13 March 2009.

"Elections in Israel – February 2009," *Israel Ministry of Foreign Affairs* <http://www.mfa.gov.il/MFA/History/Modern+History/Historic+Events/Elections_in_Israel_February_2009.htm>, accessed 14 March 2009.

Elkin, S. and Soltan, K.E. (eds) (1999), *Citizen Competence and Democratic Institutions* (University Park: Penn State University Press).

Elster, J. (1998), *Deliberative Democracy* (New York: Cambridge University Press).

Emshwiller, J., "Questionable Enron Deals May Date to Early 1990s; Transactions Raise New Questions About Roles Played by Former CEO and CFO," *Globe and Mail*, 30 September.

"E.F. Schumacher Society," *E.F. Schumacher Society* <http://www.schumachersociety.org>, accessed 19 August 2007.

Epstein, L. (1986), *Political Parties in the American Mold* (Madison: University of Wisconsin Press).

Esterling, K.M, Neblo, M.A. and Lazer, D. (2005), "Home (Page) Style: Determinates of the Quality of the House Members' Web Sites," *International Journal of Electronic Government Research* 1:2, 50-63.

Etzioni, A. (1992), "Teledemocracy," *Atlantic*, October, 36-9.

European Commission (2008), *Preparing Europe's Digital Future: i2010 Mid-Term Review* (Luxembourg: Office for Official Publications of the European Communities).

Evelyn, J., "Nontraditional Students Dominate Undergraduate Enrollments, U.S. Study Finds," *Chronicle of Higher Education* <http://chronicle.com/weekly/v48/i40/40a03401.htm>, accessed 4 June 2002.

Fallows, D., "China's Online Population Explosion What It May Mean for the Internet Globally…and for U.S. Users," *Washington, DC: Pew Internet and American Life Project* <www.pewinternet.org/pdfs/China_Internet_July_2007.pdf>, accessed 10 November 2008.

Farrell, H., Lawrence, E. and Sides, J. (2008), "Self-Segregation or Deliberation? Blog Readership, Participation, and Polarization in American Politics," *Annual Meeting of the Midwest Political Science Association*, 1-29.

Fathi, N. (2002), "Taboo Surfing: Click Here for Iran," *New York Times*, 4 August.

Feldman, A., Halderman, J.A. and Felten, E., "Security Analysis of the Diebold AccuVote-TS Voting Machine," *Princeton University: Center for Information Technology Policy* <http://citp.princeton.edu/voting/>, accessed 6 June 2008.

Fisher, B., Margolis, M. and Resnick, D. (1996a), "Breaking Ground on the Virtual Frontier: Surveying Civic Life on the Internet," *The American Sociologist* 27:1, 11-29.

Fisher, B., Margolis, M. and Resnick, D. (1996b), "Surveying the Internet: Democratic Theory and Civic Life in Cyberspace," *Southeastern Political Review* 24:3, 399-429.

Fishkin, J.S. (1991), *Democracy and Deliberation: New Directions for Democratic Reform* (New Haven: Yale University Press).

Fishkin, J.S. (1992), *Democracy and Deliberation: New Directions for Democratic Reform* (New Haven: Yale University Press).

Fishkin, J.S. and Laslett, P. (eds) (2003), *Debating Deliberative Democracy* (Malden: Blackwell).

Fogg, P., "Colleges Have Cut Proportion of Full-Time Faculty Members, Study Finds," *Chronicle of Higher Education* <http://chronicle.com/weekly/v48/i10/10a01701.htm>, accessed 2 November 2001.

Foot, K. and Schneider, S. (2006), *Web Campaigning* (Cambridge: MIT Press).

Foster, A.L., "Energy Department Seeks to Close Web Site That Searches Journal Abstracts," *Chronicle of Higher Education* <http://chronicle.com/free/2002/08/2002081401t.htm>, accessed 14 August 2002.

"Foundation for Tolerance International," *Foundation for Tolerance International Website* <www.fti.org.kg>, accessed 10 November 2008.

Fountain, J.E. (2001), *Building the Virtual State: Informational Technology and Institutional Change* (Washington, DC: Brookings Institution Press).

Franklin, R., "Hate Directory," *Hate Directory* <www.hatedirectory.com>, accessed 4 November 2008.

"Freedom of Expression and the Internet in China," *Human Rights Watch* <http://www.hrw.org/backgrounder/asia/china-bck-0701.htm>, accessed 9 August 2002.

"Friends of Falun Gong USA," *Friends of Falun Gong* <www.fofg.org>, accessed 4 November 2008.

Galbraith J.K. (1973), *Economics and the Public Purpose* (Boston: Houghton Mifflin Company).

Gamson, W. (1968), *Power and Discontent* (Homewood: Dorsey Press).

Gibson, J., Cotter, C., Bibby, J. and Huckshorn, R. (1985), "Whither Local Parties? A Cross-sectional and Longitudinal Analysis of the Strength of Party Organization," *American Journal of Political Science* 29:1, 139-60.

Gibson, J., Freindreis, J. and Vertz, L. (1989), "Party Dynamics in the 1980s: Changes in County Party Organizational Strength," *American Journal of Political Science* 33:1, 67-90.

Gibson, R., Margolis, M. and Ward, S. (2003), "Election Campaigning on the WWW in the US and UK: A Comparative Analysis," *Party Politics* 9:1, 47-76.

Gibson, R., Nixon, P., Ward, S. (eds) (2003), *Political Parties and the Internet: Net Gain?* (Routledge: London).

Gibson, R.K., Römmele, A. and Ward S.J. (2004), *Electronic Democracy: Mobilisation, Organization and Participation via New ICTs* (London: Routledge).

Gilens, M. (2001), "Political ignorance and collective policy preferences," *The American Political Science Review* 95:2, 379-397.

Gladieux, L.E. and Swail, W.S. (1999), *The Virtual University and Educational Opportunity: Issues of Equity and Access for the Next Generation* (Washington, DC: The College Board).

Godfrey, D.G. (1999), "CBS Reports," in Murray (ed.).

Goldman, S., Booker, A. and McDermott, M. (2008), "Mixing the Digital, Social, and Cultural: Learning, Identity, and Agency in Youth Participation," in Buckingham (ed.).

Goldsmith, J. and Wu, T. (2006), *Who Controls the Internet? Illusions of a Borderless World* (New York: Oxford University Press).

Gore, A. (2001), "Remarks on Global Information Infrastructure' the International Telecommunications Union," in Hester and Ford (eds).

Graber, D. (2006), *Mass Media and American Politics*, 7th edition (Washington, DC: CQ Press).

Graf, J., "The Audience for Political Blogs," *Institute for Politics, Democracy & The Internet, George Washington University, Graduate School of Political Management* <http://www.ipdi.org/UploadedFiles/Audience%20for%20Political%20Blogs.pdf>, accessed 7 May 2008.

Greenstein, F. (1965), *Children and Politics* (New Haven: Yale University Press).

Grimes, A. (2000), "A Matter of Degree," *Wall Street Journal*, 17 July.

Guillen, M.F. and Suarez, S.L. (2005), "Explaining the Global Digital Divide: Economic, Political and Sociological Drivers of Cross-National Internet Use," *Social Forces* 84:2, 681-708.

Gutmann, A. and Thompson, D. (2004), *Why Deliberative Democracy?* (Princeton: Princeton University Press).

Habermas, J. (1962/1989), *The Structural Transformation of the Public Sphere: An Inquiry into a Category of Bourgeois Society* (Cambridge: MIT Press).

Habermas, J. (1997), "Popular Sovereignty as Procedure," in Bohman and Rehg (eds).

Habermas, J. (1998), *Between Facts and Norms: Contributions to a Discourse Theory of Law and Democracy* (Cambridge: MIT Press).

Hadenius, A. (2001), *Institutions and Democratic Citizenship* (Oxford: Oxford University Press).

"Harding Institute for Freedom and Democracy," *Harding Institute for Freedom and Democracy* <http://www.hardinginstitute.org/>, accessed 19 November 2008.

Hafner, K. and Lyon M. (1996), *Where Wizards Stay up Late: The Origins of the Internet* (New York: Simon & Schuster).

Hales, R.S. (2000), "Expectations Exploded," in Cole (ed.).

Hargittai, E., Gallo, J. and Kane, M. (2008), "Cross-Ideological Discussion Among Conservative and Liberal Bloggers," *Public Choice* 134:1, 67-86.

Harknett, R. and Cobane, C. (1997), "Introducing Instructional Technology to International Relations," *PS: Political Science and Politics* 30:3, 496-501.

Hartz, L. (1962), "Democracy: Image and Reality," in Chambers and Salisbury (eds).

"Hate Groups on the Web: Q&A with Dr. Patricia Riley," *Online Journalism Review* <http://www.ojr.org/ojr/workplace/1017968514.php>, accessed 9 September 2000.

"Hate Sites on the Internet," *Media Awareness Network* <http://www.mediaawareness.ca/ english/resources/research_documents/statistics/internet/hate_sites_internet.cfm>, accessed 20 November 2008.

Hauben, M., "Participatory Democracy From the 1960s and SDS into the Future On-line," *Columbia University* <http://www.columbia.edu/~hauben/CS/netdemocracy-60s.txt>, accessed 15 February 2001.

Hauben, M. and Hauben, R. (1997), *Netizens: On the History and Impact of Usenet and the Internet* (Los Alamitos: IEEE Computer Society Press).

Hauben, M., "John G. Kemeny: BASIC and DTSS: Everyone a Programmer," *University of Michigan Computing Club* <http://www.ais.org/~jrh/ kemeny.html>, accessed 11 August 2003.

Haynes, A.A. and Pitts, B. (2009), "Making and Impression: New Media in the 2008 Presidential Nomination Campaigns," *PS: Political Science and Politics* 42:1, 53-58.

Head, B. (1993), "Lindblom on Business Power and Public Policy," in Redner (ed.).

Hedges, C. (2008), "America the Illiterate," *Truth Dig* <http://www.truthdig.com/report/item/20081110_america_the_illiterate/>, accessed 11 November 2008.

Heilbroner, R.L. (1994), "Do Machines Make History?," in Smith and Marx (eds).

Held, D. (1993), *Prospects for Democracy: North, South, East, West* (Palo Alto: Stanford University Press)

Helmond, A., "How Many Blogs Are There? Is Someone Still Counting?," *The Blog Herald* <http://www.blogherald.com/2008/02/11/how-many-blogs-are-there-is-someone-still-counting>, retrieved 15 December 2008.

"Help America Vote Act of 2002," *HAVA Public Law 107-252 107th Congress* <http://www.fec.gov/hava/law_ext.txt>, accessed 10 October 2007.

Herring, E.P. (1940), *The Politics of American Democracy: American Parties in Action* (New York: Norton).

Hester, D.M. and Ford, P.J. (2000), *Computers and Ethics in the Cyberage* (Upper Saddle River: Prentice Hall)

Hess, R. and Torney, J. (1967), *The Development of Political Attitudes in Children* (Chicago: Aldine Publishing Company).

Hill, K.A. and. Hughes, J.E. (1998), *Cyberpolitics: Citizen Activism in the Age of the Internet* (Lanham: Rowman and Littlefield).

Hill, T.D. and Sen, K. (2005), *The Internet in Indonesia's New Democracy* (New York: Routledge).

Hindman, M. (2007), "'Open Source Politics' Reconsidered: Emerging Patterns in Online Political Participation," in Mayer-Schönberger and Lazer.

Hoffman, M.D., "Vice President and Mrs. Cheney Too Generous?," *Planned Giving Design Center* <http://www.pgdc.com/pgdc/news-story/2006/04/20/vice-president-and-mrs-cheney-too-generous>, accessed 27 March 2009.

Horrigan, J., "A Typology of Information and Technology Users," *Washington, DC: Pew Internet and American Life Project* <http://www.pewinternet.org/pdfs/PIP_ICT_ Typology.pdf>, accessed 4 June 2008.

Horton, S. (2008), "Justice After Bush: Prosecuting an Outlaw Administration," *Harper's Magazine*, December, 49-60.

Howard, M. (2001), "E-Government Across the Globe: How Will 'e' Change Government?" *Government Finance Review* 17:4, 6-9.

Howard, P. (2006), *New Media Campaigns and the Managed Citizen* (New York: Cambridge University Press).

Howard, P. and Jones, S. (eds) (2004), *Society Online: the Internet in Context* (Thousand Oaks: Sage Publications, Inc.), pp. 237-54.

Howell, W., West, M. and Peterson, P.E., "The 2008 Education Next-PEPG Survey of Public Opinion," *Education Next* <http://www.hoover.org/publications/ednext/26380034.html>, accessed 23 January 2009.

Huber, R.M. (1992), *How Professors Play the Cat Guarding the Cream : Why We're Paying More and Getting Less in Higher Education* (Fairfax: George Mason University Press).

Hyde, J., "GM's 'Engine Charlie' Wilson learned to live with a misquote," *Detroit Free Press* <http://www.freep.com/article/20080914/BUSINESS01/809140308/>, accessed 27 March 2009.

"Income, Expenditures, Poverty and Wealth," *The 2009 Statistical Abstract: The National Data Book* <http://www.census.gov/compendia/statab/cats/income_expenditures_poverty_wealth.html>, accessed 30 March 2009.

"Independent Media Center," *Indymedia* <www.Indymedia.org>, accessed 4 November 2008.

"Inside Corporate Media – Can it Tell the Truth?," session at National Conference for Media Reform, Memphis, TN, 12 January 2007.

"International Network Against Cyber-Hate," *INACH* <www.inach.net>, accessed 22 February 2009.

"Internet Voting is no 'Magic Ballot'," *NSF News* <http://www.nsf.gov/od/lpa/news/ press/01/pr0118.htm>, accessed 13 March 2001.

"Internet extends long arm of the law," *Associated Press* <http://vigilant.tv/article/1883/ap-internet-extends-long-arm-of-the-law>, accessed 22 July 2002.

"Internet and ICTs for social justice and sustainable development," *Association for Progressive Organization* <www.apc.org>, accessed 4 November 2008.

"Internet and American Life Project," *Washington, DC: Pew Center for The People and The Press* <http://www.pewinternet.org/reports.asp>, accessed 4 June 2008.

"Italy gags 'porno' Virgin Mary sites," *BBC News* <http://news.bbc.co.uk/2/hi/world/ europe/2119780.stm>, accessed 10 July 2002.

Jaeger, P.T. (2003), "The Endless Wire: e-government as global phenomenon," *Government Information Quarterly* 20:4, 323-331.

Jamieson, K.H. and Cappella, J.N. (2008), *Echo Chambers* (New York: Oxford University Press).

Jefferson, T. (1964), *Notes on the State of Virginia* (New York: Harper & Row).

Jesdanan, A, "Yahoo! Bans selling of Nazi artifacts," *The Independent* <http://www.independent.co.uk/news/business/news/yahoo-bans-selling-of-nazi-artifacts-705331.html>, accessed 3 January 2001.

Joinson, A., McKenna, K., Postmes, T. and Reips, U. (2007), *Oxford Handbook of Internet Psychology* (Oxford: Oxford University Press).

Jordan, T. (2007), "Online Direct Action: Hacktivism and Radical Democracy," in Dahlberg and Siapera (eds).

Kahn, R. and Kellner, D. (2007), "Globalization, Technopolitics, and Radical Democracy," in Dahlberg and Siapera (eds).

Kariel, H. (ed.) (1970), *Frontiers of Democratic Theory* (New York: Random House).

Kayden, X. (1989), "Alive and Well and Living in Washington: The American Political Parties," in Margolis and Mauser (eds).

Kaye, B.K. and Johnson, T.J. (2002), "Online and in the Know: uses and gratifications of the web for political information," *Journal of Broadcasting and Electronic Media* 46:1, 54-72.

Katz, R.N. and Associates (eds) (1999), *Dancing with the Devil: Information Technology and the New Competition in Higher Education* (San Francisco: Jossey-Bass).

Keefe, W.J. and Hetherington, M. (2003), *Political Parties and Public Policy in America*, 9th edition (Washington DC: CQ Press).

Kemeny, J. (1972), *Man and the Computer* (New York: Scribner).

Key, V.O. (1961), *Public Opinion and American Democracy* (New York: Knopf).

Keren, M. (2006), *Blogosphere: The New Political Arena* (Lanham: Lexington Books).

Kim, E., "Are Political Blogs a Different Species?: An Examination of Nonelite Political Blogs," *All Academic Incorporated* <http://www.allacademic.com/meta/p173097_index.html>, accessed 7 May 2007.

King, T. and Bannon, E., "At What Cost? The Price That Working Students Pay for a College Education," *Washington DC: The State PIRG's Higher Education Project* <http://www.pirg.org/highered>, accessed 6 April 2009.

Kirp, D.L. (2004), *Shakespeare, Einstein and the Bottom Line: The Marketing of Higher Education* (Boston: Harvard University Press).

Kobayashi, T. and Ikeda, K. (2004), "Does Internet Usage Increase the Amount of Social Participation? A comparison of the social use of the PC and mobile phone," *JSICR Annual Report* 2003, 39-49.

Kobayashi, T. (2006), "The Internet as a Tool for Policy Understanding: Investigating the Influence of Internet Use in Japanese Public Opinion," *Paper presented at the annual meeting of the American Political Science Association*, Philadelphia, PA.

Kobayashi, T., Ikeda, K. and Miyata, K. (2006), "Social Capital Online: Collective Use of the Internet and Reciprocity as Lubricants of Democracy," *Information, Communication and Society* 9:5, 582-611.

Kobayashi, T., "The Effect of Mobile Phone E-mailing on Socialization: The Effects of Homogeneity and Heterogeneity of Personal Networks," *Dept. of Social Psychology University of Tokyo* <http://www-socpsy.l.u-tokyo.ac.jp/kobayashi/pdf/IAMCR_Cairo_kobayashi.pdf>, accessed 5 July 2008.

Kohut, A., "Internet Users are on the Rise; But Public Affairs Interest Isn't," *Columbia Journalism Review* <http://www.cjr.org/year/00/1/kohut.asp>, accessed 4 April 2000.

Kolowich, S., "Recession May Drive More Adult Students to Take Online Classes," *Chronicle of Higher Education* <http://chronicle.com/free/2009/01/9375n.htm>, accessed 22 January 2009.

Kornhauser, W. (1959), *Politics of Mass Society* (Glencoe: Free Press).

Ladd, E.C. Jr. and Lipset, S.M. (1975), *The Divided Academy: Professors and Politics* (New York: McGraw-Hill).

"Landmark ruling against Yahoo! in Nazi auction case," *Guardian Unlimited* <http://www.guardian.co.uk/technology/2000/nov/20/internetnews.freespeech>, accessed 20 November 2000.

Laursen, J.C. and Nederman, C. (1998), *Beyond the Persecuting Society* (Philadelphia: University of Pennsylvania Press).

Lax, S. (2001), "Information, Education and Inequality: Is New Technology the Solution?," in Lax (ed.).

Lax, S. (ed.) (2001), *Access Denied in the Information Age* (Basingstoke: Palgrave Macmillan)

Lazerson, M., Wagener, U. and Moneta, L., "Like the Cities They Resemble, Colleges Must Train and Retain Competent Managers," *Chronicle of Higher Education* <http://chronicle.com/weekly/v46/i47/47a07201.htm>, accessed 28 July 2000.

Leahy, E., "Online Hate Activity Rises, Extremists Using Web 2.0 Technologies," *Smartnewtown* <http://www.smartnewtown.org.nz/index.php?option=com_content&view=article&id=21:news8&catid=3:news&Itemid=5>, accessed 20 November 2008.

"Legislation," *GAP (Government Accountability Project)* <http://www.whistleblower.org /template/index.cfm>, accessed 12 May 2008.

Lenhart, A. and Fox, S., "Bloggers: A portrait of the internet's new storytellers," *Washington, DC: Pew Internet and American Life Project* <http://www.pewinternet.org/PPF/r/186/ report_display.asp>, accessed 19 July 2006.

Leonard, D. (2000), "The Web, the Millennium, and the Digital Evolution of Distance Education," in Cole (ed.).

Lewis, B., Massey, C. and Smith, R. (2001), *The Tower Under Siege: Technology, Power and Education* (Montreal: McGill-Queens University Press).

Lessig, L. (1999), *Code and Other Laws of Cyberspace* (New York: Basic Books).

Lessig, L. (2001), "The Internet Under Siege," *Foreign Policy* <http://lessig.org/blog/ ForeignPolicy.pdf>, accessed 8 October 2007.

Lichtbau, E. (2008), *Bush's Law: The Remaking of American Justice* (New York: Pantheon).

Lindblom, C.E. (1977), *Politics and Markets: The World's Political-Economic Systems* (New York: Basic Books).

Lips, C., "'Edupreneurs': A Survey of For-Profit Education," *Washington DC: Cato Institute Policy Analysis* <http://www.cato.org/pubs/pas/pa-386es.html>, accessed 20 November 2000.

Lipset, S.M. (1959), *Political Man: The Social Bases of Politics* (Garden City: Doubleday).

Lippmann, W. (1922), *Public Opinion* (New York: Macmillan).

Lively, K., "Northwestern U. Professor Loses Breach-of-Contract Lawsuit Over Pay," *Chronicle of Higher Education* <http://chronicle.com/che-data/articles.dir/art-44.dir/issue-47.dir/47a0902.htm>, accessed 6 April 2009.

Livingston, S., Couldry, N. and Markham, T. (2007), "Youthful Steps towards Civic Participation: Does the Internet Help?," in Loader (ed.).

Loader, B. (ed.) (2007), *Young Citizens In The Digital Age: Political Engagement, Young People and New Media* (New York: Routledge)

Loomis, B.A. (2007), "Does K Street Run Through Capitol Hill? Lobbying Congress in the Republican Era," in Cigler and Loomis (eds).

López-Pintor, R. and Gratschew, M. (2002), *Voter Turnout Since 1945: A Global Report* (Stockholm: International Institute for Democracy and Electoral Assistance).

Loundy, D., "Lawyer's Electronic Ads Leave Bad Taste," *Chicago Daily Law Bulletin* <http://www.loundy.com/CDLB/Spam.html>, accessed 9 March 1995.

Lowi, T.J. (1994), "Toward a Responsible Three Party System," in Shea and Green (eds).

Lyman, J., "How Terrorists Use the Internet," *NewsFactor Network* <http://www.newsfactor.com/perl/story/7731.html>, accessed 12 September 2001.

Mackie, G. (2003), *Democracy Defended* (New York: Cambridge University Press).

"Maintaining the Momentum: The Search for UC's Next President," *University of Cincinnati* <http://www.uc.edu/presidentialsearch>, accessed 7 April 2009.

Malbin, M., "REALITY CHECK: Obama Received About the Same Percentage from Small Donors in 2008 as Bush in 2004," *Washington, DC: Campaign Finance Institute* <http://www.cfinst.org/pr/prRelease.aspx?ReleaseID=216>, accessed 27 March 2009.

Mangalindan, M. (2002), "No More Free Lunch," *Wall Street Journal*, 15 April.

Mann, H., "Report No. 12 of the Massachusetts School Board," *U.S Department of State, Basic Readings in U.S. Democracy* <http://usinfo.state.gov/usa/infousa/facts/democrac/16.htm>, accessed 6 April 2009.

Mansbridge, J. (1980), *Beyond Adversary Democracy* (New York: Basic Books).

Mansbridge, J. (2003), "Re-Thinking Representation," *American Political Science Review* 97:4, 515-528.

Marginson, S. and Considine, M. (2000), *The Enterprise University: Power Governance and Reinvention in Australia* (Cambridge: Cambridge University Press).

Margolis, M. (1973), "The New American Government Textbooks," *American Journal of Political Science* 17, 457-63.

Margolis, M. (1979), *Viable Democracy* (New York: Penguin Books).

Margolis, M. (1983), "Democracy: American Style," in Duncan (ed.).

Margolis, M. (2004), "The Withering of the Professoriate: Corporate Universities and the Internet," in Odin and Manicas (eds).

Margolis, M. and Mauser, G. (eds) (1989), *Manipulating Public Opinion: Essays on Public Opinion as a Dependent Variable* (Pacific Grove: Brooks/Cole).

Margolis, M. and Resnick, D., "Third Voice: Vox Populi Vox Dei?," *First Monday* <http://www.firstmonday.dk/issues/issue4_10/margolis/index.html>, accessed 22 February 2003.

Margolis, M., Resnick, D. and Wolfe, J. (1999), "Party Competition on the Internet: Minor Versus Major Parties in the UK and USA," *Harvard International Journal of Press/Politics* 4:4, 24-47.

Margolis, M. and Resnick, D. (2000), *Politics as Usual: The Cyberspace "Revolution"* (Thousand Oaks: Sage Publications, Inc).

Margolis, M., Resnick, D. and Levy, J. (2003), "US Elections and the Internet: Major Parties Dominate, Minor Parties Struggle," in Gibson, Nixon and Ward (eds).

Markoff, J. (2005), *What the Dormouse Said* (New York: Viking Penguin).

Marshall, M., "American Opinion Leaders Rank BBC News As One of the Most Objective and Credible U.S. News Sources," *BBC America* <www.press.bbcamerica.com/press/newsdetail.jsp?news_id=78>, accessed 30 November 2008.

Mathewes, C.T. (2008), "An Interview with E.J. Dionne, Jr.," *The Hedgehog Review* 10:2, 92-101.

"Mayfly Politics – e-Democracy," *The Hansard Society* <http://hansardsociety.org.uk/blogs/edemocracy/archive/2008/03/19/mayfly-politics.aspx>, accessed 7 April 2008.

Mayer-Schönberger, V. and Lazer, D. (2007), *Governance and Information Technology: From Electronic Government to Information Government* (Cambridge: MIT).

McKenzie, R.T. (1966), *British Political Parties: the Distribution of Power within the Conservative and Labour Parties* (New York: Praeger).

McLaughlin, S., "The Use of the Internet for Political Action by Non-State Dissident Actors in the Middle East," *First Monday* <http://firstmonday.org/htbin/cgiwrap/bin/ojs/index.php/fm/article/view/1096/1016>, accessed 4 November 2008.

McMains, A., "Why Clients Withhold Ad Spending Online," *Adweek* <http://www.adweek.com/aw/esearch/article_display.jsp?vnu_content_id=1003641204>, accessed 17 September 2007.

"Media Awareness," *Media Awareness Network* <http://www.mediaawareness.ca/english/resources/research_documents/statistics/internet/hate_sites_internet.cfm>, accessed 20 November 2008.

Mencken, H.L. (1926), *Notes on Democracy* (New York: Knopf).

Meisel, J. (1962), *The Myth of the Ruling Class: The Myth of the Ruling Class; Gaetano Mosca and the "Elite"* (with the first English translation of the final version of *The Theory of the Ruling Class*) (Ann Arbor, MI: University of Michigan Press).

Milbrath, L. (1965), *Political Participation* (Chicago: Rand-McNally).

Mill, D. (2006), *Deliberation, Social Choice, and Absolutist Democracy* (New York: Routledge).

Mill, J.S. (1963), "Inaugural Address at St. Andrews," in *The Six Great Humanistic Essays of John Stuart Mill* (New York: Washington Square Press).

Mill, J.S. (1989), *On Liberty and Other Writings*, ed. by S. Collini (Cambridge: Cambridge University Press).

Mill, J.S. (1991), *Considerations on Representative Government* (Buffalo: Prometheus Books).

Miller, A. (1974), "Political issues and trust in government: 1964-1970," *American Political Science Review* 68:3, 951-972.

Miller, D. (1983), "The Competitive Model of Democracy," in Duncan (ed.).
Miller, D.V. (1993), "Deliberative Democracy and Social Choice," in Held (ed.).
Mills, C.W. (1957), *The Power Elite* (New York: Oxford University Press).
Mintz, M. and Cohen, J. (1971), *America Inc.: Who Owns and Operates the United States?* (New York: Dell Publishing).
Mooney, A. and Evans, B. (2007), *Globalization: The Key Concepts* (London: Taylor & Francis Routledge).
Moreno-Riaño, G. (2002), *Political Tolerance, Culture, and the Individual* (New York: The Edwin Mellen Press).
Morris, D. (1999), *Vote.com: How Big Money Lobbyists and the Media are Losing their Influence, and the Internet is Giving Power to the People* (Los Angeles: Renaissance Books).
Murray, M.D. (1999), *Encyclopedia of Television News* (Phoenix: Oryx).
NASULGC [National Association of State Universities and Land-Grant Colleges] (2007), *Online Learning as a Strategic Asset: A Survey of Presidents and Chancellors* (Washington, DC: NASULGC-Sloan National Commission on Online Learning).
Nederman, C. (2000), *Worlds of Difference: European Discourses of Toleration, c. 1100-c. 1550* (Pennsylvania: Pennsylvania State Press).
Nelson, M. (ed.) (2009), *The Elections of 2008* (Washington: CQ Press).
"Net Neutrality," *Wikipedia, The Free Encyclopedia* <http://en.wikipedia.org/wiki/Network_neutrality>, accessed 13 March 2008.
Newman, J.H. (1996), *The Idea of a University* (New Haven: Yale University Press).
"Newspaper Preservation Act of 1970," *Wikipedia, The Free Encyclopedia* <http://en.wikipedia.org/wiki/Joint_operating_agreement>, accessed 18 October 2008.
Nichols, J., "Dick's Special Interest in $87 Billion," *The Nation: Blogs: The Beat* <http://www.thenation.com/blogs/thebeat/1010>, accessed 27 March 2009.
Noble, D.F., "Digital Diploma Mills: The Automation of Higher Education," *First Monday* <http://www.firstmonday.dk/issues/issue3_1/noble/index.html>, accessed 6 April 2009.
Noble, D.F., "Digital Diploma Mills, Part IV: Rehearsal for the Revolution," *Universal Service Administration Company* <http://communication.ucsd.edu/dl/ddm4.html>, accessed 22 August 2002.
"No Child Left Behind," *U.S. Department of Education* <http://www.ed.gov/nclb/landing.jhtml>, accessed 24 July 2006.
Noelle-Neumann, E. (1984), *The Spiral of Silence: Public Opinion – Our Social Skin* (Chicago: University of Chicago Press).
Noelle-Neumann, E. (1992), "The Contribution of Spiral of Silence Theory to an Understanding of Mass Media," in Rothman (ed.).
Norris, P. (2001), *Digital Divide: Civic Engagement, Information Poverty, and the Internet Worldwide* (New York: Cambridge University Press).

Norris, P. (2004), "The Bridging and Bonding Role of Online Communities," in Howard and Jones (eds).

Northrop A. and Kraemer, K.L., "The Information Age: Which Nations Will Benefit?," *Center for Research on Information Technology and Organizations* <http://repositories.cdlib.org/crito/business/154>, accessed 19 June 2008.

"Northern Lights Internet Solutions," *Northern Lights Internet Solutions* <http://www.lights.ca/freenet/>, accessed 9 September 2008.

Nownes, A., Thomas, C.S. and Hrebenar, R. (2008), "Interest Groups in the States," in Gray, Virginia and Hanson (eds).

Oates, S. (2008), *Introduction to Media and Politics* (London: Sage Publications).

Oberdiek, H. (2001), *Tolerance: Between Forbearance and Acceptance* (Lanham: Rowman and Litttlefield Publishers, Inc).

Odin, J.K. and Manicas, P.T. (eds) (2004), *Globalization and Higher Education* (Honolulu: University of Hawai'i Press).

O'Loughlin, B. (2001), "The Political Implications of Digital Innovations: Trade Offs of Democracy and Liberty in the Developed World," *Information Communication and Society* 4:4, 595-614.

Olsen, F., "'Virtual' Institutions Challenge Accreditors to Devise New Ways of Measuring Quality," *Chronicle of Higher Education* <http://chronicle.com/free/v45/i48/48a02901.htm>, accessed 6 April 2009.

"Online Degrees & Distance Learning Programs," *Petersons* <http://www.petersons.com/ distancelearning/>, accessed 7 February 2009.

"Online Hate and Free Speech," *Media Awareness Network* <http://www.media-awareness.ca/english/issues/online_hate/hate_and_free_speech.cfm>, accessed 20 November 2008.

"Online Teens Say their Schools Don't use the Internet Well," *Washington, DC: Pew Internet & American Life Project* <http://www.pewinternet.org/releases/release.asp?id=48>, accessed 21 August 2002.

"Our Fading Heritage: Americans Fail a Basic Test on Their History and Institutions," *Intercollegiate Studies Institute* <http://www.americancivicliteracy.org/>, accessed 2 December 2008.

"Overview of the Schools and Library [E-Rate] Program," *Universal Service Administration Company* <http://www.universalservice.org/sl/about/overview-program.aspx>, accessed 27 January 2009.

Page, B. and Shapiro, R. (1992), *The Rational Public: Fifty Years of Trends in Americans' Policy Preferences* (Chicago: University of Chicago Press).

Papacharissi, Z. (2002), "The Virtual Public Sphere: The Internet as a Public Sphere," *New Media and Society* 4:2, 5-23.

Parijs, P.V. (1999), "Contestatory Democracy Versus Real Freedom for All," in Shapiro and Hacker-Cordon (eds).

Pasek, J., Kenski, K., Romer, D and Jamieson, K.H. (2006), "America's Youth and Community Engagement: How Use of Mass Media Is Related to Civic

Activity and Political Awareness in 14- to 22-Year-Olds," *Communication Research* 33:3, 115-135.

Pateman, C. (1970), *Participation and Democratic Theory* (London: Cambridge University Press).

Pearlstein, S. (1999), "WTO Talks Said to Send 'Grim Message'," *Washington Post* 8 December.

Peterson, D.J. (2005), *Russia and the Information Revolution* (Santa Monica: RAND Corporation).

Phipps, R. and Merisotis, J. (1999), *What's the Difference? A Review of Contemporary Research on the Effectiveness of Distance Learning in Higher Education* (Washington DC: The Institute for Higher Education Policy).

Pibel, D., "Safeguarding the Vote," *Yes!* <http://www.yesmagazine.com/26courage/pibel.htm>, accessed 12 May 2008.

Poisoning the Web: Hatred Online," *Anti-Defamation League* <http://www.adl.org/poisoning_web/poisoning_toc.html>, accessed 4 November 2008.

"Political Parties," *Yahoo!* <http://dir.yahoo.com/Government/U_S__Government/Politics/ Parties/>, accessed 17 September 2002.

Pool, I.D.S. (1973), *Talking Back: Citizen Feedback and Cable Technology* (Cambridge: MIT Press)

Postman, N. (2006), *Amusing Ourselves to Death: Public Discourse in the Age of Show Business* (New York: Penguin Books).

Prensky, M. (2001a), "Digital Natives, Digital Immigrants," *On the Horizon* 9:5, 1-6.

Prensky, M. (2001b), "Do They *Really* Think Differently?," *On the Horizon* 9:6, 1-7.

Prior, M. (2007), *Post-Broadcast Democracy. How Media Choice Increases Inequality in Political Involvement and Polarizes Elections* (New York: Cambridge University Press).

"Protecting and Advancing Freedom of Expression and Privacy in Information and Communications Technologies," *Global Network Initiative* <www.globalnetworkinitiative.org>, accessed 4 November 2008.

Putnam, R. (2000), *Bowling Alone: The Collapse and Revival of American Community* (New York: Simon & Schuster).

"Question Search: 'News Source National International,'" *Washington, DC: Pew Center for The People and The Press* <http://people-press.org/questions/>, accessed 22 December 2008.

"Race, Religion and Ethnic Origin," *Canadian Human Rights Commission* <http://www.chrc-ccdp.ca/client/site/includes/print.asp?lang=en&print=1&url=%2Fpublications%2F1997_ar%2Fpage4-en.asp>, accessed 17 December 2008.

Ramasastry, A., "Can Europe Block Racist Web Sites from its Borders?," *CNN.com* <http://www.cnn.com/2003/LAW/02/06/findlaw.analysis.ramasastry.cyberlaw/index.htm>, accessed 25 November 2008.

Rawls, J. (1971), *A Theory of Justice* (Cambridge: Harvard University Press).

Ray, B. and Marsh, G.E. "Recruitment by Extremist Groups on the Internet," *First Monday* <http://firstmonday.org/htbin/cgiwrap/bin/ojs/index.php/fm/article/view/834/743>, accessed 10 November 2008.

Rayport, J.F. and Jaworski, B.J. (2002), *Introduction to e-Commerce* (New York: McGraw Hill).

"Recent Litigation Events," *National Access Network, Teachers College, Columbia University* <http://www.schoolfunding.info/litigation/recent_decisions.php3>, accessed 7 April 2009.

Redner, H. (1993), *An Heretical Heir of the Enlightenment: Politics, Policy, and Science in the Work of Charles E. Lindblom* (Boulder: Westview).

Reed, M., "Better Data on Student Borrowing Needed," *The Higher Ed Watch Blog* <http://www.newamerica.net/blog/higher-ed-watch/2008/guest-post-better-data-student-borrowing-needed-7886>, accessed 28 January 2009.

Reed, M. et al., "Student Debt and the Class of 2007," *The Project on Student Debt* <http://projectonstudentdebt.org/pub_home.php>, accessed 29 January 2009.

Reich, C.A. (1971), *The Greening of America* (New York: Bantam Books).

Resnick, D., "The Virtual University and College Life: Some Unintended Consequences for Democratic Citizenship," *First Monday* <http://firstmonday.org/htbin/cgiwrap/bin/ojs/ index.php/fm/article/view/781/690>, accessed 22 February 2003.

Rheingold, H. (1993), *The Virtual Community: Homesteading on the Electronic Frontier* (Reading: Addison-Wesley Publishing Company).

Riley, S., "USC's Online Teaching Master's Called Cybereducation Milestone," *Investor's Business Daily* <http://www.investors.com/editorial/IBDArticles.asp?artsec=17&artnum=1&issue=20090225>, accessed 15 March 2009.

Riker, W. (1982), *Liberalism Against Populism* (New York: Waveland Press).

Robinson, J., Neustadtl, A. and Kestnbaum, M. (2004), "Technology and Tolerance: Public Opinion Differences Among Internet Users and Nonusers," in Howard and Jones (eds).

Rosen, J. (2008), "Censor? Google's Gatekeepers," *New York Times Magazine*, 30 November.

Rousseau, J.J., "Emile, or On Education," *New York: Institute for Learning Technologies, Columbia University* <http://www.ilt.columbia.edu/Projects/emile/emile.html>, accessed 7 April 2009.

Roszak, T. (1969), *The Making of a Counter Culture* (Garden City: Doubleday Anchor).

Rothstein, E., Muschamp, H. and Marty, M.E. (2003), *Visions of Utopia* (New York: Oxford University Press).

Rothman, S. (ed.) (1992), *The Mass Media in Liberal Democratic Societies* (New York: Paragon).

Ruby, R., "Special Report: Public Attitudes," *The State of the News Media, 2008* <http://www.stateofthenewsmedia.org/2008/narrative_special_attitudes.php?cat=1&media=13>, accessed 12 December 2008.

Sandel, M. (2003), "What Money Shouldn't Buy," *The Hedgehog Review* 5:2, 77-97.

Saris, W. and Sniderman, P. (eds) (2004), *Studies in Public Opinion: Attitudes, Nonattitudes, Measurement Error, and Change* (Princeton: Princeton University Press).
Sartori, G. (1987), *The Theory of Democracy Revisited* (Chatham: Chatham House Publishers, Inc.).
SaveTheInternet.com (2008),<http://www.savetheinternet.com/>, accessed 7 July 2009.
Sassenberg, K. and Jonas, K. (2007), "Attitude Change and Social Influence on the Net," in Joinson, McKenna, Postmes and Reips (eds).
Schattschneider, E.E. (1942), *Party Government* (New York: Holt, Rinehart and Winston).
Schattschneider, E.E. (1960), *The Semisovereign People: A Realist's View of Democracy in America* (Hinsdale: Dryden Press).
Schudson, M., "The Limits of Teledemocracy," *The American Prospect* <http://www.prospect.org/cs/articles?article=the_limits_of_teledemocracy>, accessed 9 August 2007.
Schumacher, E. (1975), *Small is Beautiful: Economics as if People Mattered* (New York: Harper and Row).
Schumpeter, J.A. (1962), *Capitalism, Socialism and Democracy*, 3rd edition. (New York and Evanston: Harper & Row).
Sedgwick, P.H. (1999), *The Market Economy and Christian Ethics: New Studies in Christian Ethics* (Cambridge: Cambridge University Press).
Selwyn, N. (2007), "Technology, Schools and Citizenship Education: A Fix Too Far?," in Loader (ed.), pp. 129-142.
Shaiko, R.G. (2005), "Making the connection: Organized Interests, Political Representation, and the Changing Rules of the Game in Washington Politics," in Herrnson, Shaiko and Wilcox (eds).
Shapiro, A.L. (1999), *The Control Revolution: How the Internet is Putting Individuals in Charge and Changing the World We Know* (New York: Public Affairs)
Shapiro, I. and Hacker-Cordon, C. (1999), *Democracy's Edges* (Cambridge: Cambridge University Press).
Shea, C., "Visionary or 'Operator'? Jorge Klor de Alva and His Unusual Intellectual Journey: Controversial Anthropologist Gives up a Chair at Berkeley to Lead the U. of Phoenix," *Chronicle of Higher Education* <http://chronicle.com/che-data/articles.dir/art-44.dir/issue-43.dir/43a00101.htm>, accessed 7 April 2009.
Shea, D.M and Green, J.C. (eds) (2006), *The State of the Parties: The Changing Role of Contemporary American* (Boulder: Rowman and Littlefield).
"Secretaries of the Treasury: Andrew W. Mellon," *U.S. Department of the Treasury* <http://www.ustreas.gov/education/history/secretaries/awmellon.shtml>, accessed 27 March 2009.
Simon, H., Smithburg, D. and Thompson, V. (1959), *Public Administration* (New York: Knopf).

Slevin, J. (2000), "Publicness and the Internet," in Slevin.

Slevin, J. (2000), *The Internet and Society* (Cambridge: Polity Press).

Smelser, N.J., and Baltes, P.B (eds) (2004), *International Encyclopedia of the Social and Behavioral Sciences* (Oxford: Elsevier)

Smith. A. (1933), "All the Ills of Democracy…" Speech. Albany, NY.

Smith, M.R. and Marx, L. (eds) (1994), *Does Technology Drive History? The Dilemma of Technological Determinism* (Cambridge: MIT Press)

Sniderman, P. and Bullock, J. (2004), "A Consistency Theory of Public Opinion and Political Choice: The Hypothesis of Menu Dependence," in Saris and Sniderman, (eds).

Sperber, M., "End the Mediocrity of Our Public Universities," *Chronicle of Higher Education* <http://chronicle.com/free/v47/i08/08b02401.htm>, accessed 7 April 2009.

"Social Networking and Videos Take Off: Internet's Broader Role in Campaign 2008," *Washington, DC: Pew Center for The People and The Press* <http://www.pewinternet.org/pdfs/Pew_MediaSources_jan08.pdf>, accessed 11 January 2008.

"State of the Blogosphere Report 2008," *Technorati* <http://technorati.com/blogging/state-of-the-blogosphere/>, accessed 2 December 2008.

Statistical Abstract "2001 Statistical Abstract of the United States," *Washington, DC: U.S. Census Bureau* <http://www.census.gov/prod/2002pubs/01statab/stat-ab01.html>, accessed 7 April 2009.

Statistical Abstract "2008 Statistical Abstract of the United States," *Washington, DC: U.S. Census Bureau* <http://www.census.gov/compendia/statab/cats/education.html>, accessed 27 January 2009.

Steiner, P. (1993), "On the Internet, No One Knows You're a Dog," *New Yorker*, 5 July.

Stephens, M. (1994), "The Theologian of Talk," *Los Angeles Times Magazine*, October, 26-30.

Stetler, B. (2008), "On Local News, Familiar Older Faces Fade Out," *New York Times*, 1 December.

Stouffer, S. (1955), *Communism, Conformity, and Civil Liberties* (New York: Doubleday).

Sullivan, W.M., "The University as Citizen: Institutional Identity and Social Responsibility," *Council on Public Policy Education* <http://www.publicpolicy-educouncil.org/publications_program/iisr.html>, accessed 7 April 2009.

Strolovich, D.Z. (2007), "A More Level Playing Field or a New Mobilization of Bias? Interest Groups and Advocacy for the Disadvantaged," in Cigler and Loomis (eds).

Sullivan, J.L., Piereson, J. and Marcus, G. (1982), *Political Tolerance and American Democracy* (Chicago: The University of Chicago Press).

Sullivan J.L. and Riedel E. (2004), "Efficacy: Political," in Smelser N and Baltes, P. (eds).

Sunstein, C.R. (2001), *Republic.com* (Princeton: Princeton University Press).

Sunstein, C.R. (2007), *Republic.com 2.0* (Princeton: Princeton University Press).

Sykes, C.J. (1988), *ProfScam: Professors and the Demise of Higher Education* (New York: St. Martin's Press).

Taylor, C., "Beyond the Banner: Online ads have come a long way since the birth of the Web," *Adweek* <http://www.adweek.com/aw/esearch/article_display.jsp?vnu_content_id=1885682>, accessed 12 May 2003.

Taylor, K.S., "Higher Education: From Craft-Production to Capitalist Enterprise?," *First Monday* <http://www.firstmonday.dk/issues/issue3_9/taylor/index.html>, accessed 7 April 2009.

"Teaching Tolerance," *Southern Poverty Law Center* <www.tolerance.org>, accessed 4 November 2008.

"Television Licence," *Wikipedia, The Free Encyclopedia* <http://en.wikipedia.org/wiki/Television_licence>, accessed 30 November 2008.

Terkel, S. (1997), *My American Century* (New York: The New Press).

"The Bayh-Dole Act: A Guide to the Law and Implementing Regulations," *Council of Governmental Relations* <http://www.cogr.edu/bayh-dole.htm>, accessed 2 November 2002.

"The International Network Education for Democracy, Human Rights and Tolerance," *International Tolerance Network* <www.tolerance-net.org>, accessed 11 November 2008.

"The Internet Freedom Fight goes to Washington," *SavetheInternet.com* <http://www.savetheinternet.com/=coalition>, accessed 1 May 2008.

"The State of the News Media, 2008," *Washington DC: Pew Project for Excellence in Journalism* <http://www.stateofthenewsmedia.org/2008/>, accessed 12 December 2008.

"The USA PATRIOT Act Six Months Later: A Statement by Members of the Free Expression Network," *Free Expression Network* <http://www.freeexpression.org/patriotstmt.htm>, accessed 25 April 2002.

"The Well," *The Well* <www.well.com>, accessed 3 June 2008.

"The Whistleblower Protection Program," *OSHA (Occupational Health & Safety Administration)* <http://www.osha.gov/dep/oia/whistleblower/index.html>, accessed 12 May 2008.

Thomas, J.C. and Streib, G. (2003), "The New Face of Government: Citizen-Initiated Contact in the Era of E-Government," *Journal of Public Administration Research and Theory* 13:1, 83-102.

Tobias, G. and Foxman, A., "ADL Press Release Commending Yahoo!," *ADL Press Release* <http://www.adl.org/PresRele/Internet_75/3735_75.htm>, accessed 3 January 2001.

Tocqueville, A. (1953), *Democracy in America* (New York: Oxford University Press).

"Top 25 Censored Stories for 2009," *Project Censored* <http://www.projectcensored.org/top-stories/category/y-2009>, accessed 3 January 2009.

"Trends in Political Values and Core Attitudes: 1987-2007," *Washington, DC: Pew Research Center for People and the Press* <http://people-press.org/reports/pdf/312.pdf>, accessed 2 June 2008.

Trippi, J. (2004), *The Revolution Will Not Be Televised: Democracy, The Internet, and the Overthrow of Everything* (New York: Regan Books).

Trow, M. (1997), "The Development of Information Technology in American Higher Education," *Daedalus* 126:4, 297-314.

Truman, D.B. (1951), *The Governmental Process: Political interests and Public Opinion* (New York: Alfred A. Knopf).

Tunstall, J. (1977), *The Media are American* (New York: Columbia University Press).

Turban, E., King, D., Lee, J.K. and Viehland, D. (2004), *Electronic Commerce: A Managerial Perspective* (Upper Saddle River, NJ: Pearson Prentice Hall).

Turner, F. (2006), *From Counterculture to Cyberculture* (Chicago: The University of Chicago Press).

Tusa, J., "1968, The Year of Revolutions," BBC Radio 4 series – Real Player <http://www.bbc.co.uk/radio4/1968/yearofrevolutions.shtml>, accessed 18 March, 29 April, 19 and 26 August 2008.

Twigg, C.A., "Who Owns Online Courses and Course Materials? Intellectual Property Policies for a New Learning Environment," *National Center for Academic Transformation, Rensselaer Polytechnic Institute* <http://www.thencat.org/Monographs/Whoowns.html>, accessed 31 January 2008.

Urbinati, N. (2006), *Representative Democracy: Principles and Genealogy* (Chicago: University of Chicago Press).

"Understanding Prejudice," *Understanding Prejudice website* <www.understandingprejudice.org>, accessed 4 November 2008.

Van Aelst, P. (2002), *New Media, New Movements? The Role of the Internet in Shaping the 'Anti-Globalization' Movement* (Boston: American Political Science Association, Annual Meeting).

Vandenberg, A. (2000), "Cybercitizenship and Digital Democracy," in Vandenberg (ed.).

Vandenberg A. (ed.) (2000), *Citizenship and Democracy in A Global Era* (Basingstoke: Palgrave Macmillan).

Varis, T., "eLearning and higher education," *eLearning Papers* <http://www.elearningeuropa.info/files/media/media11006.pdf>, accessed 27 January 2009.

Ventkatesh, S. (2009), "Feeling too Down to Rise Up," *New York Times,* 29 March.

Verba, S. and Nie, N. (1972), *Participation in America: Political Democracy and Social Equality* (New York: Harper & Row).

Verba, S., Schlozman, K.L. and Brady, H.E. (1995), *Voice and Equality: Civic Voluntarism in American Politics* (Cambridge: Harvard University Press).

Vernon R. (1971), *Sovereignty at Bay* (New York: Basic Books).

"Virtual Revolution: The e-Government Imperative," *Paris: Organization for Economic Co-operation and Development* <http://oecdobserver.org/news/fullstory.php/aid/1096/ virtualrevolution.html>, accessed 6 April 2008.
"Voting Technology Project," *CALTECH/MIT* <http://www.votingtechnologyproject.org/ index.html>, accessed 26 May 2008.
Vromen, A. (2007), "Australian Young People's Participatory Practices and Internet Use," in Loader (ed.), pp. 97-113.
Walker, J.L. (1966), "A Critique of the Elitist Theory of Democracy," *American Political Science Review* 60:2, 285-95.
Walzer, P. (2008), "Landmark agrees to sell Weather Channel," *Roanoke Times* <http://www.roanoke.com/news/breaking/wb/168503>, accessed 6 April 2009.
Wallace, P. (1999), *The Psychology of the Internet* (Cambridge: Cambridge University Press).
Wakefield, J., "BBC and ISPs clash over iPlayer," *BBC News Online* <http://news.bbc.co.uk/2/hi/technology/7336940.stm>, accessed 9 January 2008.
Watson, R.T. and Mundy, B. (2001), "A Strategic Perspective of Electronic Democracy," *Communications of the ACM* 44:1, 27-30.
"Web 2.0," *Wikipedia, The Free Encyclopedia* <http://en.wikipedia.org/wiki/Web_2.0>, accessed 24 March 2009.
"Website Traffic Comparisons," *Alexa* <www.Alexa.com>, accessed 10 April 2008.
Weil, N., "Who Owns the Internet?," *The Industry Standard* <http://www.thestandard.com/article/display/0,1151,12545,00.html>, accessed 7 April 2009.
Weling, K. and Wei, K.K. (2004), "Successful E-Government in Singapore," *Communications of the ACM* 47:6, 95-99.
Wessels, J., "Read All About It While You Can," *City Beat* <http://www.citybeat.com/cincinnati/article-16154-read-all-about-it-while-you-can.html>, accessed 15 October 2008.
West, D.M., "Assessing E-Government: The Internet, Democracy, and Service Delivery by State and Federal Governments," *Taubman Center Release* <http://www.brown.edu/ Departments/Taubman_Center/polreports/egovtrelease00.html>, accessed 17 September 2002.
West, D.M. (2005), *Digital Government: Technology and the Public Sector* (Princeton: Princeton University Press).
West, D. (2007), "Global Perspectives on E-Government," in Mayer-Schönberger and Lazer (eds).
"Where trade unionists start their day on the net," *LabourStart* <www.LabourStart.org>, accessed 4 November 2008.
White, S. (1988), *The Recent Work of Jürgen Habermas* (Cambridge: Cambridge University Press).

White, F., "Digital Diploma Mills: A Dissenting Voice," *First Monday* <http://www.firstmonday.dk/issues/issue4_7/white/index.html>, accessed 7 April 2009.

White, J.K. (2001), "Reviving the Political Parties: What Must be Done?," in White and Green (eds).

White, J.K. and Green J.C. (2001), *The Politics of Ideas* (Albany: SUNY Press)

Wiklund, H. (2005), "A Habermasian Analysis of the Deliberative Democratic Potential of ICT-enabled services in Swedish Municipalities," *New Media and Society* 7:2, 247-270.

"William M. Tweed," *Wikipedia, The Free Encyclopedia* <http://en.wikipedia.org/wiki/William_Marcy_Tweed>, accessed 30 March 2009.

Wilson, R., "Georgia State U. to Replace Part-Timers With Full-Time, Untenured Professors," *Chronicle of Higher Education* <http://chronicle.com/weekly/v45/i40/40a01801.htm>, accessed 7 April 2009.

Wingfield, N. (2003), "Can Webvan Founder Succeed with Online Archives?," *Wall Street Journal*, 21 July.

—— (2002), "Yahoo's China Concession," *Washington Post*. 19 August.

Woody, T., "Higher Earning: The Fight to Control The Academy's Intellectual Capital: Universities are facing a revolution over intellectual property as technology blurs the lines between good business and good education," *The Industry Standard* <http://www.thestandard.net/articles/article_print/0,1454,874,00.html>, accessed 7 April 2009.

Woodly, D. (2008), "New Competencies in Democratic Communication? Blogs, Agenda-Setting, and Political Participation," *Public Choice* 134:1, 109-123.

Yablon, Y. (2007), "Feeling Close from a Distance: Peace Encounters via Internet Technology," *New Directions for Youth Development* 116: 99-107.

"Yahoo! Nazi auction ban welcomed," *CNN* <http://www.cnn.com/2001/WORLD/europe/01/03/net.hate>, accessed 3 January 2001.

"Yahoo! Risks Abusing Rights in China," *Human Rights Watch* <http://www.hrw.org/press/2002/08/yahoo080902.htm>, accessed 9 August 2002.

Yang, G., "Activists beyond Virtual Borders: Internet–Mediated Networks and Informational Politics in China," *First Monday* <http://firstmonday.org/htbin/cgiwrap/bin/ojs/index.php/fm/article/view/1609/1524>, accessed 14 November 2008.

Yankelovich, D. "Ferment and Change: Higher Education in 2015," *Chronicle of Higher Education* <http://chronicle.com/weekly/v52/i14/14b00601.htm>, accessed 7 April 2009.

Young, J., "A Study Finds that Web Users are More Tolerant Than Non-Users," *Chronicle of Higher Education* <http://chronicle.com/free/2001/06/2001061501t.htm>, accessed 15 June 2001.

Young, J.R. "Research Universities Team Up to Create a 'Portal' to On-Line Education," *Chronicle of Higher Education: Daily News* <http://chronicle.com/free/99/06/99061001t.htm>, accessed 7 April 2009.

"Youth Partnership Web Portal," *Youth Partnership* <www.youth-partnership.net>, accessed 22 October 2008.

"Youth Making Media," Global Action Project <www.global-action.org>, accessed 22 October 2008.

"YouTube Taps ADL As Partner In Fight Against Hate," *Anti-Defamation League* <http://www.adl.org/PresRele/Internet_75/5416_75.htm>, accessed 15 December 2008.

"Yes Men," *Yes Men* <http://www.theyesmen.org>, accessed 19 November 2008.

Yudof, M.G., "Is the Public Research University Dead?," *Chronicle of Higher Education* <http://chronicle.com/weekly/v48/i18/18b02401.htm>, accessed 7 April 2009.

"Zapatistas," *Ejército Zapatista de Liberación Nacional* <www.ezln.org.mx/index.html>, accessed 4 November 2008.

Zinn, H. (1997), *A People's History of the United States* (New York: Harper-Collins).

Zinn, H. (1999), *A People's History of the United States: 1492-Present*, 20th Anniversary Edition (New York: Harper Collins).

Zuckerman, E. and McLaughlin, A., "Introduction to Internet Architecture and Institutions," *Harvard Law* <http://cyber.law.harvard.edu/digitaldemocracy/internetarchitecture.html#infra>, accessed 3 May 2008.

Zukin, C. et al. (2006), *A New Engagement? Political Participation, Civic Life, and the Changing American Citizen* (New York: Oxford University Press).

Index